'Mavericks drive progress and the world needs many more – this book shows why.' SIR JAMES DYSON

'Inspirational and aptly reflective of the current global environment, *Mavericks* affirms the importance of ordinary people taking action. We are very proud to have several Brookings Echidna Global Scholars featured as exemplars of Maverick leadership in this book. They truly inspire all of us to tap into our own inner Maverick and lead our society towards a better, improved tomorrow.' JOHN R ALLEN, PRESIDENT, THE BROOKINGS INSTITUTION

'I love everything about this book. The world needs more Mavericks!' JULIA HOBSBAWM, FOUNDER, EDITORIAL INTELLIGENCE

'Release your inner Maverick – this ground-breaking book gives everyone a manual for how to make a difference at work and in society.' JAMES PURNELL, PRESIDENT AND VICE-CHANCELLOR, UNIVERSITY OF THE ARTS LONDON

'*Mavericks* is a very different take on the type of leadership we need if we are going to tackle the monumental challenges we face. It is one I recognize and heartily endorse. The book is a refreshing, exhilarating read whether you want to use it for personal inspiration or to assess the world in which you operate on a day-to-day basis. It is also practical and gives you the tools to nurture your own inner Maverick, or those of the people around you.' GARY LUBNER, CEO, BELRON INTERNATIONAL

'Reading this delightful and incisive book, I recalled a line Henry David Thoreau wrote in *Walden*: "If a man does not keep pace with his companions, perhaps it is because he hears a different drummer. Let him step to the music which he hears, however measured or far away." All of us are capable of being Mavericks – those who see a gap between what is and what could be. The five characteristics of Mavericks herein are profound, a guiding light you can refer to over and over to avoid fatalism. By fusing all five of these traits, you will transform into an effective rebel with a cause, contributing to a flourishing life for all.' RONALD J BAKER, HOST, THE SOUL OF ENTERPRISE PODCAST, FOUNDER, VERASAGE INSTITUTE AND BESTSELLING AUTHOR OF *IMPLEMENTING VALUE PRICING*

'*Mavericks* is an optimistic book about how we can do better. When something is wrong and we don't stand up for improvement, we fail ourselves and everyone. This book shows how Maverick leaders who are "normal" people (like us) use their belief, determination and courage to ameliorate the world; it also discusses creating an environment for such change. Much needed right now; no other book challenges us like this, for the good of all.' DIANA AMBACHE, FOUNDER, AMBACHE CHARITABLE TRUST AND PIONEER OF THE REVIVAL OF CLASSICAL MUSIC BY WOMEN

'This book is truly liberating! Armed with a Maverick mindset, ordinary people can become inspirational leaders. Packed full of practical examples, this is a ground-breaking toolkit that awakens the characteristics within, so you can become an inspirational and Maverick leader. *Mavericks* gives you the inspiration to say "I can" and the confidence to say "I will". Bravo!' JEZ GROOM, FOUNDER, CEO COWRY CONSULTING

'I was declared a Maverick in the mid-nineties in the brand new (read charmless, uncomfortable and desperately boring) boardroom of a multi-national corporation. That day, my boss used this term to qualify my contribution to the collective efforts of our European board. Twenty-five years of Maverick-ability later, I know that this is not a title of glory, nor an actual job title but a desperate attempt by many executives to escape the status quo and corporate nonsense. A Maverick attitude is a little thing that makes a big difference. Society and organizations are suffering from a huge appetite for conformity and a subsequent lack of "fantaisie". Make your voice heard and join the Mavericks club, it's never too late.' CHRISTOPHE GILLET, PROGRAMME DIRECTOR, CEDEP AND FORMER DIRECTOR OF BUSINESS INNOVATION, SONY BUSINESS EUROPE

'With *Mavericks*, Lewis, Goddard, and Batcheller-Adams have identified the essence of entrepreneurship. They demonstrate that innovation and creativity can occur anywhere so long as one person remains, as they put it, "undeterred in the face of ridicule, resistance and outright hostility". The book itself creates a movement, just like the Maverick leaders identified therein. I hope to join this movement and change our world for the better.' ED KLESS, HOST, SAGE THOUGHT LEADERSHIP PODCAST AND CO-HOST, THE SOUL OF ENTERPRISE PODCAST

Mavericks

How bold leadership changes the world

David Lewis

Jules Goddard

Tamryn Batcheller-Adams

KoganPage

Publisher's note
Every possible effort has been made to ensure that the information contained in this book is accurate at the time of going to press, and the publishers and authors cannot accept responsibility for any errors or omissions, however caused. No responsibility for loss or damage occasioned to any person acting, or refraining from action, as a result of the material in this publication can be accepted by the editor, the publisher or the authors.

First published in Great Britain and the United States in 2022 by Kogan Page Limited

2nd Floor, 45 Gee Street
London
EC1V 3RS
United Kingdom
www.koganpage.com

8 W 38th Street, Suite 902
New York, NY 10018
USA

4737/23 Ansari Road
Daryaganj
New Delhi 110002
India

Kogan Page books are printed on paper from sustainable forests.

ISBNs
Hardback   978 1 3986 0441 4
Paperback 978 1 3986 0439 1
Ebook   978 1 3986 0440 7

British Library Cataloguing-in-Publication Data
A CIP record for this book is available from the British Library.

Library of Congress Control Number
2021058602

Typeset by Hong Kong FIVE Workshop
Print production managed by Jellyfish
Printed and bound by CPI Group (UK) Ltd, Croydon CR0 4YY

Jennifer and David Lewis
Joan and Herald Goddard
Vicky and Keith Coats

Contents

List of figures and tables x
About the authors xi
Foreword xiii
Acknowledgements xvii

Introduction 1

01 Belief: We should do better 17

No long-range missile is going to prevent a crippling cyberattack 17
An awakening 18
Taking matters in your own hands 21
Mobilizing others 22
You learn as you go 22
Going to school in a wheelbarrow 23
What keeps you going? 24
Why am I here? 25
True stories 27
Ordinary people 28
Extraordinary journeys 30
The Maverick leader mindset 31
'Maverick' and 'leader' 32
The Maverick leader within 32

02 What makes a Maverick leader? 35

We are born creative, explorative and challenging – and then? 36
A performance mindset or a master mindset? 38
It is never too late 40
From wanting to win, to wanting to do good 'for people and
    planet' 42
The catalyst: when competence and circumstances connect 44
The right thing to do 45
Our Maverick spirit can be stirred at any point in life 46

03 Resourcefulness: Connecting people, ideas and assets 49

Breadth of early life, depth of later life 49
Freedom with belonging 52
Connecting the dots 57
Three kinds of capital 58
The social functioning of the brain 59
Are we living in the age of connection? 61
The Maverick as maven 63
A behavioural theory of networking 63

04 Nonconformity: The instinct to question 69

Truth to one's mission 70
Self-efficacy 72
Do it your way 73
Originality 76
Fertile ground 77
Playfulness 79
Personhood 83
Collaborate with others 85

05 Experimental: Learning through trial and error 89

Question, hypothesize, experiment and learn 89
We discover by doing 92
Failure is hard but necessary 93
Trial and error 94
Curiosity and playfulness 96
Think for yourself 98
Bending, breaking and blending 100
Learning 101

06 Undeterred: Resisting opposition 105

Still striving 105
Higher-order goals 106
Life philosophy 108
The professional is personal 110
A blank canvas 113

Go together 114
Life philosophy and higher-order goals 116
Resilience 118
Invest in yourself 120
We all have it within us 121

07 Maverick styles of leadership 123

Leadership is in our DNA 124
Organizational distortions of leadership 124
Non-hierarchical forms of leadership 126
The emergence of the Maverick leader 129
The Maverick leader's relationship to the concept of leadership
    itself 133
What sets the Maverick leader apart? 135
Leading with intent 135
Leading oneself 137
Leading the movement 139

08 Maverick forms of organization 145

The organizational challenge 147
The First Machine Age and its bureaucratic culture 147
Managerialism in crisis 150
The Maverick hemisphere 150
The Second Machine Age and its technocratic culture 152
The Maverick organization and its adhocratic culture 153
The choice of architecture of a Maverick culture 157

09 Maverick states of society 161

What enhances human accomplishment? 161
Back to the future 162
The Maverick leader's sense of responsibility 164
Taking personal responsibility 166
The Maverick leader's sense of community 170
Where business fits in 173
Summary 174

10 Becoming a Maverick leader 177

We need to be more resourceful 179
Curiosity 180
Building a diverse and open network 180
Engage your network with curiosity 181
The ladder of inference 184
We need to be more nonconformist 185
We need to be more experimental 187
Strengthening your resolve 190
Higher-order goals and life philosophy 191
Summary: becoming a Maverick leader 192

References 193
Index 201

List of figures and tables

Figures

Figure 0.1 What makes the Maverick leader different 5
Figure 0.2 The adaptive organization and the Maverick characteristics 9
Figure 0.3 The desire for more Maverick leadership 9
Figure 4.1 The relative dominance of different behaviours 84
Figure 6.1 Maverick leader characteristics drive innovation 111

Tables

Table 6.1 Maverick leadership fosters positive emotions 111
Table 6.2 The absence of Maverick leadership increases negative emotions 112

About the authors

David Lewis has 35 years of experience in business and academia. He is a consultant and sought-after speaker working with global business leaders. In 2019, David was cited on Thinkers 50 Radar of top global management thinkers. David's research with co-author Alison Reynolds focuses on diversity and performance – the ability of teams and organizations to thrive in the face of new, uncertain and complex situations. With Alison, David developed the Qi Index, a tool to help leaders understand and enhance the quality of interaction between people to better formulate and execute groundbreaking strategies. David is a programme director at the London Business School and adjunct faculty at Hult International Business School.

Jules Goddard has spent most of his career at London Business School, first as a Professor of Marketing and latterly as an architect of its action learning programmes for corporate clients. He served as the inaugural Gresham Professor of Commerce, and is currently on the faculty of CEDEP, Fontainebleau, France. He is a member of the Council of the Royal Institute of Philosophy.

Tamryn Batcheller-Adams is a psychologist, leadership presenter, consultant and coach working internationally with TomorrowToday Global. As a practising psychologist with two Masters' degrees in psychology, Tamryn focuses on leadership, team and individual development. Having worked with leaders across 20 countries, Tamryn utilizes frameworks with a focus on building adaptability, emotional agility, resilience, stress management, self-awareness, social awareness and team cohesion to enhance personal, professional and collective growth. She co-designs, facilitates and coaches in Senior Executive Leadership Programmes and is a registered Enneagram (personality) specialist based in Cape Town, South Africa. Tamryn works with the Brookings Institution, supporting a network of global leaders invested in the field of girls' education.

Foreword

I suppose I've always been a bit of a silent rebel from my school days on. I resented authority. I resented all kinds of rules and prescriptions which I saw as somehow chains on my freedom. After reading this book, I've promoted myself to a Maverick which sounds more respectable than rebel. I also realize from the book that the term Mavericks gives me a social purpose in life, one which I've always been keen to associate myself with. Unfortunately, it was still a feeling of frustration rather than any action.

That all changed when I went to work for Shell in Malaysia. In my first three years there, I was just told to roam the country, learn the language, and make myself familiar with how Shell did its business. In the process, I discovered a yawning gap – Shell distributed its product in 50-gallon drums in unwieldy old lorries which kept breaking down on the jungle tracks in that country. 'Why are they ignoring the railway line that runs through the heart of the country?' I thought to myself. I approached the railway company and they confirmed that they could lease us their bulk carrier waggons which would bring the oil products to a railhead where the local dealers could bring their drums and decant the oils into them. The dealers could then drive them back to where they needed to be, accessible to their customers.

I got a quotation from the railway company. I prepared a neat little case. I put it in a file, put a half page summary of my proposals attached to it and put it on the desk of the Operations Manager in Singapore.

I soon got a message to go and see him. When I entered, he pointed to my file lying on his desk and said, 'Very interesting Handy, I'll take a look at it. By the way,' he said, 'how long have you been here with us?'

'Three years, sir,' I replied.

'And how long do you think the company has been working in Malaysia?'

'Oh, I think 50 years, sir.'

'No,' he said. 'One hundred and twenty years, and do you really think that in your three years you know better how to distribute our products in the country than we who have been here at least 20 times as long as you?'

'N-n-n-no no, sir,' I stammered. 'Of course not, sorry sir.'

'Well, Handy,' he said, 'you are obviously very bright, but do remember, sometimes experience is better than brilliance. It is OK to consult those who have been here longer than you before you write any more reports.'

'Yes sir, thank you sir,' I said as I left, thinking, silly old fool.

But that's the trouble with Mavericks – their proposals don't always fall on welcome ears. Indeed, sometimes they are made to suffer for their originality.

But top of Aristotle's list of virtues is courage by which he meant the courage to persevere with what you believe to be right, no matter what the consequences. So, to be a Maverick, you need to be brave, and if you want to be influential, you need to encourage others to follow you. I hope that by my actions, other young employees of Shell might also look for gaps in the system that could be filled by their ideas. In which case, I suppose I could call myself a Maverick leader having encouraged others to follow my example.

Lewis and Goddard describe, in some detail, all the characteristics of a Maverick, but the book comes alive when they describe some of the many Mavericks they encountered around the world. Like me, many of them became models for others and so, in effect, became Maverick leaders. They may not be as boastful as me in proclaiming that.

The book ends by becoming something of an appeal for a culture change in organizations and in society. If more of us released our Maverick tendencies which the authors believe lie dormant in all of us, and if more of us encouraged others to follow our example, the world would be full of Maverick leaders.

It is an exciting vision of a stimulating, entrepreneurial society, first to be found, I hope, in businesses such as Shell who are still rooted in their standard procedures and practices, thinking that the status quo is the way forward, and that any kind of innovation is some kind of disruption to the smooth processing that they are used to.

So, was I not only a Maverick, but a Maverick leader, and maybe even some kind of missionary or prophet of the kind of world that we might come to; one of open experiment, of questioning, of taking nothing for granted, of experiment and excitement rather than of standardization, and rules and procedures?

It is an exciting vision, and I could see my short-lived experience in Shell in Malaysia when things started to hum along much more openly and interestingly than when I first arrived there. So, the more people that read this book, the better should we all be and the better should all our organizations be. Mavericks of the world unite and change everything for the better.

I can heartily recommend this book to everybody who has ever felt at all frustrated by life in organizations or in society at large. Believe me, there is room for your ideas; believe me, have the courage to promote them, to stick with them, to encourage others to follow your example. Read this book and act on it.

Charles Handy

Acknowledgements

Fello Atkinson, Ruth Attenborough, Geoff Batcheller-Adams, Joss Batcheller-Adams, RP Beckinsale, Nick Binedel, Julian Birkinshaw, Donald Blankertz, Thierry Bonetto, Julie Brennan, John Byrne, Clare Chandler, Keith Coats, Géraldine Collard, James Crow, Pierre Deheunynck, Sir James Dyson, ASC Ehrenberg, Jane Farran, Gohar Goddard, Peter Gorley, Sebastian Hamers, Ian Hardie, Gay Haskins, Ashok Hegde, Terry Hill, Tim Hornblow, FX Houghton, Dominic Houlder, Ian Hunt, Linda Irwin, Isaac Lewis, Jacob Lewis, Joseph Lewis, Joshua Lewis, Liz Lewis, Sarah Lewis, Zachary Jules, Imogen Maya, Franck Mougin, Alastair Nicholson, Nigel Nicholson, David Ogilvy, Greg Orme, Mike Placko, Rick Price, Denis Pym, Alison Reynolds, Franck Riboud, AA Robertson, Richard Robertson, Claire-Marie Robilliard, Sir John Rose, Nick Roy, Bob Sadler, Kenneth Simmonds, Frank Smith, Zeldi Storni, Chris Styles, Paul Taylor, Bill Weitzel and all our interviewees: Luciano Cirinà, Patrick Collister, Andy Craggs, Guatam Duggal, Adefunke Ekine, Janna El-Hadad, Giles Ford, Masanori Hashimoto, Nick Hine, Khadim Hussain, Annmarie Lewis, Oscar Corona Lopez, Mmusi Aloysias Maimane, Jens Meyer, Yusuke Mizukami, Armene Modi, Salim Mokhtari, Andre Norman, Christine Apiot Okudi, Samar Osama, Barry Oshry, Damaris Seleina Parsitau, David Pearl, Suman Sachdeva, Urvashi Sahni, Madalo Samati, Nasrin Siddiqa, Hannah Silverstein, Rory Sutherland, Akin Thomas, Jan Vablinder and Rik Vera.

Introduction

Let no one be discouraged by:
… the belief there is nothing one man or one woman can do against the
enormous array of the world's ills – against misery, against ignorance,
or injustice and violence… Few will have the greatness to bend history,
but each of us can work to change a small portion of events. And in the
total of all those acts will be written the history of a generation.
ROBERT F KENNEDY, 1966

Must do better

When we consider the well-being of people across the world, we see that nearly half the world's population live on less than $5.5 a day (World Bank, 2018) and at the same time 2.8 million adults die each year as a result of being overweight or obese (World Health Organization, 2021). In a period of unprecedented wealth creation, prison populations have doubled, trebled and even in some countries quintupled. We could go on: about 37 per cent of young people between the ages of 12 and 17 have been bullied online (Patchin, 2019); millions of people are at risk of severe flooding due to global warming…Yet, more than at any time in our history we have the resources, the ingenuity and the technology to enable everyone on earth to live a fulfilling and flourishing life. The question is: where are these resources and why are they not being fully deployed for the benefit of us all? Where are our best brains? Who owns the latest technology? To what end is our human ingenuity, creativity and innovation being utilized?

Most of us either work directly, as salaried staff, or indirectly, as contractors, for organizations – commercial businesses, social enterprises, government departments, NGOs, established charities. And this is where almost all our resources are owned – in our organizations. And what are our organizations doing with these precious resources? Not enough! Why not? Because we, the people that populate these organizations, are not doing enough. We are failing ourselves and others in so many ways. We allow bureaucratic red tape to grow and strangle innovation in our organizations and institutions. We treat each other as human resources rather than resourceful humans, the consequence of which is reported in employee engagement surveys recording more people feeling disengaged at work than ever before.

Despite there being more than 15,000 books on leadership in print today, most organizations and most leaders show very little leadership. For many, leadership means seniority, seniority means responsibility, and responsibility means don't screw up. Don't rock the boat.

Maverick leaders

But for some this is simply not good enough. Some of those for whom this is not good enough work from within our organizations, others operate from outside organizational boundaries. These are the Maverick leaders who strive for and bring about positive progress. These are the people who are determined that we must do better, that we can do better and that we will do better. And they come in all shapes and sizes and from every walk of life: middle managers, shopfloor workers, philosophers, artists, teachers, politicians, soldiers, scientists, entrepreneurs and senior executives. The world does not need any more managers; the world needs many more of us to become Maverick leaders.

In this book we meet some of these Maverick leaders and attempt to learn from them how we can release the Maverick leader that we believe lives within all of us. We will explore their stories and distil the mindset and the skillset that they have developed and that we can adopt if we want to be Maverick leaders. The mindset and skillset that we need if we want not just to notice and become frustrated by the incompetence, the injustice and the complacency around us, but to do something about it.

Everyone wants to make the world a better place

Have you ever wondered why things are the way they are in your organizations or in your community when it seems pretty obvious that things could be a lot better? Of course you have; of this, we the authors are confident. In our research for this book, we conducted a study with people from over 50 different organizations from different sectors and countries. Of the people in our study, 100 per cent agreed that, 'the way things are done in our organization and the outcomes achieved could be much better'. The question is: why do so few of us do so little about it? Or to put it more positively, what can we learn from those who not only recognize the need for improvement but set about, and succeed in, making it happen?

To understand this, we need to think about what it takes for a person to make positive change happen. This is not about organizational change methodologies, the many variants of which mostly boil down to a six- to eight-step model: create a sense of urgency; role-model strong sponsorship; build a compelling vision; secure widespread buy-in, etc.

Neither is it about project and programme management methodologies: clearly scoped projects aligned to defined benefits; red/amber/green (RAG) status reports; weekly, monthly project and programme board meetings... . All of these methods, when trying to make change at scale, have their part to play. But it is not a compelling vision or a project RAG report that makes change happen, it is people. Creating positive outcomes for more people, as we will see from the stories of our Maverick leaders, means confronting vested interests, challenging cultural norms and letting go of established comfortable habits and conventions.

When Samar Osama, whom we will meet in Chapter 1, had to confront her male colleagues to get a desk in the shared office instead of having to do her work sitting on the stairs outside, there was nothing trivial about the challenge she faced – open hostility and ridicule from her male colleagues. No methodology is going to make that happen; Samar made that happen. And why was it so important? Because Samar was breaking the mould in establishing the acceptance for women to work in what was a male preserve in the factory in which she worked. It was not just about the desk; it was about getting the respect and acceptance of her male colleagues, and that meant changing their mindset.

When Khadim Hussain, a boy in a remote village in Northern Pakistan, started trying to persuade the parents of young girls to allow them go to school, those of us looking in from other cultures may well have responded with outrage at the idea that education was the preserve of young boys. But neither our outrage nor any methodology is going to change the cultural norms at play. But Khadim, whom we will also meet in Chapter 1, did bring about that change.

When Rik Vera, a Belgian carpet salesman, took over a polluting, loss-making carpet factory, it changed his attitude and approach to business entirely, from winning in business and treating business as a game, to creating businesses that are good for 'people and planet'. No brand management method told him how to do this; he worked it out as he set about it.

From these stories and many more we see that it is people that make change for the better happen. It is people that change other people's mindsets and assumptions, that change organizational and cultural norms and conventions. We call these people Maverick leaders.

The etymology of the word Maverick comes from a Texan rancher in the 1800s who declined to brand his cattle. Most other ranchers did. It was accepted practice. His name was Samuel Maverick. Maverick has come to mean independent minded and nonconformist. We add to the word Maverick the word leadership because we are not simply interested in people who refuse to conform for the sake of it – rebels without a cause. We are interested in rebels with a cause, people who strive for better outcomes for others. And why do we add Maverick to the word leadership? Because to lead for the betterment of others means challenging the status quo, the norms, conventions, vested interests and rules that govern how things currently are.

During our research for this book, we interviewed over 30 Maverick leaders. What became clear from our interviewees was that, despite their very different personalities and situations, these Maverick leaders shared a common set of characteristics. We identified five core characteristics:

1 a passionate belief that things should be better
2 resourcefulness: the ability to connect people and ideas to create momentum towards a better outcome
3 preparedness to challenge the status quo and act in unorthodox and nonconformist ways to get things done
4 the ability to learn and make progress through trial and error, through experimentation

5 the ability to remain undeterred in the face of ridicule, resistance and sometimes outright hostility

Five Maverick leadership characteristics: purposeful belief, resourceful, nonconformist, experimental and undeterred.

What differentiates the Maverick leader?

As part of our quantitative research, we asked a control group of executives from organizations across the world to rank themselves with respect to these five mindset/skillset characteristics. We then compared their results to how our Maverick leaders ranked themselves on the same five characteristics. The outcome is shown in Figure 0.1.

FIGURE 0.1   What makes the Maverick leader different

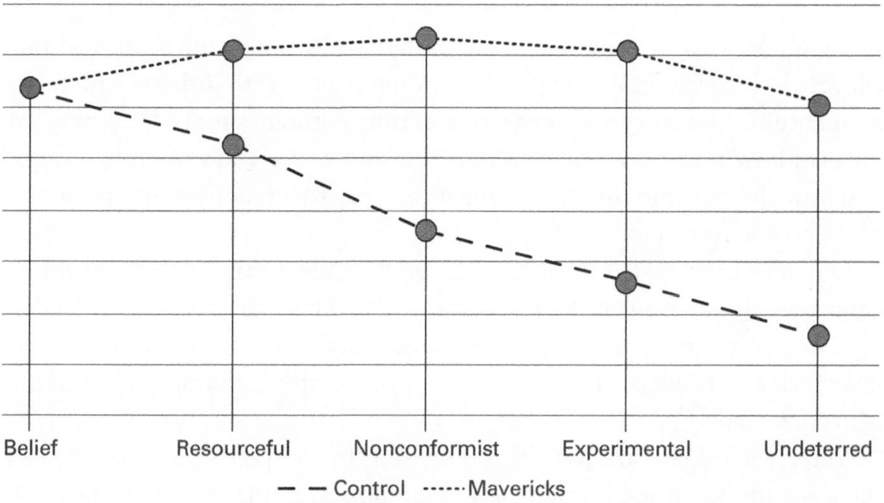

The Mavericks and the control group both have a strong **Belief** that things should be better. On the next characteristic, **Resourcefulness**, a gap emerges. Our Mavericks see themselves as more resourceful – 10 per cent more resourceful than our control group. On the next characteristic, **Nonconformist**, a bigger gap emerges. Our Mavericks see themselves as more nonconformist – in fact 20 per cent more nonconformist than our control group. On the next characteristic. **Experimental,** a still bigger gap emerges. Our Mavericks see themselves as more experimental – 25 per cent more experimental than our control group. On the final characteristic. **Undeterred,** you see the biggest gap. Our Mavericks see themselves as more undeterred by 27 per cent.

This data confirms our opening observation: *almost everyone, Maverick and non-Maverick alike, believes that in their organization or community things could be better.* What differentiates the Maverick from the non-Maverick is the extent to which they are resourceful, nonconformist, experimental and undeterred. This is what makes the difference, the difference between those of us that simply complain and those of us that actively endeavour to make things better.

> Maverick leaders and non-Maverick leaders share a belief that things should be better. What differentiates Maverick leaders is that they strive to make things better through resourcefulness, challenging convention, experimentation and persisting in the face of resistance.

In Chapters 3 to 6, we explore this difference through the stories of our Maverick leaders. How they create connections with others and build momentum; how they challenge convention without simply becoming an outcast; how they experiment to find new and better ways of doing things; and how they sustain their drive when they meet with consistent and sometimes hostile resistance.

Our aim is to reveal how our Maverick leaders think and to examine what they do, so we can learn what it takes to become a Maverick leader. We examine the research on growth mindset, self-efficacy, life stage development, grit and resilience that can help us to develop the characteristics of the Maverick leader.

Maverick leaders are not born. For each of the people we interviewed there is a unique story. A unique set of circumstance that stirs the Maverick spirit within. The same spirit we see in all children who naturally experiment, test boundaries and use their imagination and creativity to make-believe. It is the same spirit that is tamed as the child learns to conform, to fit in, to collaborate. But it never dies. The Maverick leader learns to harness that Maverick spirit, not simply to make-believe in an imaginary world, but to make what they believe come true in the real world. And to do this they exercise their freedom to balance conforming with nonconforming; experimenting with preserving; they pick their battles and create allies.

Maverick leaders exercise their freedom for the good of the collective

Georg Wilhelm Friedrich Hegel, the 19th-century German philosopher, analysed history and concluded, in his major work, *The Philosophy of History*, that history is the inexorable progress towards freedom (Hegel, 1899). He also took care to define freedom, not as unrestrained egotistical trampling over all others in pursuit of self-gratification – in other words, the freedom to do as you please, come what may. Instead, Hegel built on Immanuel Kant's categorical imperative which commands us to 'act in such a way that you always treat humanity, whether in your own person or in the person of any other, never simply as a means, but always at the same time as an end' (Kant, 1785). Hegel describes freedom as only having meaning in the context of our membership of and duties to our community, to other people – i.e. the Kantian categorical imperative: '...always treat humanity... never simply as a means, but... as an end [in its own right].'

Hegel put it like this: while duty may appear to us as a restriction on our natural or arbitrary desires, the truth is that 'in duty, the individual finds her liberation, from mere natural impulses. In duty the individual acquires her substantial freedom' (Hegel, 1820). In short, Hegel's argument is that to act solely in accordance with our impulse, our base desires, is not to act freely but to be driven by our animal instincts; equally, to act having been subjected to conditioning (or in the modern world, advertising) is also not to act freely – but is to conform. To act freely is to act from our reason, our sense of what is right and wrong. One has to be conscious of and strive to act in accordance with what is right, not solely in accordance with what is expedient. That is to act as liberated persons. To act freely.

A Maverick collective

While one of our objectives in this book is to help individuals to recognize and harness their Maverick spirit and freedom to make happen the change they want to see, we also want to shed light on what we can do to create an environment in which more people release their inner Maverick in our organizations and communities for the greater good. Organizations, like civilizations, ultimately decline when the dominant practices and culture no longer serve the well-being of their members. Maverick leaders are people prepared to challenge the status quo, build connection with others, experiment with new practices and remain undeterred by the resistance and hostility of others. These characteristics are the foundation for the successful continuation and development of organizations and communities small and large.

Increasingly, organizational leaders call upon us to be more innovative and agile, community leaders call upon us to do more for each other, and political leaders call upon us to take more responsibility. And rightly so, if we are to address the challenges presented at the start of this Introduction, and many more that need our ingenuity, compassion and perseverance. But it is not enough simply to call on others to act if we are failing to act ourselves and when we are not doing everything we can to create an environment in which Maverick leaders can flourish, rather than be ignored, marginalized or met with an impenetrable wall of silence and bureaucracy.

The Maverick organization

Returning to our quantitative research, Figure 0.2 shows the responses of our control group of executives to the question: to what extent do you see Maverick leader characteristics present in your organization? The dotted line shows the responses of those in an organization who see their organization as static – specifically, poor at innovation, not agile and unable to respond effectively to both challenges and opportunities. The dashed line represents the responses of those who see their organization as adaptable – specifically, good at innovation, agile and able to respond effectively to both challenges and opportunities.

What you see is that the more people see Maverick leadership characteristics around them, the more they see their organization as innovative, agile and adaptive.

Furthermore, when we ask people the extent to which they think Maverick leadership characteristics are desirable within their organization, compared to the extent to which they experience Maverick characteristics in others, the same gap emerges (Figure 0.3).

FIGURE 0.2   The adaptive organization and the Maverick characteristics

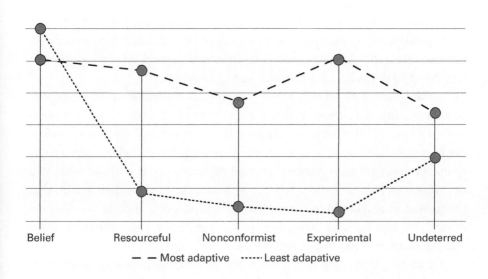

Belief   Resourceful   Nonconformist   Experimental   Undeterred

— — Most adaptive   ······ Least adapative

FIGURE 0.3   The desire for more Maverick leadership

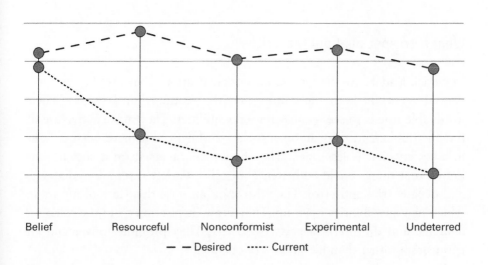

Belief   Resourceful   Nonconformist   Experimental   Undeterred

— — Desired   ······ Current

The Maverick leadership principle

We are born Maverick in nature, unique and independently minded. We are born questioning, exploring, experimental, resourceful and determined. We become Maverick leaders when our inherent natural Maverick spirit is harnessed to the belief that things should be better.

At the heart of this book is the principle that anyone at any time can become a Maverick leader. It is not a question of genetics; it is not a question of a special 'Maverick' upbringing. It is a choice and once the choice is made, it is a continuous journey of development. It is not about earth-shattering, globally transformational change programmes. It is about what you do, whatever your situation, when you notice, as you inevitably will, that things should and could be better. Do you simply complain, do you become cynical, do you become compliant, or do you ignite your Maverick spirit and set about making things better?

Our motive in writing this book is our belief that the world needs more of us, if not all of us, to be Maverick leaders. All of us, in whatever way we can, to be more Maverick and to take the initiative to lead in small, medium or large ways to imagine and create the world we want for ourselves and others.

What is so special about Mavericks?

Maverick leaders are the foundations of civilization. They are the entrepreneurial agents in both the culture and the economy of a society. Their invaluable role is to see – and seize – possibilities. They make active use of the liberties extended by an open society and fight to achieve what is right in a society that is less open. They find encouragement in a society that knows that things could be better. They relish variety of opinion, dialogue and debate, trial and error. They thrive on an unsettled state of affairs in which new possibilities open up. They draw inspiration from the tolerant, anarchic and disorderly aspects of society. They promote movements of enthusiasm rather than hierarchies of obedience.

They remind each of us of the Maverick that lurks within. They challenge us to be true to ourselves, and to find and act upon our autonomous view of the world. They nourish the pioneering spirit.

How do we recognize a Maverick?

Mavericks are the brave souls that are prepared to fail personally in order to succeed collectively. They are the movers and shakers. They can't, and won't, sit still. They are the irritants in a society that has turned complacent. They have an agenda. They are the doers that tire of endless commentary. They place effective deeds ahead of worthy thoughts. They are more interested in why and how than what and where. They're suspicious of hierarchy and sceptical of bureaucracy.

In today's parlance they embody the growth mindset, a term introduced by US psychologist Carol Dweck (Dweck and Leggett, 1988) and abjure the fixed mindset. They are adaptive but never defeatist. They judge by outcomes rather than just intent. Their optimism is often irrational. What they fear is not failure but fatalism.

Mavericks are defined less by their skills than by their intent. What sets them apart is not their talent so much as their state of mind. For example, they are recognizable less by their personality than by their character. Their hopes and aspirations, more than their anxieties and fears, precede them.

> We all recognize the seeds of the Maverick within ourselves. Nothing in the Maverick character is entirely foreign to us. Equally, we recognize those factors that inhibit or censor our innate Maverick nature.

What kind of leader is a Maverick leader?

Mavericks prefer to cast themselves as leaders of ideas and initiatives more than of people and plans. Mavericks are leaders who seek out fellow adventurers rather than followers. They would be embarrassed by a fan base. They would prefer to learn from others rather than to be admired by others. They form movements, not institutions. It is the cause they serve – and the manner in which they serve it – that attracts interest and affiliation.

They don't want their relationship with others to be hierarchical. The whole panoply of managerialism is antithetical to their way of working. Concepts of master and servant, boss and subordinate, master and apprentice, leader and follower are unhelpful and unattractive to them. Far more congenial is the notion of a gang of fellow reprobates, adventurers, volunteers, change agents, catalysts or pioneers, all united by a cause.

Who are our exemplars?

We make little reference to the recognized groundbreaking Mavericks. We don't tell the story of Steve Jobs, or Oprah Winfrey, or Jack Ma, or Jacinda Ardern, or Elon Musk, or David Hockney, admirable though they all are. We have chosen to feature a more humble, less well-known variety of Maverick: people like us. Those to whom we have spoken and whose stories we tell are 'normal people' in normal surroundings in normal circumstances, but aspiring, however humbly, to do abnormal things in abnormal ways with abnormal results.

They are people drawn from across the world.

Why now?

In a polarizing world, we need mavens, connectors, bridge-builders – people capable of decentring and seeing the world through the eyes of others. In a homogenizing, standardizing world we need original opinions and dissenting voices – if only to remind ourselves of the virtue of heresy. In an illiberal, culture-cancelling world we need more pluralism and an enriched enjoyment of diversity and debate.

In an increasingly egocentric and arrogant world, we need greater acknowledgement of human fallibility, and a more experimental approach to the future. In a short-term world, we need to cultivate more visionary possibilities. This is where Mavericks play a key role.

What is the structure of the book?

The first half of the book (Chapters 1 to 6) examines what we see as the five defining qualities of Mavericks. The second half (Chapters 7 to 10) looks at the environment in which Mavericks make their contribution, whether the environment is conducive or hostile to their efforts. In particular, we examine different concepts of leadership, dissimilar forms of organization and varied states of society. We argue that the Maverick is not just an accident of genetics; he and she are also the construct of the setting in which they build their life and exert their influence.

Introduction to the chapters

In the following chapters we explore with real-life stories and research what it takes to be a successful Maverick leader. What is the mindset/skillset needed, once that inner Maverick has been stirred, to persist and make progress in a worthy cause? We focus on five characteristics that have emerged from our interviews with the wide range of Maverick leaders featured in this book: the duty they feel they have towards improving the state of the world (Belief), the extent of their creativity (Resourcefulness), their flair for finding unconventional solutions (Nonconformity), the zestful joy they take in experimenting with ideas (Experimental), and the resilience of their willpower (Undeterred).

BELIEF: WE SHOULD DO BETTER
In Chapter 1, we explore the first mindset characteristic of a Maverick leader: the passionate belief that things should be better and that through our actions we can make things better. We see how in the face of what seems to be systemic, ineffective and unjust outcomes, individuals resolve to take action to make things better.

WHAT MAKES A MAVERICK LEADER?
In Chapter 2, we examine how the inner Maverick spirit that resides in all of us can be awoken and put to work, whatever circumstances surround us and whatever our stage of life.

RESOURCEFULNESS: CONNECTING PEOPLE, IDEAS AND ASSETS
In Chapter 3, we explore the second mindset characteristic of a Maverick leader: being resourceful in creating momentum by connecting people, ideas and assets. We see how, through curiosity, Maverick leaders identify opportunities to connect people, ideas and assets that to others may seem unconnected or even at odds, in a coalition for positive change.

NONCONFORMITY: THE INSTINCT TO QUESTION
In Chapter 4, we explore the third mindset characteristic of a Maverick leader: nonconformity – a natural instinct to question, a refusal to believe that just because this is how we've always done it, it is the best way; or just because it hasn't broken yet, doesn't mean that by breaking it we could not put something better together.

EXPERIMENTAL: LEARNING THROUGH TRIAL AND ERROR

In Chapter 5, we explore the fourth mindset characteristic of a Maverick leader: being experimental – progressing and learning through trial and error. We see how the recognition that there is no proven path to a better future motivates Maverick leaders to take the first step, learn and work out how to get there along the way, while others simply give up.

UNDETERRED: RESISTING OPPOSITION

In Chapter 6, we explore the fifth mindset characteristic of a Maverick leader: the ability to be undeterred by ridicule, dismissal or even attack. We see how in the face of resistance, expressed as personal ridicule, undermining and political manoeuvring, or even outright hostility, Maverick leaders persist in striving to make things better through the force of their own will.

MAVERICK STYLES OF LEADERSHIP

In Chapter 7, we look at the implications for leadership. How do we need to challenge assumptions and conventions around what leadership is in the modern organization, in order to move away from managerialism, maintaining the status quo with incremental improvements, to tackling the major challenges and opportunities we face, in a way that is both more human and more worthy?

MAVERICK FORMS OF ORGANIZATION

In Chapter 8, we examine how organizational structure and culture can facilitate or hinder the expression and execution of Maverick leadership at all levels. To enable those in the best position, with the best grasp of what is happening to do what is best for others, our colleagues, our customers and our communities.

MAVERICK STATES OF SOCIETY

In Chapter 9, we confront the wider societal context within which we all live: the cooperation and collaboration across communities and organizations that decides who are to be included and who are to be excluded. How do we create a society in which everyone is included?

BECOMING A MAVERICK LEADER

In Chapter 10, we bring together the learning, the insights and the practical approaches of our Maverick leaders in a guide to help everyone of us, whatever our circumstances, release and develop our inner Maverick spirit to pursue things we want to change, to make the world we live in for us and those around us, a better place.

CHAPTER ONE

Belief

We should do better

No long-range missile is going to prevent a crippling cyberattack

In 2017, the National Health Service in England (NHS England) was brought to its knees by a cyberattack. Emergency patients were desperately relocated from stricken health centres. NHS staff had to use pen and paper and personal mobile phones to maintain a basic service. The NHS was not the only organization to be affected; several organizations across the world were also targeted. While it is still not certain to this day where the attack emanated from, or what the motive was – North Korea is cited by the BBC as the most likely culprit (Corera, 2017) – the attack was a clear indication that you do not need a nuclear warhead to bring a country to its knees.

Meanwhile, as the NHS and many other organizations across the world were grappling with the devasting threat and consequences of the attack, the UK Ministry of Defence was arguing with the Treasury to secure sufficient funding to add more complex warheads to an existing fleet of long-range missiles. The spend on cyber was a tiny percentage of the defence budget. As Vice Admiral Nick Hine, who at the time of writing was the Second Sea Lord, number two in the British Navy, put it to us, 'No long-range missile is going to prevent or help to recover from a cyberattack.' The nature of, and the arena in which, the defence of a nation state can be secured, has changed. And it changed some time ago.

Nick and his boss, the then First Sea Lord Admiral Sir Tony Radakin have been instrumental in the latest UK government defence plans, announced in March 2021, indicating a significant rebalancing of defence spend towards 'space' and 'cyber'. In making their argument over the years, they faced resistance and even hostility as their reasoning threatened established practice and convention. Yet they remained steadfast and undeterred. Why? Because they kept front of mind the purpose of defence: that is, to be ready for, and effective in the face of, current and near future threats, not to build ever more sophisticated equipment to fight historical wars. They knew what 'better' looked like in terms of the purpose of national defence. They risked and incurred personal ridicule and coordinated resistance from their own organization to argue for and to initiate change. They recognized that the world had changed, that the old ways would not adequately protect any nation state. As a result of their persistence the UK government finally acted on the need to shift its focus.

An awakening

Annmarie Lewis has worked within criminal and youth justice fields for over 25 years with 'end to end' justice experience. Simply put, Annmarie has worked at local, national and international levels across most areas within youth justice. From a young age Annmarie had a deep sense of justice and fighting for those who were often rejected, excluded, harmed or marginalized in society. She witnessed many young people from poorer backgrounds, under-represented and under-served communities, often with disproportionate life outcomes, especially within the education, criminal and youth justice systems. In her early life and teens, Annmarie personally experienced and witnessed both friends and family being negatively affected by harsh, punitive and unjust systems. This sparked a curiosity and a questioning in Annmarie to not only learn more about these systems but also what she could do to change them.

Annmarie completed studies in criminal justice (specializing in juvenile justice and psychology). In 1999, she joined the prison service as an officer in a young offenders' institution in the UK. She was 22 years old and the first black female to take up this position. Coupled with her own personal experiences, Annmarie saw first-hand that many of the kids who ended up in young offender institutes suffered higher levels of complex trauma and mental health needs, multiple levels of dysfunction, discrimination and/or disadvantage, disrupted education, were in the care of the welfare system for much longer periods, and were often not aware of, or afforded, the same rights and protections as their counterparts.

Annmarie has seen a lot of appalling things throughout her work within youth justice that left an indelible mark:

> When you cut a young 15-year-old down from hanging in his cell, it changes everything you see and think you know about the system. You're never going to think this is normal, acceptable or OK – it changes you, on the inside.

After nearly four years' service, the event that finally pushed Annmarie over the edge, over the tipping point, was in the early 2000s. A young man was brought into the prison, extremely weak and unable to physically support himself, stand or walk unaided. 'I looked at this young man and thought, how on earth is he in prison in this condition?' Annmarie and her colleague were given charge over him, and Annmarie began questioning him about his situation. The young man had been on hunger strike for some time, protesting his innocence. The nurses who brought him into the healthcare unit were crying, saying, he is literally going to die. Annmarie asked him, why are you doing this, why are you starving yourself, putting yourself through so much pain? He replied, 'I know no other way, I am innocent and I'd rather die than go to jail for something I didn't do.'

Annmarie described to us the experience of meeting and being with this young man:

> From what I can recall, his actual alleged offence was a non-violent one and he was being kept on remand until his trial. I've never seen anybody intentionally starve themselves, knowing it could be unto death. I thought you would not put yourself through this at 16 or 17 years old, if you really did not believe you were innocent. His organs were actually shutting down, he was in excruciating pain. He was crying out in pain and yet he was so malnourished that no tears could appear.

Annmarie often found herself acting against regulations when she opposed draconian and outdated practices. In response to the young man's pleading to not have his cell door shut overnight, and (in an environment where everyone else was white) to be with someone of the same colour as him, she and her colleague sought agreement to stay with him during the night and keep the door open. And during the night, talking to him and singing to him, she persuaded him to take a few sips of water. She remembers vividly how he struggled desperately and could not sit up, but with their assistance lifted his head to swallow the water. The next morning, she determined to have the young man transferred out of prison and back to the hospital. What they had to go through to make this happen was Kafkaesque. This was her watershed; this experience is forever imprinted on her mind.

Moved by compassion, Annmarie's conclusion (which is not really the right word – ever since these events, it is more like her 'calling') is driven by the realization that the system was, and still is, deeply and irrevocably flawed. Experiencing this, and remembering the young man she cut down from hanging, alongside innumerable other experiences, led Annmarie to the realization that has driven her in everything she has done since. As she puts it, 'The system has to change, and I have to be one that changes it.'

The impact of these experiences was an awakening – a point of embarkment, of no turning back, a realization that the youth justice system was broken. A conviction that to react instinctively to help in the face of a specific crisis is not enough; the real need is to challenge and transform the entire system that brought the crisis about. Annmarie has spent the best part of 25 years doing just this. In 2010 she established her own award-winning social enterprise, Rainmakers Worldwide, specifically supporting young people who had been incarcerated, placed in the care system and impacted by homelessness. She has undertaken national and international research in entrepreneurship and system change within justice-related fields, and later established The Rainmakers Group, a business, social justice and leadership consultancy to bring about systemic, cultural and national change within these fields. With each tipping point or moment of awakening, Annmarie reviews and adapts to meet current needs and remain relevant to the cause. As such, she has undertaken a restructuring within her social enterprise. Several beneficiaries now make up the core leadership group and are currently planning their re-launch and new direction of travel in 2022.

While of course she does not negate the seriousness of some of the offences children have committed, Annmarie made it clear that nearly 40 per cent are summary offences, which means they are less or non-violent, or less serious. Annmarie remains steadfastly committed to understanding the context of children's criminal behaviours, rather than focusing on punishment alone, seeking effective, trauma-informed and supportive alternatives to custody while simultaneously transforming the experience of those subject to custodial sentences, in the same vein. She reflected that:

Many of these children need protecting from the harm society has done to them, rather than society needing protection from the harms they've done, which are arguably not commensurate with the punishments they receive.

Annmarie is the first to acknowledge that an awakening is more than a simple moment in time, a flash of inspiration in which you change your entire mindset. It's just the beginning; the beginning of a journey that starts with challenging yourself before you can be successful in challenging others or challenging the system.

We share these stories, the story of Annmarie's awakening, the story of Nick's battle with the establishment, not because they are exceptional or extreme – although they are in some respects – but because they are also, albeit not with the same life-threatening consequences, everywhere you look. Because, everywhere you look, the ascendancy of bureaucracy, 'jobsworthy' behaviour and conformity trumps treating people with respect and understanding, trumps overturning outdated practices and attitudes to address the challenges and opportunities today.

Taking matters in your own hands

In 1991, Rick Rescorla, who at the time was Vice President for Security for Dean Witter Corporation, was concerned that the Twin Towers, the World Trade Centre in New York, were vulnerable to attack by a bomb planted in the underground carpark. He warned the authorities, but no action was taken, and in 1993 such a bombing took place.

Later Rick warned that the Twin Towers were vulnerable to attack from the air. This time he urged Dean Witter, now merged with Morgan Stanley, to move out of the Twin Towers as there was no way he could protect staff from such an attack. His seniors declined to move because their rent wasn't expiring until a few years later. So, Rick took matters into his own hands and drilled, regularly and incessantly, all the staff of Dean Witter/Morgan Stanley in evacuation procedures. He faced criticism and ridicule as he forced people to drill. Repeatedly, he'd set off the alarm and stand over people as they practised the evacuation process. When the air attack predicted by Rick actually came on 11 September 2001, 2,700 people from Dean Witter/Stanley Morgan got out alive just before the Twin Towers collapsed. Having re-entered the building to find the six remaining Dean

Witter/Morgan Stanley staff still in the building, Rick was killed as the buildings collapsed (Stewart, 2002).

In the absence of leadership from others, in the face of the complacency, irritation and even hostility of others, Rick never abandoned his duty as he saw it, and that was to do whatever he could to protect the people he was responsible for.

Mobilizing others

In 2010, Adefunke Ekine asked herself a question: 'Why do so few girls take up science in their education and in their careers?' She knew that it was not because they were not scientific or did not have scientific abilities. Was it because the way science was taught did not connect and engage them? She set about exploring her hypothesis that by integrating the way science and maths was taught into the real world and into games and stories, more girls would connect with and pursue science and maths. She saw stories as not only a means of teaching young children language, but also as a means of teaching maths and science.

But this realization on its own was not enough. If she could not mobilize others, persuade and engage others, she knew she could achieve little on her own, even if she could command and direct others. She needed the willing engagement, contribution of ideas and commitment of others. And doing this meant being open to feedback on her own behaviour, her own ideas and finding ways to connect the ideas of others behind a common goal. She told us:

> I've found out that as a leader, if you want followers with you, to actually go along with you and to surpass your expectations, you must be human, you must understand them, you must empathize with them, you must invite and act on their feedback.

You learn as you go

In late 2013, Oscar Corona Lopez started his own company, an agency for a large Mexican insurance company. He soon realized that while his own business managed to succeed, 90 per cent of start-up agencies failed, with devastating consequences for the people who put their money, their houses and their futures at risk. The 'mother company', the big insurer that sold their policies through the agencies, was not worried; it cost them almost nothing when an agency failed and they picked up anything of value from the remnants (new agents, plus premiums, plus new business). Oscar believed the problem with the start-up agencies was that they were forced to adopt the recruitment practices and 'culture' of the mother company, stifling the innovation, the human touch, the fun and the energy that are the ingredients of a successful sales organization.

In early 2019, Oscar went to the senior management of the mother company with a proposal to create an agency with a different recruitment process and a different culture. His proposals were rejected, and he was told to stick to the existing business model. Using £250,000 of his own money, he decided to create an alternative model anyway, alongside his existing business, unbeknown to the mother company. His plan was that in time, by demonstrating success over two years, he would be able to go back to the senior executive team and get support for a new way of doing business. A new way that was not only more successful and more fun, but would increase the success rate of start-ups and reduce the collateral human damage of failure.

But creating a new agency model is not plain sailing. Finding new ideas is relatively easy; finding new ideas that work is harder. Oscar recognized that he had to experiment. He had to do what he thought would be better, but he had to be open to changing his mind in the light of the results. To get new ideas Oscar enrolled on programmes at Harvard and the London Business School that challenged conventional thinking and encouraged experimentation. He told us:

> I learnt quickly there is no one predetermined guaranteed path to a new business model for agencies. There is only a series of business experiments from which you learn, construct your next experiment and in so doing move closer to your desired outcome and further away from the failing model you left behind.

Going to school in a wheelbarrow

Khadim Hussain was born in the mountain region of Karakoram in a remote village in northern Pakistan. As a young child he contracted polio and lost the use of his legs. When it came time to go to school, his friends took him to school in a wheelbarrow. The teacher sent him home, the message being, 'School is not for you!' The next day his friends took him to school again in the wheelbarrow. Khadim was not to be deterred.

As a child with a disability, at that time, in that place, most people referred to Khadim not by his name but by his disability. Sometimes with indifference; sometimes with hostility. We asked Khadim if he ever felt angry about this, and his response was immediate: 'No, I felt sad. I understood that it came from their mindset, their way of thinking, and with a smile on my face, I determined that I would change their mindset.' Khadim embarked on a journey to introduce schools for girls in his remote village; girls who, like him, were considered by others to be unworthy of education. He faced more resistance, undermining and hostility from many in his community, including the Imams, the people who lead Muslim worshippers in prayer, the heads of the Muslim community. Again he was undeterred.

What keeps you going?

Armene Modi had been teaching English in Japan for several years when a Peace Education course she enrolled in for her MA programme at Teachers College, Columbia University changed the direction of her life. She tells the story like this:

> When I started to introduce peace issues into my curriculum for my Japanese university students, the response was tremendous, motivating many of them to campaign for various human rights issues. For my part, I often wondered that while I was motivating my students to take action, was I myself doing enough to make a difference? It was then that I came across a shocking statistic in India's 1991 census that only 39 per cent of women in India were literate. It was a wake-up call that made me decide at 50 to give up my job in Japan, return to India, and launch a non-profit to educate and empower marginalized women.

Armene went on to promote literacy and financial autonomy for rural women as well as the education and empowerment of girls in Shirur County of Pune District in Maharashtra State in India. To arrest the high rate of child marriages, she introduced a bicycle bank to encourage girls to go to school and augment their education with life skills, and created scholarships to get more young women into higher education. We asked Armene how she maintained her energy and drive. She is now 73 years old and still an active Maverick leader. She replied:

> When you are able to help vulnerable women find their voice to fight injustice, help girls gain agency, and achieve some of their dreams and potential, it just

gives you a feeling that you are on the right path, you are contributing, in a small way, to making a positive difference and being, in Gandhi's words, 'the change that you want to see in the world'.

Why am I here?

Barry Oshry is a softly spoken, introverted 89-year-old, who has dedicated much of his life to helping people to see. To see the power they have; to see how the misuse of and blind use of power not only damages others, but damages themselves; and to see how to use power constructively, for the benefit of others. Barry is known for many things. To us, the authors, Barry is the person who, through his groundbreaking thinking, encapsulated in his book *Seeing Systems* (Oshry, 2007), has helped many thousands of people to dismantle the barriers of the single narrative – the categorization of a whole group of people into one set of characteristics, good, bad or indifferent – and instead treat them as individuals. And in so doing, to know one another, to learn from one another and start to create value rather than maintain an oppressive status quo.

Did Barry know as a 13-year-old that this was what his life was going to be about? No. Among other things, early in his career, Barry was a professor in human relations at Boston College; a consultant enjoying fat fees for a couple of hours work, followed by a boozy lunch; and later still, a bartender. In each job he was moderately to very successful, but eventually walked away. Why?

At 13 years old, Barry certainly didn't know what the future held for him. But something happened when he was 13 that would inform his raison d'être for the rest of his life, the answer to the question 'Why am I here?' He was made aware of the Holocaust. Simply put, his reaction to learning about the horror was ANGER – 'How could people do this to other human beings?' – and INQUIRY – 'How could people do this to other human beings?' Same question, different inflection. The first is in rage at ignorance, evil, stupidity. The second is cool, scientific, getting beneath the surface. How does this happen? What leads to what?

This combination of anger and inquiry stayed with Barry. The horrific reality that one human being could see another human being as so clearly in a different category of human being to themselves – a category with lesser or non-existent human rights – that they could be vanished, could not be ignored. Later, at the age of 16 he recalls the retort of a pony trap driver in Central Park waiting for him and his friends to make up their minds whether they could afford a trip: 'People like you are a dozen to the dime' – dispensable! Again Barry's response was anger: 'Don't make a category out of me: I am a unique individual. SEE ME!' The driver was not a bad person; quite the contrary, he was a good person. Barry's anger shook him out of reflex. He apologized.

Looking back, Barry sees both these events as formative in his later dedication to peeling away layers of ignorance – ignorance of others, ignorance of one's own blindness. Barry never held a senior position in a big organization and to this day is reluctant to think of himself as a leader, but through his writing and through his facilitation of experiences in which people see power and the impact it is having, he has changed the mindset and behaviour of thousands for the better. And what does better mean? For Barry, it means recognizing the power you have, organizing with others to strengthen the power you have and using that power for the benefit of all.

Anger and Inquiry underlie all Barry's work. *Seeing Systems* and the work that led up to it were driven by both. Early on, Barry was struck by the observation that organizations, despite having the best people and the best intentions, keep repeating the same old destructive scenarios – burdened Tops (senior executives), oppressed Bottoms (staff), torn Middles (middle managers), and righteously done-to (screwed) Customers. The cost this blindness incurs for individuals and relationships is so wasteful and dehumanizing. 'So my reaction has been anger – How does this happen? – and inquiry – How does this happen?'

In our conversations with Barry, he stopped a number of times to reflect on the question, the question he often asked himself as he found himself in new situations: Why am I here?:

> As a deep introvert, my preference is to be left alone. One day at a meeting
> and feeling WHY AM I HERE, I resolved, wherever I am I will strive to make
> a useful contribution. I don't believe that any higher power has sent me on a
> mission to the people. I do believe I have stumbled across a huge insight, and it
> is my responsibility to share it for the harm it can avoid and the good it can do.

This is the moment, the moment when we ask ourselves, why am I here, why me, what difference can I make, what does it matter what I do, the moment when we have the opportunity to find ourselves. And this is the beginning of the journey of a Maverick leader. In Barry's own words:

Much of my life was spent in discovering what I didn't want to do, without knowing what I should be doing. The path I ultimately fell into is who I am. It was not always an easy path. I am far from those who say they wake up every day glad and happy to get at it again. I often wake up in a panic. Oh no! Another day to work with another group of strangers. But happiness was never the ultimate criteria. Are you giving what only you can give?

True stories

These stories are modern parables: the story of Khadim Hussain, creating opportunities for girls in remote villages in northern Pakistan to go to school; the story of Nick Hine, transforming the approach to national defence in the UK; the story of Adefunke Ekine, transforming the educational outcomes of girls in Nigeria; the story of Rick Rescorla saving the lives of 2,700 Dean Witter/Morgan Stanley staff; the story of Oscar Corona Lopez experimenting his way away from an old, failed model to discover a new, more human model for business; the story of Annmarie Lewis transforming the approach to the youth justice system in the UK; the story of Armene Modi, still working at the age of 73 to see more young women in India reach their full potential in their education and professional careers; the story of Barry Oshry turning from one thing to another until the answer to the question, why am I here, became apparent.

These are just some of the stories we will explore in building our understanding of what it is to be a Maverick leader – someone who sees injustice, incompetence, mediocrity, human waste, prejudice – any gap between what is and what could be – and acts to make the 'what could be', the 'what is'. We will encounter the stories of many more people, from all parts of the world, from all walks of life and at different stages in their journey.

> The Maverick leader – someone who acts to fill the gap between what is and what could be to make the world a better place.

Ordinary people

What we have learnt through meeting, reading about and talking to these amazing people is that they are ordinary people. This is not a book about great leaders. It is a book about ordinary people doing extraordinary things. It's not about great figures of history, people the history books remember. It's about the people history books didn't even notice, the people we will never know about. To revisit the quote from Robert F Kennedy, it is about — 'each of us [who] can work to change a small portion of events. And in the total of all [our] …acts will be written the history of a generation.'

In 1976 Andre Norman was an ordinary young black boy growing up in Boston when the school bus he travelled on passed through a white neighbourhood and the bus was pelted with stones, thrown by young white people. When he got home he asked his Dad, why are they throwing stones at us? His Dad had no answer. It was as if, to Andre's Dad, this was just how it was and there was no answer, other than 'that's just how it is'. This and other inexplicable hostile experiences become part of Andre's everyday life. How is any young boy or young person going to respond? By taking matters into their own hands and finding ways to protect themselves.

For Andre it was the beginning of a journey that in 1991 culminated in him being contained in solitary confinement in a top security prison as one of, if not the most, feared prisoner in the Boston prison system. And it was then that Andre, at the very point where he had reached the top of the prisoner hierarchy, the most feared, the most powerful, the most entrepreneurial, the point at which he was about to be crowned No 1, on top of the pile, that he suddenly realized he was actually not the victor but the prime victim, 'the prime sucker'. He was actually the biggest loser, sitting atop a hierarchy of other losers, other victims. This had not been a life of his choosing; this had been a life determined by events and others. With this realization, Andre chose a very different life, a life of his making. A life that from that day he started working on, step by step, to make his own.

Today Andre is an ordinary person doing extraordinary things, because he chose to. Today he is an inspiration and support to people of all ages. Helping people to find the greatness that lies within them, by reclaiming the right to choose, consciously, the life they want, irrespective of circumstances and what others may have determined for them. If a company wanted to make change, putting Andre on the board of directors would be step one.

Samar Osama is a 36-year-old mother of two, who loves her family and her cats. She was born in Saudi Arabia, spent her youth between Saudi Arabia and Egypt, and now lives in Dubai. She is an ordinary woman who takes pleasure in ordinary things. But Samar has never conformed to the expectations of those around her. With a passion for science, for the application of science to the production of quality solutions to health and well-being, Samar found herself at the age of 22 working in a pharmaceutical manufacturing plant, responsible for quality control. Her colleagues and superiors were almost entirely men, older men, who were not about to take instructions from a young woman on when and how they should operate 'their' machines.

The hostility and rejection of her right to be among them and to undertake her responsibilities and duties, to ensure quality control, manifested in many ways. To start with, the men refused to give her any space in the office area, so she conducted her notetaking, report writing, analysis and planning activities sitting on the factory stairs. In those early days, Samar spent many evenings in tears, and who wouldn't in response to such unfair and unjustified hostile treatment? But despite her tears, there was a steel to Samar. A determination to do her job, to ensure quality outcomes for the recipients, the customers of their products.

One evening she cleared a corner in the office, found herself a desk and set up her equipment and notebooks. The men laughed at her, but she stayed put. Six months later, through determination, focusing not on the barriers and the hostility, but on the quality of what they were all there to produce, by connecting with her colleagues as people, showing an interest in them, and showing them that what she wanted and what they wanted were mutually supportive, she eventually achieved a mindset shift in her colleagues. In so doing, she learnt an important lesson. If you want to change things you have to find a way of connecting with and earning the respect of those who are comfortable in the status quo.

Today Samar is continuing to challenge convention in quality production and health product regulation. And more, she is applying her energy and challenging instincts beyond her professional discipline, into the arena of diversity and inclusion. Samar is a Maverick leader in the making.

The Zulu greeting *Sawubona* means 'I see you' and the response *Ngikhona* means 'I am here'. Central to the exchange is the sense that until you saw me, I didn't exist. But it is more than simply recognizing another person's existence; it is a recognition of their importance, that they count. The

Maverick leader constantly asks the question: Are we doing things in a way in which the results are that each and every one of us, irrespective of our background and circumstances, counts?

Extraordinary journeys

In our Introduction we listed a few of the challenges and opportunities that we face. We have begun to share the stories of people who are challenging convention and persisting in the face of opposition in the belief that we should do better. While every individual brings their own personality to the challenges they face and the improvement they want to make happen, these Maverick leaders share a common mindset and skillset.

These characteristics are not a set of genetically inherited features that some have and some do not. They are forged through experience, through context, and through the inspiration and support of others. As many have done, or will do in time, they witnessed unfairness, myopia and inadequacy. And they embarked on a journey to make things better. For many of us that journey is yet to begin. Our ambition is that by sharing the stories of Andre, Samar and the others, by exploring the mindset and skillset that character-ize their journeys, many more of us will initiate our own journeys in recognition that things should be better and that we can play our part in making them better.

Rory Sutherland, Vice Chairman of advertising agency Ogilvy, tells the story of when he was recruited as a graduate entrant to Ogilvy. There were about 20 applicants for four places. Rory was later told how the conversa-tion between the selectors had proceeded: 'Well, we've selected three, and they all look, sound and think pretty sound; what say you we take a punt on the oddball?' They did, and ever since Rory has been challenging conven-tion and traditional thinking. We asked him why he is always challenging: is it is simply that he is a contrarian? He answered: 'If we are prepared to be creative... there are far more good ideas out there than rational approaches will ever uncover – including many that might be much simpler to enact.' And he went on to say:

> The requirement to appear rational massively narrows the potential creative solution space for any problem. In short, there are far more good ideas out there that you can post-rationalize than there are good ideas you can pre-rationalize.

The Maverick mindset or skillset stands in stark contrast to accepted wisdom and established tradition, as well as most careers advice and the majority of recruitment and talent management programmes. There are those whose fear of failure impedes the exploration of new ideas; there are others whose irritation with the status quo motivates them to explore alternatives and risk setbacks. The former invariably dominate organizational life; the latter are the Maverick leaders who, when they find the tried and tested lacking, unjust or simply second-best, embrace the risk of failure in pursuit of something far better.

The Maverick leader mindset

So what is the Maverick leader mindset and skillset? From our discussions with Maverick leaders we have identified five attributes that characterize the Maverick leader. We describe them using the pronoun 'I':

- **Belief:** I believe that things should be better, I can make things better and I have a sense of what better looks like. The Maverick leader, in the face of what seem to be systemic, ineffective and unjust outcomes, resolves to take action to make things better. They assess options, seize opportunities and side-step barriers with an absence of ego, the need to be right or personal preference. Rather, they act informed by a vision of what better looks like.
- **Resourceful:** I create momentum by connecting people, ideas and assets. The Maverick leader, through curiosity, identifies opportunities to connect people, ideas and assets that to others may seem unconnected or too bothersome to engage in.
- **Nonconformist:** I am prepared to act in an unconventional and original way. The Maverick leader challenges orthodoxy, not for the sake of being obstinate or contrary, but to break out of the box and create something better.
- **Experimental:** I progress and learn through trial and error. The Maverick leader recognizes that there is no proven path to a better future, yet is determined to take the first step, learn and work out, along the way, how to make progress while others simply give up.
- **Undeterred:** I am undeterred by ridicule, dismissal or even attack. The Maverick leader persists in striving to make things better, in the face of difficulty, resistance and even outright hostility, through the force of their

own will. In the face of setbacks and little or no indication of success, they find ways to stay energized and garner support when needed.

'Maverick' and 'leader'

When Samuel Maverick declined to brand his cattle, his stated reason was that he did not want to inflict pain upon them. And while it may be stretching a point, experience suggests that to be constrained and unable to act in accordance with your independent mind is in and of itself a source of pain to be avoided. We chose the word Maverick to describe the kind of leader we want to celebrate in this book and to inspire others to liberate their independent mind and act accordingly, both consciously and deliberately.

For some the word Maverick simply means unconventional, contrarian or uncontrollable. This is why we talk not just about Mavericks, we talk about and explore the stories of Maverick leaders. For it is the combination of the Maverick spirit *and* the sense of responsibility and duty that is inherent in the act of leadership that this book is about. Leadership for us is an endeavour to guide oneself and others to a better place.

The Maverick leader within

In our careers as management consultants, researchers and educators, we are yet to meet a frontline worker, a middle manager, a senior executive or a CEO, a community worker, a social entrepreneur, a philosopher or indeed anyone, who openly or in confidence has not expressed deep dissatisfaction with how things are. That is not to say they are full of negativity or unable to recognize and celebrate positive aspects of their life and the lives of those around them. But it is a manifestation of the human condition that, in response to the suffering, unfulfilled potential and downright stupidity we see around us, we can't help but notice and remark upon it.

This is the stirring of the Maverick leader within all of us. And if more of us can move from a stirring to an activation, to live the active life (*vita activa*), as the philosopher Hannah Arendt described it in her book called *The Human Condition* (Arendt, 1958), we will get closer to creating a world in which all can flourish. A world in which we can all live up to the challenge laid down by, among others, the 18th-century German philosopher Immanuel Kant: 'God has set us on the stage where we can make each other happy, it rests with us, and us alone to do so' (Kant, 1997).

In secular terms, our moral obligation is to serve each other's fulfilment in life.

Maverick leaders are inspired by a problem in need of a solution, a change that needs to be made, an opportunity to right a wrong. Who among us has not had this feeling? Maverick leaders are animated by everyday issues that demand a solution and are motivated by the possibility of making progress towards it.

In the next chapter we ask the question, what makes a Maverick leader? Is it our upbringing, is it genetics or is it the choices we make along the way? Drawing on the stories of our interviewees, research on early years development and the development stages we go through in later life, we see how the inner Maverick that lies within us all can be brought to life at any point in our journey from childhood to old age.

CHAPTER TWO

What makes a Maverick leader?

H annah Silverstein has always been fiercely independent. As a child, she got herself to school, made sure she had what she needed, got herself fed, kind of brought herself up:

> Myself and my siblings almost raised ourselves... I didn't really have much parental guidance, I didn't really have any rules... no one knew where we were, it was like a freedom to learn for yourself what was right and wrong.

With this independence and maturity, Hannah took it upon herself to lend a hand at her local youth centre and to help out at school. From the age of 11 to 16 she ended up as a voluntary youth worker helping to improve and develop a successful youth centre for other young people.

Hannah is driven by helping people to learn, grow and do better as human beings. As an adult her career has taken her into the world of creative consultancy, where she works with brands to positively change the world and shape the future. Today, Hannah is a Creative Consultant at Fluxx and magneticNorth. Fluxx are all about supporting organizations to bring about change and innovation through products and services – in essence, solving big business challenges with ideation, insight and a human-first approach. It is here that Hannah found a space to bring forth her Maverick ways, executing independent thought to develop the projects she works on.

The question is: What has made Hannah the Maverick leader she is? Was it the freedom in her upbringing? Or genetics? Perhaps it was the choices she made along the way, her accumulated experience and/or the inspiration of others? This is the question that we are going to explore in this chapter. Drawing on the stories of our interviewees, research on early years development and the development stages we go through in later life, we see how the inner Maverick that lies within us all can be brought to life at any point in our journey from childhood to old age.

We are born creative, explorative and challenging – and then?

Apparently, the five-year-old daughter of one of us authors is a creative genius. Well, if genius involves drawing pictures of barely recognizable animals in our first-edition copy of Charles Dickens' A Tale of Two Cities; or blocking the overfill outlet in the bath, filling the bath to the brim and beyond, leaving the taps on and running downstairs to see the water dripping through the living room ceiling and exclaiming in delight, 'It's raining inside!' – then she is without doubt a genius. A very disruptive, costly, thoughtless and messy genius. Thankfully, the research tells us that by the time she is 10 she is much more likely to be a normal, average dullard who draws pictures in drawing books and takes baths without flooding the living room.

George Land and Beth Jarman conducted a study into creative genius by assessing a group of children at 5 years of age, then again at 10 and again at 15 years of age (Land and Jarman, 1992). They defined creative genius as the ability to come up with new, different and innovative solutions to problems. The result showed a dramatic decline in creative genius as we get older, from 98 per cent at 5 years old, to 30 per cent at 10 years old and 12 per cent at 15 years old. And it gets worse! George and Beth administered the assessment to approximately one million adults with an average age of 31, and found that creative genius levels had dwindled to just 2 per cent. What is going on?

Ask yourself the question: How many times in a day does your one-year-old, two-year-old, three-year-old, hear the word 'no'? 'No, don't do that'; 'No, not like that, do it like this'; 'No, you can't'; or simply 'No! No! No!' Should we as parents and teachers feel guilty as the main culprit in extinguishing the Maverick spirit in each of our children by the age of 10? Well, let us offer you a 'get out of jail' card. On one rainy afternoon, when one of us was stuck indoors with a three-year-old, we noticed that the three-year-old said no to the one-year-old on average 10 times a minute – phew, we parents are in the clear – it's the siblings! There is of course a very serious point here.

Children have to learn to fit in, not to rock the boat, avoid conflict. In many instances this is critical; children have to be protected from dangers inside and outside the home. But a lot of the time we are simply, with good intentions, 'teaching' them the 'right' way to do things. Do as I tell you and things will work out better. We find ourselves correcting play activities so that our child puts the wooden blocks together to build a house the way a conventional house looks, or drawing a picture of a person the way a conventional person looks. Picasso never found fame by doing that! The point is, children are just playing, there is no right way to play. That is why it is called play, engaging in activity for enjoyment and learning, through curiosity, rather than following a pre-planned process in pursuit of a prede-termined outcome – that is called work. What is even more alarming to the average parent is that by the time the child reaches toddler age and is barely speaking, parents hear the word 'no' more times than they would care to shake a stick at, from their children – we wonder where they got that from.

Subconsciously, or indeed deliberately, we are focusing the minds of our children on the idea of what is right, what is correct, what is logical and repeatable. What we want and what we don't want. It is well known that many breakthroughs come from accidental discoveries of things that don't work out as planned, or happen coincidentally – Post-it notes, penicillin. What if we could reignite our playful mind, experiment without preconcep-tions, break the rules, notice what is happening rather than being frustrated by what was *supposed* to happen but is not happening!

Thomas Edison, inventor of the electric light bulb, is famous for having attempted 10,000 different approaches before finding success. But interest-ingly, he did not see his 10,000 previous attempts as failures. As he is widely reported to have said, 'I have not failed, I've just found 10,000 ways that won't work' (Elkhorne, 1957). This is play, the Edison version: 'I never did a day's work in my life. It was all fun.' An efficient mind, a work mind, limits distractions, looks for the path of least resistance and sees the unexpected or unintended as mistakes – not so for Edison. For those of us less playful and experimental than Edison, by focusing on right answers and efficiency, we create a barrier to creativity; serendipity passes us by. While we may have, and we think most of us do, a growing sense that things just 'ain't right', we are too distracted by the pursuit of getting it right, to do anything about it.

From the stories shared in Chapter 1, it would seem that creativity, seeing things differently, having the imagination and confidence to try new things, combined with a positive view of one's own abilities and an approach to problems and challenges based on learning and seeking mastery, is a prerequisite for a Maverick leader. So, despite the evidence from Beth and George that growing up is, at least in part, a process of transitioning from creative genius to compliant drone, the question is, *can we reignite our Maverick spirit?* To answer this question, we start by asking: Are Maverick leaders the result of nature or nurture?

A performance mindset or a master mindset?

Researchers Carol Dweck and Ellen Leggett started investigating why people behave in certain ways when confronted with a challenge (Dweck and Leggett, 1988). Some people rise to the challenge with enthusiasm, creativity and vigour while others seem to shy away from the challenge or become quickly overcome with emotions that impair their ability to function effectively. Most of their research was conducted with children.

Dweck and Leggett explain that a helpless behavioural response is characterized by avoidance of challenges, a decrease in self-confidence, decreased self-competence in the face of a challenge, and increased anxiety. Children who adopted a helpless response readily began speaking negatively about themselves and their ability to complete the task. They seemed to quickly spiral into a negative emotional cycle of self-doubt and inadequacy that then impaired or reduced their ability to complete the tasks successfully.

In contrast, the mastery-oriented behavioural response is characterized by individuals who are undeterred by failure and continue to seek out new challenging tasks. During the task itself, these children did not show the same sense of aversion to the challenges presented to them, nor (and importantly!) did they attribute any failures that did occur to themselves personally. Rather they externalized the challenge (and any failures) and saw it as something to overcome, separate from their own personal ability.

There is a story about the 18th-century mathematician Carl Friedrich Gauss. The story goes like this. As a boy at school Gauss was in a class when the teacher, fed up with the noise and distraction, set the whole class a difficult, laborious exercise to keep them quiet for as long as possible. The task was to add all the numbers between 1 and 100. All the children, including Gauss, started by trying to add up the numbers as follows: 1+2=3, 3+3=6,

6+4=10, 10+5=15, 15+6=21, and so it went on until most children lost interest, or had to start again as they got lost. Gauss, like his fellow pupils, started in the same way, but very quickly decided it was too difficult. Not that the problem was too difficult, but that the way he was approaching it was too difficult. Instead of giving up he decided to look for a different way of doing it. So instead of adding up the numbers in sequence, he tried adding up the numbers in pairs: 1+100=101, 2+99=101, 3+98=101, which led him to the idea that there are 50 pairs of numbers, which with this approach, always add up to 101. Since there are 50 pairs of numbers, the answer must be 50×101 which is 5,050 – which is the correct answer. He kindly shared the answer with the teacher just a couple of minutes after the exercise was set. Sadly for the teacher, this Maverick behaviour, challenging the approach rather than continuing to struggle with an almost impossible approach (in other words complying with convention) meant that the ingenious plan to keep the entire class silent for as long as possible was unravelled in an instant.

The point being made by Dweck and Leggett, and the story of Gauss, is the difference between seeing barriers or failure as limitations of the individual, as opposed to seeing failure and barriers as limitations of the approach, the system or convention. This is an important distinction, because to those children with a mastery approach, failures, when they did occur, did not become internalized as 'I am' statements, e.g. 'I am not smart enough to do this' but rather they remained separate and external, e.g. 'this is really hard'. Any set-back is motivation to look at the challenge in a different way, to master the problem at hand, through persistent effort. These children with the mastery mindset, in Dweck and Leggett's research, tended to be more solution-focused, optimistic in their ability to find a solution, spoke more positively about themselves, and monitored their own effort as they worked. Mastery-oriented children viewed the task not as a performance of their ability, but as an opportunity to engage with a challenge and 'learn something new'.

Perhaps most interestingly, children who adopted a mastery-oriented approach to problem solving seemed to learn from each failed attempt, and with every new attempt they improved their strategy for solving the task. These children learnt to 'fail forwards', which meant failure was not an event but rather a crucial and expected part of the process of discovering the solution. This is in sharp contrast to the helpless response – children who, upon the first failure, reverted to avoidance of the task and distraction tactics which were significantly less likely to yield a solution. The question is, what led children to adopt either a mastery-oriented or helpless response in the first place?

What the researchers discovered was that the behavioural response was related to the perception that the child held in relation to their ability to solve the challenge at hand. Even when matched for ability and intelligence, children adopted different behavioural responses in the face of a presented challenge. When the challenge was viewed as a performance task, in which the goal was to achieve, impress or gain approval, children who had a positive view of their abilities adopted a mastery-oriented approach and persisted in the task. However, those with a low perception of their own ability were more vulnerable to feeling insecure and afraid of failing in the task, and therefore more likely to adopt a helpless pattern of behaviour, seeking to avoid the challenge.

So, the research suggests that early childhood experiences have a lot to do with which mindset a child adopts: a positive view of their abilities or a negative view of their abilities. *Those who receive consistent and valuable feedback around their competence and abilities internalize a more competent sense of their abilities.* As a result, they are more likely to show an openness to new learning opportunities and adopt a mastery-oriented response, choosing tougher tasks, based on the perception that they could learn through doing them. So, it seems it is nurture rather than nature that has a big impact on a child's willingness and ability to confront and tackle the problems with confidence and creativity. But is that it? Does this mean it is all over by the time we are five: we are either a Maverick leader in the making or a compliant drone because of the way we are nurtured as a child? *Or can this mastery-oriented response to new challenges be resurrected later in life, and in so doing our inner Maverick reignited?*

It is never too late

From the research we have explored so far, it seems that the characteristics of a Maverick leader are psychological attributes. They relate to our personality composition which largely stems from our childhood, our early life experiences and the interactions we have with our environment. Our experiences by the time we are seven years old, the place in which we grew up, the context in which we grew up and the ways in which others (family, peers, society at large) treated us, are all ingredients that have culminated in developing our personality structure. While a large part of this is developed in the formative years (our childhood), the question is: Is the journey complete at, say, age six, seven or eight? *Thankfully, further studies tell us the journey is not complete until adulthood and even then, continues to develop into late adulthood.* So, as we shall see, personal growth and development remains viable until old age, and this is good news for any of us wanting to develop, sustain or regain our internal Maverick, regardless of our current life stage.

In order to explore this life stage approach to growing your inner Maverick, we draw on the theory of developmental psychologist and psychoanalyst Erik Erikson. Erikson's theory of psychosocial development explores how human beings develop a sense of identity across their lives (Robinson et al, 2017). His work built on the ideas of Freud, who highlighted the importance of childhood in moulding one's personality. However, Erikson expanded Freud's work by suggesting that identity is developed over the course of the human lifespan and through facing and resolving a key 'crisis' that emerges in each stage of development.

Erikson suggested that there are eight stages of development, each with its own nuanced challenge which needs to be resolved in order to integrate a new skill and build a platform to face the next life challenge. Erikson's eight life stages are:

- Stage One: Infancy – the ability to rely on the continuity of caregivers and ultimately oneself.
- Stage Two: Early childhood – the development of increased independence and ability for 'free choice'.
- Stage Three: Preschool age – the ability to approach what one desires with increased accuracy, planning and energy (purposeful goal).
- Stage Four: School age – learning to work, be productive and be a potential provider to others.
- Stage Five: Adolescence – the development of a new sense of 'continuity and sameness' in one's own eyes while being aware of the 'eyes of others', e.g. peer pressure.
- Stage Six: Young adulthood – the ability to commit to others in partnership and maintain this even at the cost of compromise and sacrifice, e.g. friendships, family relationships and intimate relationships.
- Stage Seven: Middle adulthood – developing a career characterized by commitment, compensation, contentment and competence.

- Stage Eight: Late adulthood/old age – the acceptance and emotional integration regarding one's own life, the human life cycle and one's own place in culture and history.

The eight stages and the corresponding 'crises' arise as a result of psychosocial forces which Erikson referred to as 'hazards of existence' (Sneed et al, 2006). These hazards will not always impact all of us at the exact same time, nor in the exact same way, hence there is room for individual differences in the journey across these eight stages of development. In fact, it may be much more of a cyclical process for many of us, rather than a purely linear process. It is also important to note that a crisis needn't be a catastrophe. *Rather, a crisis in this context is the emergence of a novel and different way of viewing the world that arises through some form of interaction with others and the world itself.*

This moment of insight can result in tension or internal conflict (cognitive dissonance) as the insight challenges our core belief system and the ways in which we have been relating to or engaging with others and our environment to date. These crises essentially result in a heightened state of curiosity, a state of questioning yourself and the world around you. When you are in this questioning state it can often result in feeling disconnected from yourself because you are re-evaluating that which you thought you knew for certain. These states of crisis therefore give rise to the opportunity for existential reflection and self-examination. While this may bring discomfort initially, it can also offer a tremendous opportunity for developing new insights and allow for new learning about yourself and your environmental context.

From wanting to win, to wanting to do good 'for people and planet'

Rik Vera is a dad and a grandad, successful in business and an agitator for doing good for people and the planet. But he was not born that way. Neither was he nurtured that way. To this day, Rik's dad is still trying to come to terms with why he did not pursue his outstanding talents as a poet, painter and a writer, having won national competitions in Belgium in all three categories as a youth.

Needs must! As a married man with a baby on the way he lost his job as a teacher when the school where he worked had to close. He took a job in sales. He was successful, because he had good relational skills and the imagination and creativity required – and he was never too concerned about following convention. But by his own admission, he did not have a purpose, other than to provide for his family and to win in sales. He saw business simply as a sport, a sport in which he fully intended to win.

That is, until he was invited to join a Belgian family firm making carpets and carpet tiles. For the first time, Rik found himself responsible, not just for sales, but for the factory, the production machine. When he walked into the factory he was shocked. He found working conditions that he thought had vanished with the passing of the era of his grandparents. He saw a factory polluting the air across the town, the town that was not only home to the factory but was also home to the workers' families. At that moment, Rik's inner Maverick was stirred into action. Business was no longer simply a game to be won. What he did and how he did it mattered. He was either going to contribute to the well-being of people and the planet or not. He had a choice to make. Did he see business as simply a means to make money, to win in the marketplace, or as the means of solving critical problems and creating outcomes 'good for people and planet'?

In Erikson's terms, Rik had hit a transition point, from one life stage to another, a crisis that needed resolution – the emergence of a novel and different way of viewing the world that arises through some form of interaction with others and the world itself. The choice was either to retreat and continue to play business as a game, or to apply his winning mindset to the challenge of transforming a polluting business into a sustainable business, doing good for people and the planet. Rik choose the latter. His inner Maverick was ignited and directed to transforming the entire life cycle of the company's products.

And it took a Maverick spirit to achieve the transformation of the company from a polluting, loss-making operation to a profitable company, breaking new ground in sustainable production. Rik told the company owners that there was market research to support a sustainable transformation. 'But there was no market research and I'm pretty sure that if I had done market research, the market would have said don't do it.' And Rik was not interested in 'greenwash'. He would tell his customers: 'To be very transparent, this is work in progress, we haven't figured it all out yet – this part of the process is OK, but this part of this production line is not OK, but we are working on it.' Maverick leaders know they cannot act alone and to bring others with them, honesty and transparency are prerequisites.

The catalyst: when competence and circumstances connect

Returning to the work of Dweck and Leggett: the researchers discovered that the responses different children had to the challenge at hand was related to the perception that the child held in relation to their ability to solve the challenge. What was important to note was the fact that participants assessed their own ability prior to the task, as well as assessing the goals of the task itself. If they felt they had the competence to achieve the task *or* they felt that the task was a learning opportunity rather than a pure performance-driven task, they adopted mastery-oriented approaches.

When participants viewed the task as performance-oriented, only those with a higher level of self-confidence (those who believed they had the abilities to achieve the task) adopted a mastery-oriented approach. Those who viewed themselves as inadequate opted for a helpless response. Hence, in the evaluation of the task, participants had already assessed their own ability. And as explained earlier in this chapter, those who had received consistent and valuable feedback around their competence and abilities had internalized a more competent sense of their abilities and therefore were more likely to show an openness to new learning opportunities through adopting a mastery-oriented response, or by choosing tougher tasks with the perception that they could learn through them.

But the process of receiving or indeed asking for feedback, or simply noticing that we are good at something does not end in childhood. As we go through our life stages we accumulate experience, we discover the contexts in which we thrive and those in which we do not. If we believe that our destiny is in our hands, we make choices. Choices to either change or leave those environments that stifle us and create or seek environments in which we can grow. Choices to surround ourselves with people who build our confidence as opposed to those that undermine us. And, as we grow, we develop our abilities and our confidence. Whatever our life stage, there will be many occasions when the confidence we have in our abilities and the inadequacy of the circumstances that confront us, connect. This is a moment, a catalytic moment in which not only can the inner Maverick be stirred, but it will give rise to a whole new purposeful pursuit of ethical change.

The right thing to do

Akin Thomas is a black man in his fifties. Twenty-five years ago, as a senior local government officer in London, with a young family, he was taking part in a training programme (an action learning set) organized by his employer when something snapped. That same day he went to his boss and resigned. A month later he left without a job to go to. It was not apparent to him, or anyone else immediately, why he had left or what had snapped. He spent the next month sitting at home. Looking back, he describes it as, 'It just felt right, [like it was] absolutely the right thing to do.' But there was a motivation, obscured at first but soon given voice to. 'I'm sick of the narrative around our people [black people], I'm going to change it, I'm going to create this amazing brand, this kind of global brand and I'm going to show people what we can do.' This is the birth of a Maverick leader. The stirring of the inner Maverick into action.

There must have been many accumulated experiences that led to the snapping point. Brought up in a social housing estate in Havant in the south of England, one of only two black children in the neighbourhood, Akin learnt early on to hold his own. During his time in local government, he noticed how many more of his black colleagues than his white colleagues ended up in some kind of disciplinary process or investigation. Including himself, investigated because the 'powers that be' could not understand how he could afford to send his children to private school. What was their assumption? In the answer to that question, you can see the narrative Akin and his black colleagues were subject to.

In the last 20 years Akin has built a company, AKD Solutions, in the belief that 'everyone has the right to shine'. The company is predominantly staffed by black people, not because of a deliberate recruitment policy but because seeing what Akin was doing, black people have stepped forward and asked to join, seeing it as a place where they can shine and help others to shine. A place with a different narrative. And AKD is changing the narrative through being the best at what they do.

Akin was not born a Maverick leader any more than any of us. He was not a Maverick leader at the age of 7 or 20 or 27. At 30 he was pursuing a successful local government career and dabbling in property investment to enhance the wealth of his family. But his understanding of what 'good' looks like, his recognition of a negative narrative affecting him and other black people, his determination that his children should live lives free of such undermining narratives, and his growing confidence that not only should things be better but that he could make them better, gave birth to a Maverick leader in his thirties.

Our Maverick spirit can be stirred at any point in life

In this chapter we have explored what makes a Maverick leader. We started with the idea that all children are born as Mavericks in the sense that they are creative, they test the rules, they break the rules, in fact they start off unaware of the rules. This is the very attitude that is the foundation for growth and development. We also recognized how the need to fit in, the concern for safety and well-being, the instruction from elders on the right way to do things, over time constrains and contains the Maverick spirit. Nonetheless, the Maverick spirit is part of being human. Of course, no one child's experience is the same as another's, in the extent to which that Maverick spirit is either given free rein or tempered with controlling guidance. The result is, as children, we have varying degrees of confidence in our abilities and in our appetite for trying new things, irrespective of our actual competencies.

We don't want to give the impression that breaking the rules, refusing to acknowledge any constraints, or living a life in denial of anything that might constitute a fact, is what being a Maverick leader is all about. One of the most insightful books we have read in many years is a book called *Curious* by Ian Leslie (2015). In it, he argues that the debate about learning, which pits curiosity and playfulness against learning facts, is about as useful as a skyhook. For those of you who don't know what a skyhook is, it is the first piece of equipment that the apprentice painter and decorator is asked to go and purchase from the ironmongers in order to hook horizontally opening windows up to the sky in order to allow the painter to paint the inner window frame without the inconvenience of having to hold up the window – do you get it?

Leslie's point is that the combination of learning facts, having knowledge and being curious fuels innovation. Curiosity without knowledge is ill-informed; knowledge without curiosity is stagnation. For example, an understanding of history in terms of sequence/flow of events, understanding people in terms of personality types, understanding Darwin's theory of evolution, understanding photosynthesis... all this knowledge, when combined with curiosity, can create new ways of thinking about the problems and opportunities that confront us.

Our experiences in childhood, the collision of nature and nurture, leads to unique outcomes for each of us. And one dimension in which we, as children, uniquely vary, is our confidence in our abilities to tackle new challenging tasks. These differences and the implications have been demonstrated through the research of Dweck and Leggett. So we asked the question: Is that it? By the time you are five, six or seven, has your life journey been determined in terms of the degree to which you could ever be, or ever will be, a Maverick leader?

To answer this question, we turned to the stories of Rik, Akin and Hannah. Before we recap on those stories, we should remind ourselves of what we mean by Maverick leadership. It is not simply a question of being counter-cultural, nonconformist, persistent and determined, although these are important qualities if you're ever to succeed as a Maverick leader. These qualities have to be harnessed to a cause, a purposeful, worthy cause to improve outcomes for people. As Rik Vera put it, 'good for people and planet'. As Akin Thomas put it, 'to change the narrative about our people'. And as Hannah Silverstein put it, 'to use brands to do good in the world'.

In exploring how and when each of our protagonists, Rik, Akin and Hannah, became Maverick leaders, there is no deterministic preordained route to becoming a Maverick leader. It's not a case of genetics; are we born with a Maverick spirit or not? It's not a case of nurture alone; similar upbringing in style and values cannot predict when, how or whether the Maverick spirit is stirred. It's not a case of circumstances alone; as we go through life we will constantly be presented with circumstances that need Maverick leadership action to improve outcomes for people, and yet so often we do nothing.

The Maverick leader is born at the moment our inner Maverick connects with our life experiences – our transition through life stages – and we are confronted by circumstances where we feel compelled to act, to change things for the better. And this can happen at any time to any of us at any stage in life.

This idea, that our Maverick spirit can be stirred at any point in life, irrespective of our early life experiences, is not just wishful thinking. It is underpinned by the research and thinking of Erikson. Erikson, as presented earlier in the chapter, describes eight life stages where our understanding of the world, our role in it and what it takes to succeed, is questioned by new demands, challenges and needs, creating a crisis in which we need to adjust our worldview and our identity, in order to continue to develop as a human being. As with all attempts to understand the complexity of what it is to be human and live a flourishing life, eight stages is a simplification – nonetheless useful in making a point. We argue, and see in the people we interviewed for this book, that *life is a concatenation of many stages and that any transition between one to another can give birth to a new Maverick leader.*

Over our careers, having talked to and met many hundreds of what we now call Maverick leaders, we have come to the conclusion that the nature/ nurture debate is completely the wrong debate. It is neither nature, i.e. some people are born Mavericks and others not, nor nurture, i.e. some people are brought up to be Mavericks and some are not. There is, in our view, a Maverick spirit inherent in the human condition, apparent immediately at birth and increasingly obvious through early years. *Whatever happens next, beyond the ages of one, two, three, four, five, six… that Maverick spirit persists – perhaps deeply buried, perhaps subordinated to a successful career following conventional skillsets and attitudes – but nonetheless lurking, ready at any moment to initiate a completely different life story for any one of us, as an individual and for those around us.*

In the next chapter we explore the first major differentiating characteristic of Maverick leaders: resourcefulness. How Maverick leaders create networks of ideas and people to give life to purposeful endeavour to change the world for the better. But no one can do this alone or as a complete outsider. Only through connecting people and ideas can we mobilize a critical mass, with sufficient insight and commitment to break down the status quo and sustain a new order.

CHAPTER THREE

Resourcefulness

Connecting people, ideas and assets

'Have you got an idea for a book?' This was the question that transformed the life of Robert Greene as he was approaching 40. He had always wanted to be a writer. But his early career as a journalist had come to an abrupt and premature end when one of his senior editors told him that he was ill-suited to a life in journalism and that he would be wise to seek a different line of work. This came as a shock. To Greene, it felt like 'a punch in the stomach' (TEDx Talks, 2013).

The resourceful person draws upon two quite different sources of inspiration. The first is *internal*, consisting of the totality of personal life experiences, the more varied the better. Seen in this way, Maverick leaders create themselves from within, transmuting breadth of experience into a particular form of mastery. The second is *external*, made up of the entire span of personal relationships, the more diverse the better. Here, Maverick leaders trade on extended networks, making connections where none existed and deriving new meaning and opportunities for growth. We return to Robert to examine internal resourcefulness.

Breadth of early life, depth of later life

After the punch in the stomach for Robert, the next few years were disjointed. He wandered the world, moving from one job to another, seemingly without any pattern or purpose. By the age of 36, he had worked in 50 different occupations. He still found time to write but his life felt rudderless. Then fate intervened. Joost Ellfers, a book packager, came onto the scene. He had read some of Robert's articles and had recognized his latent talent. He may also have recognized the lost soul that Robert had become.

It was Joost who asked Robert the question: 'Have you got an idea for a book?' Robert found himself grappling for an answer. Effectively, he was synthesizing the seemingly chaotic experiences of his earlier life. He talked about the exercise of power as a deeply embedded motive in human behaviour. He had noticed in many of the biographies he had read – and in many of the lives he had personally witnessed – that the desire for power was an overriding motive. He wanted to expose a truth about human nature that was too often repressed. There were many stories he could tell to make his case.

Joost was sufficiently impressed by the ideas that Robert was expounding so enthusiastically and spontaneously to offer to cover his living expenses while he wrote the book. *The 48 Laws of Power* was published in 1998. It sold over 1.2 million copies in the United States alone. For Robert, the act of writing the book was a huge release. The experience seemed magical. It was as though his whole life had been leading up to this achievement. Everything had come together as though pre-ordained. What had seemed like a disordered life now seemed patterned, pointed and purposeful. Since then, he has written five equally brilliant books on various aspects of human nature, all drawing upon the broad spectrum and eclectic mix of his life's experiences.

What is the moral of this story? For Robert, it suggests strongly that the mind, if given sufficient time, will make sense of experience, however disordered. What may look like – and feel like – a randomly conducted life will ultimately be given a focus and a direction, if given a chance. At a certain stage, provided one is patient and attentive, the mind will turn experience into meaning. What once may have seemed chaotic is made orderly. 'Everything clicked into place,' Robert has said. 'All my earlier experiences seemed like preparation for this achievement. I had been altered from the inside out.' Each of us, in our own way, at least to some extent, constructs ourselves from within. Robert's advice is 'to look inward'.

Robert interprets his life to mean that personal success is an internal, invisible and unplanned process. It is the haphazard result of 'many small improvements and adjustments'. It is an illusion to believe that success can be explained mainly by what can be seen happening to a person, as though it were the effect of a myriad of external causes. Personal development is not, essentially, a visible, deliberative and rational process. Every life needs an eclectic mix of experiences if it is to become something special. This cannot, of course, be a hard and fast rule for leading the life of a Maverick. There will be many exceptions – but we were struck by how many of the Mavericks we interviewed had led lives of such variety.

The lesson to be drawn from Robert Greene is that a rich life does not necessarily follow an orderly or purposeful sequence of events and experiences. It will often depart from the straight and narrow to explore further afield. It may relish diversions and get lost on purpose or pay special attention to the unusual and the diverse. The Maverick is noticeable for being particularly resourceful in drawing upon diverse experiences and finding inspiration in the unexpected.

Greene's main message, that the mastery of any particular skill is founded upon an internal journey of the mind, finds support in Anders Ericsson's famous 10,000-hour rule. This is the idea that, at a certain stage, the mind acquires a creativity and fluidity to make sense of experience and transmute it into expertise. The conscious art of living is to provide the mind with a sufficiently diverse and eclectic mix of experience out of which to construct unique interpretations and meanings.

Greene makes the point that it is through work that a productive and fulfilling life is most likely to be found. We each grow through the mastery of practical activity. In his case, it was writing. He acknowledges that this is an unfashionable point of view. Popular opinion prefers to believe that work, for the most part, is sterile and boring, and that true fulfilment is more likely to arise through spiritual exercise or psychotherapy. But Greene believes that this is a form of escapism. His message is straightforward: 'Transform yourself through your work.' Hence, to bring out the Maverick within, we should turn back the clock and pay closer attention to the (sometimes forgotten or overlooked) breadth of our early lives. We should draw upon this internal experience as a renewed source of inspiration and energy if we are to find depth and meaning in later life.

Hungarian psychologist, Mihaly Csikszentmihalyi, spent over 30 years researching creativity in the context of work productivity. As the author of *Flow*, he highlights the ways in which passion and profession come together in an intrinsic and often unconscious way to produce some of our greatest enjoyments through work (Csikszentmihalyi, 1990). In *Flow* he argues that our ability to be deeply engaged with our most creative self and simultaneously in our most productive space is enhanced when we love our work and have mastered our domain.

In our conversations with Mavericks, we realized that this combination of passion and profession, or personhood and professional identity, is inherently interwoven. It is no coincidence that, out of all the Mavericks we interviewed, a significant majority spoke about their work and their Maverick traits not as a professional identity but simply as *who they are*. Unlike many other occupations where employees try to draw clear boundaries between work life and personal life, for the Maverick leader there was an undeniable seamlessness between the professional being personal and the personal being professional. Their work is an outlet for personal expression. It is through their work that they transform both themselves and the world around them.

Freedom with belonging

Like Robert Greene, Andy Craggs has led a life of two halves and has drawn heavily on the breadth of his early life as a source for a more purposeful and resourceful vocation as a business consultant and coach today. But the road to get there has been varied, challenging and not always successful. 'From 20 to 40 I was working in a series of what may have looked like well-planned day jobs', he says, 'but I was really trying to find my place in the world of work and struggling quite a bit in the process.'

The diversity of his early years included growing up and living variously in South Africa, Canada, Switzerland, France, the United States and the UK. The son of an expatriate family, he experienced several school systems in a variety of languages, and by the age of 20 found himself having completed his studies in Johannesburg, South Africa. It was the era of apartheid and international boycotts against a country deemed a pariah by most of the rest of the world. Having experienced an international upbringing, he felt compelled to build his life without borders or prejudice. Exploring the world outside southern Africa was going to take much planning and many risks and to this day he is not sure how he found the resourcefulness to leave on a one-way ticket to New York with $200 in American Express travellers' cheques and the address of a family connection outside Manhattan:

I look back at all the people I was at school with, and I think, 'Why did I make it so complicated?' They all fell into great jobs in big companies, have a house, a pool, a spouse and three kids, a nice car, and enjoy each other's company at weekend barbeques. But somehow I had to find a way to get to where the 'action' was in the world.

To do so, he posted a hand-typed letter to the CEO of every company on the US Fortune 50 list, copying their names and addresses from an old edition in the school library. The letter proudly announced his imminent arrival upon their shores and the great value of his new bachelor's degree, so he was slightly disappointed to receive just three letters back, all of which were rejections. But this didn't stop him boarding the plane to New York in early 1985, landing with a wardrobe wholly inappropriate for January's minus 20 degrees. 'My parents thought I was crazy, but something made me do it.'

He describes his life since then as an existential journey, taking on a panoply of roles that moved from one set of responsibilities to another every five years or so. 'I was never quite doing what I thought I wanted, but then, if somebody had waved a magic wand and handed me the "perfect" job, I couldn't have told you what it was.' Nonetheless, his early experiences of languages and cultures proved to be useful as, after much badgering, he was allowed in for an interview at the *Wall Street Journal* (one of those three letters):

> It was solely because I had lived in Europe and spoke French and had briefly attended an Organizational Behaviour elective in South Africa, that a slim opportunity arose for me to be hired, not as a journalist as I had hoped, but in the personnel department at the time when the *European Wall Street Journal* was being launched.

This role soon took him to Europe for the EWSJ and Hong Kong where the Asian edition of the paper was growing:

> I was managing the expatriation contracts for a variety of young journalists including Adi Ignatius, now editor in chief of the *Harvard Business Review*, and Roger Cohen, now an author and senior columnist at the *New York Times*. We are still in touch after all these years and it has been a great inspiration following the life experiences of these remarkable story-tellers.

From the WSJ Andy moved to Watson Wyatt (WW) after having got to know them as the advisors to the WSJ on executive pay. He jumped at the opportunity to 'graduate' into the world of consultancy from HR, and once again his early experiences rather than any technical skills were what opened the door. WW was expanding their services into Europe and Andy volunteered to be part of the Paris-based team building a local client network for executive pay and HR systems:

> I had read Hemingway's *A Moveable Feast* and jumped at the opportunity
> to be a young man in Paris like him, though the reality on the ground was
> somewhat less glamourous than in the novel.

Exiled to the outer arrondissements due to his junior pay grade and working long hours to build up a fickle client base that was suspicious of US consultants, Andy rarely had time or money to be a flâneur on the terrace of *Les Deux Magots*:

> But I learnt a huge amount, including the vast cultural gap in business between
> American and European companies. Most of my later jobs were in fact versions
> of that early experience, where I was paid to be a sort of cultural ambassador
> between US HQ Executives and local management teams who were invariably
> at odds with each other about power, status or autonomy.

Subsequent ambassadorial roles took him back to California with WW as Regional Practice Leader, to Los Angeles with Walt Disney's Film and Television division, and to Europe, South America and Asia with Sony Pictures Entertainment.

Finding himself in London a few years later and at the end of his own expatriate contract with Sony, he called all the search firms he knew to once again figure out 'what was next'. With the help of Jan Hall at Spencer Stuart (another long-term networking contact and a superb mentor and coach), he joined the senior team at Egg, the first online bank in the UK. It was the height of the dotcom boom in 2001 and the start of the fintech revolution in the City of London. Part of the job was leading the bank's expansion into Germany, France and Japan:

> Again, the early cross-cultural experiences did their magic. I knew nothing
> about banking or technology, but Egg wanted to get into France, and I could
> speak the language and help build up the team.

But when the bank started to struggle – as did most dotcoms – he knew it was time to move again:

I was standing on the Eurostar platform at the Gare du Nord having just attended a meeting about selling our unsuccessful French business when the phone rang. It was the UK HR Manager at Saatchi and Saatchi, the advertising agency, whom I had met by chance at a conference a few years before.

Their industry was undergoing wholesale disruption from new digital advertising entrants like Google and Facebook, and the brief was to transform the culture of the firm to somehow respond accordingly.

Andy gratefully took the job, and under the guidance of regional CEO Richard Hytner, another highly creative leader, felt he was finally gaining some clarity about what he could contribute to the world of business:

It was a turning point. I discovered what business transformation meant. I understood the role of culture and leadership in the process of disruptive change. Over the next three years we created a series of interventions to engage our teams in change and innovation, working with brilliant people like John Pallant, our S&S Creative Director, external consultants like David Pearl, and management thinkers like Charles Handy.

Something had finally clicked for Andy in his early 40s:

Thanks to Richard, I reframed 'work' as more of a vocation and a mission. I wanted to make sense of human behaviour in the world of business. I wanted to understand the process of change and the value of diversity of thought when the future is unknown. It pulled together the cultural, creative and commercial strands that I had been playing with for 20 years.

This project, too, came to its natural end and the thought occurred to Andy, 'Maybe this is the time to do something on my own.' With a nudge from Hytner, Andy set up his own consultancy with Saatchi as his first client. 'Since then,' he says, 'a portfolio of complementary things around this theme of leadership and change has emerged and, hopefully, has begun benefiting others and contributing to social projects through my coaching and consulting.'

Once he found the confidence to go it alone, set up his own business, and trust in his own experience, he 'went back to school', completing behavioural and psychometric qualifications and then joining the Centre for Creative Leadership (CCL) and London Business School (LBS) as an Associate designing leadership programmes:

Those institutional relationships are absolutely key to continued learning. Otherwise, you're only as good as your last idea. You have to ask for feedback, learn from others, and stay abreast of what's happening if you are to stay relevant.

Building a new client network in leadership development and executive coaching over the last decade has finally made him feel he has impact as a business advisor. Working alongside educational organizations like CCL and LBS meets his need for 'freedom with belonging':

> My career had been a sequence of five-year stints, consisting of different assignments in different companies, in different parts of the world and in different languages. But I never felt an 'identity', let alone a 'destiny'.

He learnt a variety of skills, from ideation and creativity (at Saatchi), to business building (at Egg and WW), to organizational engagement (at Disney and Sony). But the moves from one job to another had been mostly unplanned. He jokes that in his early career he had just followed the advice of Yogi Berra: 'When you come to a fork in the road, take it.'

He was also deeply influenced by his father's professional life as an archetypal Company Man in the 1970s:

> Dad wore a suit every day of his life and seemed to hate every moment. Well, I decided business must be terribly boring and I certainly didn't want to go anywhere near it. But I had met people who seemed to find life interesting, creative, fun and colourful. I wanted to feel that way too but had no idea how to do it while making a living. It took 20 years, but I finally started to find a more definite direction and a more energizing purpose.

Like Greene, Andy's random journey to middle age was a necessary path to discover a personal identity and build the skills that would matter later. But many of those steps, starting with the one-way ticket to New York, involved uncertainty, regrets and anxiety. Moving away from family and home, repeated attempts at self-definition, compromises on money and security, and an uncertain reputation as 'rebel' or 'professional' were all bumps in the road that could have forced him back to a 'day job':

> I also got fired at least three times from various jobs, mostly through my own fault. Each time I had to sit back and try to ask myself the question: 'What happened, what have I learnt, and what's next?'

But undeterred, Andy now sees himself as an agent provocateur and Maverick of sorts. Having discarded what had frustrated him in work allows him to help others do the same in their own professional lives. His wide experience of organizational life, along with all its trials and tribulations, helps him empathize with those who are grappling with its realities. His management workshops are realistic and relevant. He confronts participants and clients with the everyday realities of organizational life and tests their ability to find new solutions and revise their behaviours. He is a natural coach and mentor for anyone looking for options and ideas about 'what's next' for them.

Yet he does not see himself as a Maverick leader in the 'hard' sense of the term, 'storming the gates on his own and disrupting the status quo'. He settles for 'doing things differently' but 'always with people in mind'. The values that inspire him as a 'softer' kind of Maverick are empathy, compassion and rapport.

Robert Greene and Andy Craggs exemplify the inner nature of resourcefulness. Let us now turn to examples of resourcefulness as an outward-looking skill.

Connecting the dots

Yusuke Mizukami is Chief of Staff at Bridgestone Corporation in Japan. He is not yet 40. He is influencing the global culture of the corporation through a pioneering, Maverick-like leadership development programme with London Business School.

At the age of nine, Yusuke found himself in a New York school unable to speak any English: 'I felt very miserable, not because people were making fun of me, but because I didn't understand what was going on.' Until then he'd been to school in Japan where everything seemed so well ordered. All that was required of him was to follow the rules. 'There was no necessity to think for myself.'

But now that he was in the United States, Yusuke was suddenly an outsider. He felt alone and lost. He knew he needed to find a way of exerting his presence. He had to think through everything. To feel happier, he had to form friendships.

The breakthrough came in a history lesson when the subject was Christopher Columbus. In anticipation of the class, Yusuke asked his parents to buy a book on Columbus in Japanese. He read it carefully and on the day of the history lesson he was able to enter fully into the discussion. 'That was the first day I did something well.' He was no longer the silent boy at the back, feeling lost and alone. He had become part of the group. He was connected.

He has never forgotten that moment. As a leader he sees his primary role as one of involving others in critical discussions: 'From that experience alone, I recognized that I needed to keep a wider view of the members in my team.' He sees the whole as far greater than the sum of the parts:

> I try to make a difference by connecting the dots – mainly by connecting the people in the company. It's a moral principle, I guess. Everybody may be doing the right thing on their own, but sometimes they forget there's something bigger going on outside their box.

Yusuke's leadership style hinges on inclusivity, on bringing everyone's voice into the discussion, and on building a genuine sense of team membership. He needs to ensure that none of his colleagues feels as he did before he read the book on Columbus.

Yusuke sees the challenge of building an inclusive culture as not labelling people. He is refreshingly honest with himself: 'Bias is what I fear the most right now.' He finds himself stereotyping Americans as being particularly gifted at both drawing the big picture and motivating the entire team while seeing his compatriots, the Japanese, as being better at handling the more detailed complexities. And he concludes, 'That's just labelling, and I may be wrong... I try not to do that, but it's very difficult.'

His resourcefulness is grounded in painful early memories of exclusion. He goes out of his way to connect emotionally with others in the firm. He sets aside Japanese norms of discretion and modesty to say openly:

> I want to be part of their lives and make their lives a bit better than what they are. I need to become a greater human being. I need to open my eyes to their way of thinking and make it part of my own way of thinking.

Three kinds of capital

If we step back from these stories of internal and external resourcefulness, we see that many Maverick leaders possess the entrepreneurial gift of not only spotting opportunities before others, but also bringing together the means by which these opportunities are captured. More specifically, they are skilled at exploiting any one of three forms of capital: economic, social and moral.

Economic capital is created by the trading of products and services. Mutually beneficial exchanges of commodities and cash enrich both parties to the transaction. One party places greater value on the cash; the other party on the commodity. The 'surplus' is economic capital. Since everyone has unique tastes and preferences, placing different utilities on different goods, the market is continuously nourished. Entrepreneurs are those who bring new and unique commodities to the market and thereby accelerate and deepen the exchange incentive.

Social capital is created by the exchange of intangible assets, such as ideas. Conversation tends to be the most effective medium by which information is exchanged and inferences are drawn. However, social media has radically increased the ease and opportunity for sharing stories, news and gossip, as well as knowledge. Creativity has been defined by Arthur Koestler as the bisociation of previously unrelated patterns of thought (Koestler, 1964). Social interaction thus serves as the engine of creativity. People share their unique experiences, thoughts and insights, and this generates an ambience of ideation and opportunity that can translate into social value.

Moral capital is created by acts of giving. Gifts, especially when they stimulate reciprocal acts of good will, contribute to the well-being of society.

Mavericks deal in all three forms of capital, but in different proportions. For the remainder of this chapter, we will deal with the ways in which Mavericks create social capital through their networking skills. But first let us examine the role of the brain as the agent of one's social self.

The social functioning of the brain

In the words of Aristotle, 'Society is something that precedes the individual.' He observed that 'man is by nature a social animal' and that 'anyone who either cannot lead the common life or is so self-sufficient as not to need to, and therefore does not partake of society, is either a beast or a god.' A life that is fulfilling will therefore be based on relationships. Our achievements as a species are essentially due to our cooperative instincts and collaborative skills.

Our intelligence is founded upon our ability to socialize. Across the animal kingdom, brain size is typically related to body size, but humans are the exception to the rule. In pioneering studies of primate behaviour, Robin Dunbar explained this anomaly by showing that the size of a species' neocortex, the part of the brain that is responsible for cognition, is more accurately correlated with the size of the social group that can be maintained as a cohesive, inter-related community (Dunbar, 1992). For human beings, he estimated this number to be about 150. In other words, the human brain has the cognitive capacity to form stable relationships with about 150 other individuals. He found this number (now known as Dunbar's Number) replicated across many different kinds of community throughout history, from hunter–gatherer tribes to the modern workplace. As a refinement, Dunbar has argued that social relationships can be tiered according to the level of intimacy: 5 loved ones, 15 good friends, 50 friends, 150 stable contacts, 500 acquaintances and 1,500 people you can recognize. The main point is not the precise numbers but that the brain is wired to be social. It is the centre of one's social self. We are 'in our element' when we are among friends and colleagues. Humans have a very strong need to belong to a group, to find their identity in companionship, and to engage in collaborative activity. E O Wilson, a socio-biologist, has said, 'To be kept in solitude is to be kept in pain and put on the road to madness' (Wilson, 2016).

Economists, true to their spirit, have attempted to put a monetary value on inter-personal relationships. For example, the simple act of volunteering for social work at least once a week has been estimated to increase happiness by the same amount as an increase in salary from $20,000 to $75,000. By the same token, meeting up with a good friend on a few days each week is worth $100,000 a year, while getting on well with your neighbour is valued at $60,000 a year. Conversely, the loss of a valuable social tie can be devastating. We don't have to take these exact numbers too seriously to recognize that the utility (and pleasure) of social belonging is often undervalued (Smith, 2013).

Neuroscientists, as well as anthropologists like Dunbar, have discovered the inherently social orientation of the human mind. For example, when the mind takes a break from an intensive activity, such as problem solving, it does not idle. It engages its 'default network'. This involves directing the imagination towards others – to what they may be thinking, or feeling or desiring. In other words, the reflex when we relax is to turn our minds to thinking of those around us, to place ourselves in their world, and to see things through their eyes. The simple act of connecting with others, even if only in our mind's eye, is a source of pleasure. Our brain, even in its quieter moments, remains attentive to our social situation. As Matthew Lieberman, a neuroscientist, explains, 'Evolution has made a bet that the best thing for our brain to do in any spare moment is to get ready for what comes next in social terms' (2013). It would seem as though we never switch off entirely from those around us.

Are we living in the age of connection?

Emotional intelligence expert, Daniel Goleman, highlighted research showing that, across 121 international companies, 67 per cent of the competencies required for excellence are related to emotional skills rather than technically based skills. Emotionally intelligent leaders account for two-thirds of top performers:

> At the top executive levels, everyone needs cognitive skills, to a certain extent, but being better at them does not make a star leader. Rather, emotional competence made the crucial difference between mediocre leaders and the best... On average, up to 90 per cent of their success in leadership was attributed to emotional intelligence (Goleman, 1998).

Maverick leaders know themselves and want to understand others. They have worked intentionally on developing their Emotional Quotient (EQ). Across our interviews there was a repeated theme of the importance of self-awareness. This was for two reasons: first, Mavericks often have to face resistance or 'go it alone' – they need to know themselves well enough to believe in what they are doing and why they are doing it; and second, Mavericks know the value of networking – they need to know how to engage others so as to be heard. Thus, they are able to build sustaining relationships across multiple different networks – the more diverse the better. Interestingly, our research with Mavericks showed that part of their network has often included one or more 'significant others'. These are individuals who have come alongside Mavericks to encourage, challenge, motivate or 'think with' them. They were made up of friends, coaches, mentors and other Maverick minds. There was no set type. But there was a pattern. Our Mavericks would deliberately seek out a significant other – a strategic influencer – someone who could help shape their dream and someone who would be honest enough to give them truthful feedback when they needed to hear it.

It has been said that the structural DNA of modern life is the network. All of us are members of self-forming, often self-managing groups of people held together by similar goals and ideals. Manuel Castells, a sociologist, has argued that, in today's society, power resides less in institutions, such as governments or large companies, and much more in the networks that comprise and structure our social life (Castells, 2009). Geoff Mulgan, a professor of public policy, reminds us of the wide variety of networks to which people can belong – networks of kinship, of work groups, of voluntary associations, of neighbourhoods, of influence and gossip, and of espionage or credit cliques (Mulgan, 1991).

The networked society is an ever-changing landscape. Many observers would say that the world has never been more densely connected. Digital technologies, including the internet, computers and mobile phones, have created a global infrastructure of simple, fast and cheap communication. The world's data is one click away from anyone.

This kind of mass mobile connectivity is becoming central to everything we do – and everything we are. Herminia Ibarra, an organizational theorist, describes our networked society as 'creating a fabric of personal contacts to provide support, feedback, insight, and resources' needed by anyone to get anything done (Ibarra, 2015). She distils the art of networking into three distinctive talents:

- **operational networking** involves performing a particular task – such as the 'day job' – more effectively by developing stronger relationships with the other stakeholders
- **personal networking** is concerned with leading a more fulfilling life by linking up with – and learning from – gifted individuals who are not part of the organization
- **strategic networking** is the pursuit of organizational success through the discovery of talented people whose insights and inspiration are germane to the problems and opportunities at hand

Mavericks are adept at playing all three of these games. The best Maverick leaders pay particular attention to strategic networking, which tends to be the one most neglected by most firms.

The Maverick as maven

In *The Tipping Point*, his celebrated book about how ideas catch on, how rumours spread and how fashions take hold, Malcom Gladwell gave fame and lustre to what it means to be a 'maven' (2000). Mavens are 'information brokers, sharing and trading what they know'. They are typically those who are the first to notice a new trend, usually because they have an appetite for seemingly irrelevant information and pay attention to the patterns emerging from it. They are also gifted at connecting with other mavens from different domains who share their skill in divining the future and anticipating changes. Lawrence Feick, who has written specifically about 'market mavens', sees them as 'individuals who act as hubs, gatherers and disseminators of general market information' (Feick and Price, 1987).

A behavioural theory of networking

'Your network is your net worth' (Gale, 2013).

One explanation for the performance of organizations has less to do with the raw talent of those who belong to them and much more to do with the quality of the connections between them. In other words, human capital is only part of the explanation. Social capital is the other part, and possibly the more important part.

The contribution that any individual player makes to the organization as a whole will be down to the quality of their network, the trust established across the network and the flow of ideas across it. *Indeed, a distinction is sometimes drawn between experts, who get things done because of 'what they know', and networkers, who achieve what they do because of 'who they know'.*

Four well-researched concepts are particularly useful for diagnosing the productivity of a network and the different roles that a Maverick can play in enriching it. The strength of a network depends far more on its structure than its size.

Weak ties

Every network is composed of relationships of different strengths, different frequencies of interaction and different degrees of diversity. For example, one's own network will have people who are close or remote, similar or different, familiar or strange. The size, density or homogeneity of a network is not necessarily an indicator of its productivity or creativity. Indeed, they are more likely to be indicators of stasis.

Whereas a strong tie is a relationship with someone with whom you interact on a regular bias, such as a family member, or a good friend, or a close colleague at work, a weak tie is with an acquaintance or a stranger with whom you rarely make contact, perhaps because they belong to a different organization entirely or lead a very different style of life. Weak ties can have a strong influence if they bring dissimilar people together. They can act as bridges between disparate groups with very different sources of knowledge. Conversely, strong ties can have a weakening effect if they imprison people in echo chambers of familiar and well-worn arguments and ideas.

For example, Mark Granovetter researched how people secured their first job (1973). He found that they would often refer to someone who had helped them. But on further inquiry this person would turn out to be a friend of a friend. In other words, acquaintances are more likely to be of help than one's closest mates. It turns out that the weakest ties often have the strongest influence. If you rely only on your closest friends, you literally don't get very far. They keep referring back to each other. At some stage we need to break free of these close ties, and escape into the wider network where a far greater variety of ideas and opportunities can be found. The Maverick is the one who ventures more naturally and easily beyond the 'incestuous' nature of close-knit companions.

In this respect, Mavericks are often adept at playing the role of the weak tie. They make a point of connecting with groups and individuals that are 'at the edge' of their network. They purposefully reach out to those with different experiences, interests and perspectives. In this way, the network benefits and draws upon the rich diversity of all of its members, opening up fresh opportunities and avenues for growth.

Armene Modi, a 73-year-old woman, has spent the latter part of her career campaigning for equality and empowerment for girls and women. In Chapter 1, we described how, while based in Japan, Armene came across a book that highlighted the appallingly low literacy rates for women in India – 61 per cent of Indian women were still illiterate more than four decades after independence. It was a statistic that felt like 'a wake-up call staring me in the face', she recalls. This statistic changed her life. She was determined to do something about it. At the age of 50, her inner Maverick had been ignited. 'Be the change you want to see in the world,' began ringing in her ears. After several meetings visiting existing projects and organizations, she realized she didn't want to join any of the existing NGOs and decided to start her own.

It was time to access her network. She wrote a one-page proposal and circulated it widely among friends and colleagues in Japan. The response was overwhelming. More than one thousand Japanese friends, colleagues and even strangers pledged their support. Arriving back in India in 1998, she continued to reach out to known and unknown resources.

'I started knocking on every door' she told us. Ultimately, she came across an award-winning surgeon and social activist, Dr Banoo Coyaji, who was running a project focused on women's health outside Pune where Armene was based. They were complete strangers to one another. Dissimilar in both profession and experience, Armene reflected that when they met, she 'had absolutely no background in social work'. She had an MA in teaching English to foreigners. Yet, Dr Coyaji agreed to mentor Armene, and became a vital resource in equipping her to launch her NGO, called Ashta No Kai, a Japanese phrase meaning 'for a better tomorrow'. From literacy to female adolescent education and empowerment, Ashta No Kai is still going strong 24 years later. With pride and humility Armene reflected that, 'the average age of marriage for our village girls has now risen to 19 from the earlier 13 years old.' This is a significant step forward on the journey of gender equality and educational empowerment and one only made possible by capitalizing on the weak ties that existed at the periphery of her social networks.

Structural holes

High achievers are noted for the openness of their networks. Ronald Burt, one of the founders of network analysis, believed it to be the best predictor of a successful career (Burt, 1992). Their success lies in actively seeking out relationships with individuals with whom there is no tie at all, particularly those who have complementary talents and know-how. This enables them to bridge what are called 'structural holes' in networks. These are gaps between individuals or parts of networks that are not currently connected but could benefit from being brought together. Mavericks, like entrepreneurs, are adept at noticing structural holes and brokering new relationships that span these chasms. This can have a disproportionately beneficial impact on the pace of innovation.

Structural folds

Networks are composed not just of individuals between which information flows can be managed and re-directed; they are also clusters of talent that can be blended and enriched. Whereas a 'structural hole' thwarts the flow of communication, what has been called a 'structural fold' (Vedres and Stark, 2010) inhibits the bonding of different communities of practice.

Thus, Mavericks are needed not only to create economic and social capital by emphasizing the flow of information across an existing structure but also to combine the know-how embedded in different work groups in new combinations. The first is about flow; the second is about bonding.

Samar, the young ambitious Egyptian woman we met in Chapter 1, has a passion for her work and for doing good in the Middle East. Her career started in pharmaceuticals, but her vocation was to work with the mechanical processes involved in the production of medicines. Inspired by her father and encouraged to pursue her education, Samar landed a role as a quality assurance inspector in a manufacturing company that by her own account was '99 per cent male'. Being the only female was a culture shock, for everyone. Despite being told she could not do that kind of work, and that this was not 'her place', Samar fell in love with the machines. She was fascinated by their complexity. Spending night and day, weekdays and weekends on site, Samar absorbed everything she could about the production processes. Yet despite her passion and commitment she faced significant push-back and isolation from colleagues because of her gender. She decided she needed to find a way to bridge the gap. She started by focusing on her social skills and building a rapport with her male colleagues. The idea was to develop a better understanding of their work and inform them of her role. She needed to find common ground in their shared value both to the organization and to their customers.

As described in Chapter 1, one day Samar bravely walked into the laboratory occupied by her male colleagues and announced, 'This is my space', promptly laying claim to a section of the laboratory, and refusing to be sidelined to the corner any longer. She reflected on how she went from being viewed as a policeman (due to her role) and someone to avoid, to being a friend, someone who would start each day by enquiring after her colleagues' well-being and that of their families.

Samar had the ability to identify the structural holes and folds that interrupted her productivity (and that of the organization) and purposefully worked to close the gap. This is a skillset she has used extensively since then, as she has moved from one company to another. Her capacity to see the gaps and ask herself, 'What is my competitive advantage here?' has enabled her not only to develop an impressive and diverse career history, but also to bring together disparate subgroups for the betterment of the whole, whether in the workplace or society at large.

While working for the Ministry of Health, for example, she realized she was the only person able to read stability reports for registering medications from a unique manufacturing perspective. Drawing on past experiences, her niche in-depth knowledge and technical background of how medicines are manufactured meant that at the age of 30 Samar was able to identify and fill a structural hole in the Ministry of Health and leapfrog her career in the process. Currently working at Johnson & Johnson, Samar has launched a Father's Day Celebration campaign that aims to emphasize paternity rights in an effort to encourage men to take greater responsibility for caring for family members, thereby challenging unhealthy gender stereotypes, increasing men's participation in the life of the home and encouraging women's participation in the workplace.

Samar defines herself as someone able to see the barriers in the supply chain, whether that supply chain is getting a machine to a customer or a drug to market or greater gender equality in the workplace. Samar expresses pride in her capacity to notice barriers, then break them down and then fill the gaps. By making connections beyond her immediate network, working across organizational departments and transcending expected cultural norms, Samar irons out the structural folds... and it usually takes her 'only six months' to do so, she says with a smile.

Homophily

Because like attracts like, human groups can often come to resemble peas in a pod. This is the state of homophily: everyone thinking and acting alike. Effectively, each network can easily become a caricature of itself. A healthy, creative network, on the other hand, will contain within its borders a great variety of human styles and skills that, together, amount to far more than the sum of the parts. Typically, Mavericks have an antipathy towards homophily of any kind.

So, to summarize, Mavericks are network brokers. They are masters of the weak link, enabling them to draw inspiration from a greater diversity of knowledge sources. At work, probably more than two-thirds of most managers' time is spent with no more than five colleagues, with much less attention given to those at the edge of their particular circle of acquaint-ance. Yet the evidence is that it is precisely at the periphery of each person's 'tribe of 150' where they have the most to learn and gain from getting better acquainted. This is where Mavericks typically spend much of their time.

Andy Craggs boils it down to a simple mantra: 'Re-educate yourself every five years, re-invent yourself at least once a decade. I think the skills we need to be Maverick leaders in our life are all contained in that journey.'

What can these examples of internal and external resourcefulness, and leveraging the edge of our networks, tell us about building such skills in our own lives? The key is to deliberately build our awareness and then apply all three kinds of capital with deliberate intent. In this way we too can build our resourcefulness as leaders and human beings.

In the next chapter we consider how the choiceful challenge of accepted norms, conventions, rules and procedures that bind and constrain our think-ing and behaviour is essential if we are to move from the status quo to a better place. We learn from our Maverick leaders the importance of living a life true to ourselves, true to what we really think, to our experience and our intuitions about how things need to change to be better. Not because we know all the answers, but because we know we have to question accepted wisdom if we are to continue to change the world for the better.

CHAPTER FOUR

Nonconformity

The instinct to question

To be independent of public opinion is the first formal condition of achieving anything great.

HEGEL, 1820

'Michaela pupils SMASHED it', tweeted Katharine Birbalsingh, the Founder and Head Teacher of one of Britain's newest schools (2019). Her students, all from under-privileged backgrounds, had outperformed almost all other non-selective state schools in the country. 'It's really great. When you think all of our kids are from the inner city, they are from challenging backgrounds, they are deprived kids.'

This outstanding performance at Michaela Community School did not happen by accident, nor did it happen by following the conventional establishment thinking in public-sector schools and the government department responsible for education. It came about because an individual, a nonconformist individual, used her experience and her intuition to establish new rules, new ways of working, new norms and values that would work for the young people she was responsible for.

When things aren't working, when outcomes are poor, or unfair, or simply just not as good as they could be, conforming to the status quo is not going to bring about the change required. It takes the Maverick's spirit of nonconformity to conjure new and different ways of doing things. This is why nonconformity is our next differentiating characteristic of the Maverick leader. It is not enough to want things to be better; it is not enough to connect ideas and people behind a movement to make things better, we also need to challenge and break with convention, established norms and procedures.

Truth to one's mission

Katharine Birbalsingh founded Michaela Community School in controversial circumstances in 2015, and was making national news and challenging many of the most strongly held educational orthodoxies. To those who knew Katharine, this was not at all surprising. In 2017, Ofsted, the schools inspectorate in England, had judged Michaela Community School 'outstanding' in every category, a rare achievement, particularly for a newly established school. Then, in 2021, as a compliment to Birbalsingh's achievements, another school, based on her radical principles, opened in Stevenage.

So, what exactly are these unconventional, unfashionable and contentious principles – beliefs that have disturbed the educational establishment? Around 50 years ago, they would have been treated as common sense; but today, they are anathema to most of those running the Department of Education, and more particularly, those who see themselves as the guardians of progressive education in Britain. Katharine lists the three most important principles as:

- belief in personal responsibility
- respect for authority
- a sense of duty towards others

She summarizes her vision of Michaela as 'bringing the values of a private education to young people of all backgrounds by providing a highly academic curriculum and strong discipline.' The school focuses on traditional subjects. Unlike most other state schools in London, Michaela does not offer classes in citizenship, or information and communications technology (ICT), or design and technology (DT). The school day, from 8.00 am to 4.30 pm, is longer. In the final hour of each day, specialist subjects are offered, such as Latin and Mandarin.

Ironically, she pays little attention to Ofsted ratings. She prefers to judge her achievements by her own standards, saying in her typically forthright manner that 'the rules that inspectors have about teaching are an absolute nonsense.'

Katharine's hard-won principles translate into a set of unfashionable practices. She insists on a strict dress code; for example, every child must wear a uniform, including standard shoes; no jewellery and no ear studs are allowed; the same style of pencil cases are prescribed for all; no talking is allowed as pupils move from one classroom to another between lessons; there is detention for pupils who break the rules; and in the first week of school every pupil attends a 'behaviour boot camp' to get fully acquainted with the school rules.

To some it may seem contradictory that while Katharine has established a school that does not conform with current educational establishment thinking, she is at the same time insisting on conformity in the way her students behave and are dressed. But that would be to misunderstand the point about nonconformity. Every collective endeavour establishes rules and norms to facilitate cooperation and achievement of some kind. And every nonconformist accepts and follows many of the conventions of the collective. The pupils at Michaela may decide to reject the school uniform, i.e. not to conform, but that would not make them Maverick leaders, unless they associated that rebellion with the betterment of others. They would simply be rebels without a cause.

More important than discipline, Katharine sets high expectations of her pupils. She despairs of those school cultures that lack aspiration, and instead find excuses for poor performance, slovenly behaviour or disobedient attitudes. She believes in her children and their potential: 'I've always known the school is great, because I'm here every day and the children are wonderful. What I'm most proud of is the young adults they've become. They are good people.'

As a black girl winning a place at Oxford, Katharine had always resented the paternalistic and condescending attitudes of 'white liberals' towards minority families. 'Rather than allowing black people to take responsibility for themselves... they think they must help us.' She fears that this patronizing attitude, which she sees as driven largely by white guilt, is now hard-wired into the school system. It has become, in her words, 'a culture of excuses, of low standards'.

Foolishly perhaps, she chose to air her beliefs at the Conservative Party conference in 2010. Despite a rapturous reception by the attendees of the conference, it upset the teaching profession, alarmed the educational establishment and angered the trade union of teachers. She was fired from her school. She was out of work and ostracized by her own profession.

Self-efficacy

The story of Katharine Birbalsingh is a tale of extraordinary self-belief. She practises the very same responsibility that she seeks to inculcate in her pupils. Her life is a profound learning journey. Her beliefs are born of practice, of trial and error, and of observing the impact of different approaches. She is intensely pragmatic. What she knows about good teaching comes from first-hand experience rather than received opinion. Her policies and practices are not ideological even though others have sought to make them so.

She is an exemplar of self-efficacy, the internal belief in our abilities to perform and our capacity to cope. It's a 'can-do' attitude. Having high self-efficacy means we are able to make decisions and act, believing that we will effectively manage the challenges that may arise because we have the 'internal toolkit' to do so. Self-efficacy theory, developed by Stanford University psychologist Albert Bandura, highlights how 'people's level of motivation, affective states and actions are based more on what they believe than on what is effectively true' (Bandura, 1997).

Self-efficacy can be built up or strengthened over time; it is based on our past experiences, role models, experiences of mastery, social influence and emotional states. We are, of course, influenced by events, by upbringing, by social pressures and by genetic inheritance, but above all we are the artefact of our own free will. The extent to which we believe in our own capabilities is also a strong indicator of the extent to which we can empower others. Self-efficacy is an internal belief that propels us not only into our own action, but also serves a great purpose in mobilizing others towards collective action. In Katharine's case, she must have given herself the right and the obligation, from an early age, to think for herself and take full responsibility for her own life.

Unlike self-esteem, which is a judgement of our own self-worth, self-efficacy is an existential commitment to one's own capacity to build a worthwhile life. It is a promise to oneself, not an assessment of oneself. Over the course of a well-lived life, it tends to strengthen as the sense of personal accountability also strengthens.

Bandura, argues that 'It is not enough to know stuff to be smart; we need some kind of motivation, purpose or strong desire that pulls us towards achievement.' This sense of possibility can only be furnished by the person him- or herself. Self-efficacy is the critical ingredient of personhood.

This taking of responsibility for personhood is akin to what some psychologists have called an internal locus of control. Birbalsingh was never one to make excuses for setbacks or place the blame elsewhere when things went wrong. She has always owned her own decisions.

One of Katharine's missions is to pass on something of her own self-efficacy to those under her care. She wills her students to will the best for themselves, to dream big, to embrace self-accountability and go for it. She encourages them never to cast themselves as victims. This is the Maverick leader within her – the compulsion she feels to instil a sense of aspiration in each and every one of her charges.

She herself has demonstrated self-efficacy in three crucial ways. First, she chose to meet a challenge that would test her self-efficacy to the limit. Founding a school from scratch is a daunting task, especially if it is designed to upset the status quo. Second, she has always gone out of her way to set an example for everyone she works with. She is in the school all day and every day, in the company of her students and staff. In effect, the school has become her life. Third, she sets high expectations of others that then, at least to some extent, become self-fulfilling.

In telling the story and achievements of Katharine, our point is not to suggest that there is one and only one effective way of running a school; it is to demonstrate what can be achieved when one follows one's beliefs – *beliefs that are born of practice, first-hand experience, rather than received opinion, shaped by trial and error, and by observing the impact of different approaches.*

Do it your way

Education is about creating developmental and transformational experiences for others. Transformation and development take place in relationship with others. When relating, we are very quick to recognize inauthentic, 'jobsworth', regurgitation of the rulebook. And we instinctively back away in retreat or rebellion. The opposite of the jobsworth is authenticity, genuine interest in others and the ability to think and act for oneself. None of which is dependent on school uniforms. There are many examples of great schools where school uniform is not a requirement. The point is, Katharine set about doing the job her way, based on her experience, centred on the development and transformation of the young people in her care. Inner city children who in the conventional approach to state secondary education were underperforming.

When we interact with others we can transform them and ourselves. Sometimes in a big way, sometimes in a small way. Whether we are a teacher, an engineer or a manager, whether we work in retail, in a factory or in an office, even as a passport control officer.

Our work often takes us abroad and often times we return to the UK tired and impatient to be reunited with our families. And what do we encounter, having navigated the long and convoluted corridors of Heathrow Airport, our level of stress and irritation rising? The queue for passport control. Why, we ask ourselves, is there a queue? After all, they know we are coming. One time, having queued for two hours, we were met by an unusual experience. As we finally reached the counter, the passport official, whose job it was to check our passports said, 'How are you?' He followed up with, 'Have you been anywhere interesting?' And as we disclosed the details of our trip he engaged with genuine interest, sharing his experience of the place we'd been to. Our mood changed from impatience and frustration to a much-needed sense of well-being and connection.

The way this passport officer chose to interact with us changed our mood and, it seemed to us, sustained his own positive outlook. He broke with convention, not the written rules, but with the convention of a somewhat severe, authoritarian and unfriendly demeanour adopted by most passport control officers, at least in our experience (and not just at Heathrow). His break with convention, his nonconformity, may seem trivial, but it had an immediate positive effect, not just on us, but on the many people in the queue ahead of us and behind us. And the effect was not fleeting. He role-modelled how to do a job, that by the nature of its repetitiveness is almost inhuman, in a way that was totally human – a lesson for all of us when knee-deep in the many repetitive mundane tasks that need doing.

'I enjoy blowing things up too much to do otherwise' was the excuse that Sidney Alford used to explain why, in his eighties, he was still going his own way and inventing explosive devices. Described in his obituary in *The Times* as a 'Maverick explosives expert who marched to the beat of his own drum', Alford led an extraordinarily original life (*The Times*, 2021).

Growing up in London during the Second World War, he became fascinated by bombs and ammunition. He made fireworks out of the unexploded magnesium alloy incendiary devices that he would retrieve from the bomb sites of the London blitz. At school he made bangers out of nitrogen tri-iodide and set them off under the chair of his French teacher.

Enrolling at Southampton University, he found the experience ponderous, rigid and frustrating. He dropped out. Shortly afterwards, by chance, he met a French chemistry professor who, impressed by his originality of mind, offered him a research post at the University of Paris. He went on to earn his doctorate there, studying the chemistry of plant products. From Paris he went to the University of Tokyo to continue his chemical research. Returning to Britain in the late 1960s, he was unsure as to what to do next. For a while, he researched the chemistry of the brain. Feeling somewhat lost but having learnt Japanese, he found himself at one point acting as the official interpreter for Emperor Hirohito on his visit to the UK.

His interest in explosives was re-ignited, if that is the right word, by the outbreak of hostilities in Northern Ireland and the ensuing Troubles. Working alone at home, he invented a system for destroying IRA bombs. It was called a 'water-lined shaped charge' and took the form of a 3,000 mph jet of water strong enough to pierce armour. Neighbours were suspicious of the huge bangs emanating from Alford's garage and reported him to the authorities. But instead of arresting him, the security officers who descended on his garage immediately recognized his talent and wisely chose to put him in touch with the Ministry of Defence. Here, he worked on many projects over many years, but particularly devices for destroying the mines, bombs and IEDs (improvised explosive devices) of terrorists and other assorted enemies.

In 1976, despite his growing reputation as an explosives engineer, the Royal Armament Research and Development Establishment turned down his application for employment on the basis that he was too old to be inventive. The more likely explanation is that his Maverick unconventionality aroused suspicions that he would be difficult to control, and frustrating to work with. So, in 1985, tiring of the attempt to form alliances, he set up his own business, Alford Technologies. It was here that, with others, he did his best work. His eclectic but brilliant inventions included Dioplex, a linear cutting charge for slicing sunk ships into smaller pieces to enable them to be salvaged, the Bangalore Blade to blast holes in razor wire defences, the Boot Banger to blow open the boots of booby-trapped vehicles, and the Gate Crasher for punching holes in the walls of buildings containing hostages.

He was immensely admired by the Americans with whom he worked. They loved and admired his can-do attitude and the originality of his ideas. His British clients, however, were less enthusiastic, if only because, as his son put it, his plain speaking 'put a lot of noses out of joint'. *The Times* obituary observed that:

A British establishment of which Alford was emphatically never a part did not always appreciate his creative (and destructive) genius, especially in the earlier years of this somewhat combustible character's career.

Alford was a Maverick leader par excellence. He had always been self-taught, was a natural self-starter, and was incapable of being anything other than independent minded. He disliked the feeling of being imprisoned in what he saw as the 'pointless rules and regulations' of most organizations and institutions. He preferred to set his own standards. Alford was a true original. He lived by his own rules.

Originality

The Maverick leader is an original. They are their own person; they may admire others, and they may well have learnt from others, but they take full responsibility for the person they are; they are inner-directed, taking the course that they believe is right, not the one that others have charted for them; their criteria of value and standards of performance are of their own choosing; theirs is not a second-hand life or a derivative of some other person's model of excellence, it is theirs and theirs alone.

Sidney Alford had no interest in being different for the sake of it. His obsession was solving a particular class of problems. He was only as unconventional as he needed to be to resolve the problems that intrigued him. He had no interest in deterring others from pursuing their particular interest in their own way. He was not in the least judgemental of others. All he wanted was to be allowed to follow his destiny and express his talent as he saw fit and, as a free spirit, he wanted others to be free spirits too.

His nonconformity possessed a genuine authenticity. He was utterly true to himself. There was no posturing or pomposity. He had no need of the admiration of others. He sought no reward other than the satisfaction of solving a particularly thorny problem. What motivated him was mastery in his chosen field. This was the source of his vitality. As a Maverick leader, he was as nonconformist as the problem demanded. And the problems he addressed were those that he deemed to be important. His nonconformity got most traction only when he found fertile ground, when he was welcomed and supported by his colleagues in his business and those in the United States who saw the potential in his challenge to convention.

Fertile ground

On the second day of her first job, Nasrin Siddiqa realized her vocation. Fight for the rights of the oppressed. She described her mother as a silent revolutionary, and the source of her inspiration. It was a shocking experience of being exposed to the severe inequality of women at the hands of fundamental religious leaders at the age of 24 that left Nasrin convinced that she had to do something. She realized her own agency, and her inner Maverick. 'Leadership', she argues, 'is in everyone' and 'sometimes you have to fight alone.' Yet, she reminds herself and us that being nonconformist is a delicate balance between breaking the system but also showing respect for tradition. To be a Maverick is not the same as being reckless. Her determination to address the issues of child labour in her community and Bangladesh at large have frequently put her at odds with government officials, friends and even family members. At times, it has come at great cost, but it is in these times that she reminds herself that her work is not about money, position, power or property; it is personal. As we will come to see later, for Maverick leaders, the professional is always personal.

The stories of Katharine Birbalsingh and Sidney Alford, and many of the Maverick leaders featured in this book, demonstrate the struggle that is inherent in nonconformity. The struggle to find fertile ground. To challenge convention as a Maverick leader is not to refuse to conform for the sake of it. It is not about refusing to conform to any convention. *It is the choiceful, considered rejection of convention, rules or traditions that get in the way of better outcomes for other people.* Maverick leaders are rebels with a cause. They rebel against that which impedes progress. In many ways, like all of us, they conform to social and organizational norms. To do otherwise is to reject, in totality, your community and as such become an outsider, unable to influence or impact others for good.

But even choiceful nonconformity can be so threatening to colleagues or fellow citizens that only two avenues remain open to the nonconformist: at best martyrdom, at worst futility. If we want our instinctive, intuitive, ethical and hard-earned sense of selective nonconformity to get traction, within our lifetime, we need to find fertile ground. Katharine and Sidney had to face rejection and find acceptance elsewhere to put their nonconformity into practice.

Going elsewhere to find fertile ground does not always mean leaving your organization or community. It can be as much about finding a different circle, set of connections, a different boss or community leader. A group or an individual who, even if they don't agree with you on all points, get you, get what you are trying to do and are prepared to support you and engage in the struggle with you. Studies repeatedly show the importance of peer group relationships on the socio-emotional development of young people (Pepler and Bierman, 2018). To flourish, to be able to make the most of our talents, to follow our convictions, to challenge damaging conventions, to be an effective nonconformist, we need the support, encouragement, engagement and contribution of others. Maverick leaders neither bang their head against a brick wall nor retreat into cynicism; they join forces to demolish damaging conventions.

Annmarie, whom we first met in Chapter 1, knows full well that she is not going to change the youth justice system in the UK by battling alone from within; neither is she going to change it by fighting alone from its outskirts. Annmarie is cultivating fertile ground by making connections with different stakeholder groups, in government, in business, in academia, in communities. She is going where she can get traction, where her nonconformity, her radical perspective on the youth justice system can be taken up, developed and pushed forward with others. She is building a new leadership network and Centre of Excellence, a place to connect nonconformist thinking and experimental practice with those developing and executing operational practice in the youth justice system.

Hannah Silverstein, whom we met in Chapter 2, passionate about helping people to learn, grow and do better as human beings, could not put her radical approach to marketing and brand creation into practice without joining forces with others who were willing to experiment with new approaches. To change the future of business, to provide an exemplar, to inspire others, to show what is possible, Hannah had to find fertile ground in which her nonconformist ideas could flourish. And that is what she did by joining Fluxx. In fact, the organization even calls its employees 'lovable misfits'!

Janna El-Hadad, the marketing lead for the Gulf with Johnson & Johnson Consumer Health Middle East knows what fertile ground means for her. 'What pushes me forward is the community... if the culture of the company does not fit, I leave.' Janna thrives on interaction with others, others who speak their mind, others who engage with their whole person. It is not a case of having to be with people who agree with her. Far from it, Janna actively engages with people who see things differently. It is a case of having a place within which to engage, debate, challenge and act. Janna does not conform; she challenges the status quo. She does not conform to the expectations of her as a young woman, whether that be working with the poor in Egypt, or in business in the Middle East. But equally, she needs, and she finds, a community that enables her to flourish.

There are lessons here for organizations. The consistent calls from the board and the CEO for more innovation, more risk-taking and more agility, so often fall on deaf ears, or, to use our analogy, on infertile ground. At the same time that people are calling for innovation, their organization's processes, bureaucracy and managerialism act to silence and disaggregate dissenting voices. So often the response to dissent, to challenge to convention, is to reinforce control, to isolate the 'troublemaker'. *What if we did the opposite? What if we fuelled a conversation between dissenting voices and joined in? What if we asked the question, what are some people seeing that we're missing? What if we created space for experimentation to test and challenge the conventions, the norms that some people see as barriers to betterment?*

Playfulness

One of Giles Ford's first challenges after leaving Deutsche Bank as Head of Learning and Development was to go back and fulfil an invitation to run a training programme for them on creativity and innovation through his then new company Alchemical Arts. He said he would be absolutely delighted to take it on, particularly because creativity was not only one of the bank's espoused values but also one of his personal passions.

He was allotted the Morgan Grenfell boardroom as the venue for the workshop. A handsome room, it boasted a wall-to-wall carpet that Giles described as 'four inches thick', on which stood a long, beautiful, polished table that 'you could see your face in'. On the walls hung grand paintings of 19th-century, suited, moustachioed bankers. Entering the room Giles felt a surge of dismay, thinking to himself, 'This is impossible. It can't be done. No creativity or innovation will ever happen in this place.' Giles felt viscerally that the room was an anachronistic projection of lineage, prestige and power. It exerted a form of psychological control over those whose who entered it. It was a sophisticated theatrical construct imbuing the room with the heavy weight of status and stasis – the very opposite of the energies needed to catalyse the freedom to create, to be different and to explore. Giles knew that investment banking had been founded on adventure, risk and exploration (as well as a degree of exploitation). He also knew that this environment lent itself more to impressing the bank's clients than acting as a laboratory of ideas. Moreover, it was based on a profound lie. From his time at Deutsche Bank he knew that everything moved super-fast – money, politics, economics, regimes, success and failure. Advantage in trading decisions was measured in milliseconds not millennia. Things were fragile. This was a cover up. He believed that two of the biggest obstacles to invention, ingenuity and innovation were the denial of truth and a sense of fragility.

Not to be defeated, he said to his team, 'Go to the store and get 10 rolls of bubble wrap and lots of rolls of sticky tape… you know, the one marked FRAGILE in red across it… as quickly as you can, because everyone's arriving in half an hour.' Duly equipped, he asked them to bubble-wrap every chair and every Victorian portrait in the room and cover the floor in industrial sheeting. Then they put fragile stickers on everything. He asked them to replace the investment and finance journals in the rack on the side table ('derivatives in Brazil… boring as hell') with a whole range of materials from the local newsagent ('colourful cartoons, illustrated magazines, science journals, daily newspapers and hobby monthlies') so that, while the rack might initially look familiar, its contents would surprise them, widen the spectrum of thought and de-stabilize anticipated normalities. Later he would ask the participants to cut them up and use them to create giant 10-foot collages to envision what Deutsche Bank could look, feel and be like if it were to be truly creative in the future.

While these preparations were being made, walkie-talkie-carrying, uniformed 'Security' flocked onto the scene to stop proceedings. They'd seen what was going on as an intrusion, an invasion, and a threat (which, for Giles, was the whole point of the exercise).

'Stop. What's going on? Who are you? What do you think you are doing?' Giles' response was that he was wrapping up the boardroom for the bank's protection – that the bank was in grave danger (but certainly not from them!) 'Ring my boss if you need to.' His former boss explained that this was not an activist group in action, or worse, but purely a training session. As Security was being called off, so the traders and brokers who had been invited to the session started arriving.

Colleagues had warned Giles that as soon as they entered the room, they would take one look, turn round and walk away. Yet, none of them did so. They understood immediately. They were being unshackled from convention, constraint and predictability. They literally had a blank canvas in front of them (the whole room) unimpeded by the weight of expectation. Within minutes they were on their hands and knees making works of art to represent the questions, concerns, opportunities and choices that they believed to be the performance-critical issues facing the bank.

By common consent, it turned out to be a stunning success. The participants had discarded their managerial and professional masks and were communicating as passionate human beings about their real concerns. They were raising the problems that needed to be faced and coming up with imaginative answers. After the workshop, two of them asked Giles for a job.

As Giles remarked, 'For less than £100 and totally harmlessly we had destroyed the prevailing psychic prison and created a symbolic, fun and different way of perceiving the world.'

Years later, it was the CIO Maverick leader in the bank who spotted his originality and suggested he head up the training function worldwide. Originality and the exploration of possibility are important to Giles. He is not satisfied with standard approaches to learning, development, communication or indeed anything. With his co-founder of Alchemical Arts, Giles Foreman, a brilliant acting coach, he has experimented with many fresh approaches such as:

- bringing the Myers-Briggs indicator to life for war reporters, by having them act out different character types in a variety of tricky situations – all in real time
- inviting a marketing agency to create paintings and collages that espoused and expressed the kinds of values that they would like to see informing the actions of the company
- working with middle-level managers to write and produce plays, performed by professional actors to an audience of the senior executives of the company, that psycho-dramatically mirrored the dysfunctional behaviours of the organization – to heighten awareness of what needed to change, and how

Fifteen years later (having obtained a Master's degree in both poetry and painting) Giles finds himself practising the same creative skills and contrarian techniques at London Business School, where he is perhaps the most original and effective designer of workshops for corporate clients. His programmes – each one unique and all of them an eclectic mix of creative experiences – are celebrated for their impact on participants and their performance.

Freedom is important to Giles – the freedom to be fully human, to create unfettered ideas, and, most of all, to help others to do so. As a child, his father had described him as 'feral'. To this day, Giles is uncomfortable with too much order and too little truth:

> Something tightens in my stomach and I know I'm in the wrong place. I've got to say something, do something, walk away... because I know in some way there's something wrong.

He can't help but regard systems, bureaucracies, hierarchies and power dynamics as inherently dangerous: 'I always played the opposite to the organization.'

Giles Ford finds in playfulness a route to the truth. His workshops use play to make connections. The participants open up to each other. Playfulness frees the mind, loosens inhibitions and builds trust. Things get said that need to be said. Giles walks in the footsteps of Johan Huizinga, a Dutch historian of ideas, who, in his famous book, *Homo Ludens*, discusses the significance of the element of play in society (Huizinga, 2016). He showed that play is a necessary, though not sufficient, requirement for the formation of culture. Art, sport, literature, games, humour, experimentation and philosophy all exhibit a powerful element of play. He said, 'For many years the conviction has grown upon me that civilization arises and unfolds in and as play.'

Play is intrinsic to human behaviour. Every child in every culture plays. Every adult is playful, though sometimes insufficiently so. Indeed, playfulness has, since the emergence of the human species, been an adaptive advantage enjoyed by humans more than any other species. Jerome Bruner, a cognitive psychologist, has described this faculty as the basis for man's 'flexibility of thought' and the problem-solving abilities that flow from this.

There are an increasing number of studies demonstrating the connection between early playfulness and creativity. In the 1960s, Wallach and Kogan showed that creative children were more playful than less creative ones (1965). Other studies, by Lieberman among others, have shown that the talent for divergent thinking in adults is especially associated with playfulness in childhood (Lieberman, 1965). Of the various forms of play, pretend play is particularly powerful.

Play is serious! When we play, we put 'in play' something that goes beyond the rational or the material or the deterministic. We allow the mind to float free, as it were. We give full rein to human agency. Returning to Huizinga: 'Life must be lived as play.'

In a study we have been conducting over several years, we invite people to select the behaviours that characterize their working environment. The bar chart in Figure 4.1 shows the relative frequency of the behaviours selected by over 2,000 people from over 200 organizations across the world. The most frequently selected behaviour is hierarchical. Hierarchical behaviour does not engender playfulness. So not unsurprisingly, playful is the least selected behaviour, bar one. It is no wonder that calls for innovation, to challenge the accepted way of doing things, to be more creative, are met with a deafening silence in our organizations when you look at the behaviour that dominates.

We need to give voice to the playfulness within us. We need to work towards creating organizational environments, less dominated by the traditional management behaviour of hierarchy and more inducive to playfulness. Then calls for innovation, to challenge the accepted way of doing things, to be more creative, to shake off the shackles of conformity, will be heard and acted upon.

Personhood

For the Maverick leader, a life that has meaning is one that entails personal growth. Each of us is born unique, but not everyone discovers and expresses their uniqueness. The pressures to comply with external norms and expectations are considerable. There is, of course, a balance to be struck between self-discovery and self-invention, between social mores and personal values, and between organizational rules and individual expression. In each case, the nonconformist places rather greater weight on the latter than the former.

Carl Rogers, a humanistic psychologist, calls it 'the courage to be' and the strength of will to 'launch oneself fully into the stream of life' (Rogers, 1995). He believed that when one is inwardly free, one will choose this process of *becoming* as the hallmark of a life well lived.

The good life does not need a destination. But it does need a direction. And this direction is best expressed as the experience of becoming a person. 'The good life is a process, not a state of being.' The stories we have told are tales of just this process. For each person, their nonconformity was a symptom of their authenticity, not a goal in its own right, or a style to be cultivated, or a value by which to live.

FIGURE 4.1 The relative dominance of different behaviours

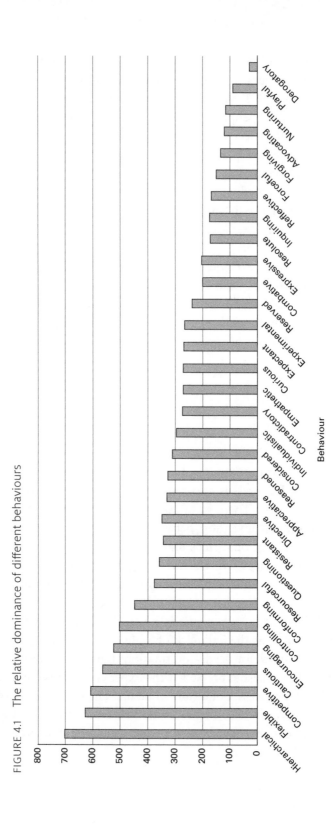

Nonconformity is the outer appearance of inner autonomy, of person-hood. It is the heartbeat of the Maverick leader. There is no potential to work for the betterment of others without the preparedness to challenge the status quo, to think for oneself and to think differently to others. Most of us have travelled on airplanes many times and are familiar to the point of taking little notice of the instruction: 'In the unlikely event of a sudden loss of cabin oxygen you must secure your own oxygen mask first, before attempting to secure the oxygen masks of others.' Why? Because if you run out of oxygen and your heart stops, you are of no use to anyone. You become an ex-person, your personhood is no more.

We entitled this chapter 'Nonconformist', perhaps erroneously. Maybe it should have been entitled 'Personhood'. To conform without question to what has gone before and what is current wisdom, is not only to merge one's individuality into an amorphous blob of conventionality, to deny others of one's unique perspective and contribution; it is also to suffocate the very essence of what it is to be the person you are. You extinguish your personhood. To be a Maverick leader we must first give voice to our noncon-formity, our expression of individuality. We must secure our own oxygen mask.

> Nonconformity is the only course of action to be true to ourselves, to live with ourselves happily and to be available to contribute to the betterment of others.

The Maverick leader is true to their mission. Their originality is no more and no less than what it takes to be true to the cause they have chosen. They have little interest in falling in line with other groups for reasons of security or companionship or fashion. But they do not go it alone, they find connec-tion with others to create momentum towards betterment.

Collaborate with others

Social deviance is roughly defined as people who do not follow the rules and values of a given society. They are often law-breakers, civilly disobedient or resistant to the predominant norms of the societal group. However:

> ...if an unjust norm or law is predominant within society or a group, then violating or resisting it – given that unjust social context – would be considered

'deviant' but it may also be regarded as a good or heroic act (Wolf and Zuckerman, 2012).

In advocating a broadening of the term deviance, Wolf and Zuckerman make a pivotal point in thinking about the nonconformist attitudes of Maverick leaders and the ways in which their attitudes and behaviours may be labelled initially as deviant, resulting in resistance by others. When their nonconformity resides within a particular epoch or context of social injustice, these Mavericks, these 'deviant heroes', are social actors who are positioned on the 'leading edge of social transformations, challenging entrenched normative environments' for the greater social and moral well-being of others. They serve as a symbol for urgent societal or organizational change. And as such they are often stigmatized and marginalized. Every attempt is made to silence their dissenting voice.

This is because there are invisible walls in society that perpetuate the status quo at the excision of equality for all. Sarah Ahmed writes about how these invisible walls are perpetuated, commenting that 'not all walls are visible to everyone'; in fact, you probably don't even realize a wall exists until you have come up against it, pushed at it or hit your head on it. 'What is the hardest [wall] for some does not even exist for others.' Ahmed highlights that being the voice who challenges the status quo does not come without personal cost (2016). It is only later in time, when awareness has been created among the majority, that the actions and behaviours of the nonconformist, of the Maverick, can be fully acknowledged and appreciated as a driving force of positive change.

In this way, the 'deviant hero has a distinct societal role... one who actively challenges and seeks to change oppressive rules, and unjust laws, at personal risk to overturn unjust social norms'. In light of this, the characteristics of the 'deviant hero' serve as a hallmark for those who are nonconformist for the benefit of broader social good. It is this aspect that resonates so aptly with the core attributes of Maverick leadership.

While the examples of heroic nonconformity given in the paper by Wolf and Zuckerman are notable, as are the examples of Maverick leadership in this book itself, one needn't feel intimidated. You can develop your own nonconformist ability in small and tangible ways. First off, to be a Maverick or to possess the qualities of a 'deviant hero', you need to develop the capacity to recognize the social structures in which you exist and be willing to challenge those which are oppressive in the hope of change for the greater good. This may come at a cost to yourself, your pride or reputation.

However, opportunities to develop this aspect of Maverick leadership surround us in everyday life, in the workplace, in our social circles and beyond. They exist in the form of racial or gender injustices that play out in your workplace, bullying, unjust practices and prejudices that often go by unchecked by others, or simply wasteful and ineffective practices.

Using your voice to challenge these daily offences or unjust values is an opportunity to develop your inner Maverick. To be bold enough to step out of the normative slipstream and face the social isolation or ridicule that may accompany being a nonconformist, for the sake of others and the greater good of society, is one way you can start harnessing your leadership capability. In developing your capacity to be nonconformist, hold in mind some wisdom from Ahmed. She highlights that being a nonconformist and 'remaining unrelenting in the face of adversity is bolstered by acting in collaboration with others'. There is a need for individuals who are pushing back on the walls in society to establish relationships with one another as a means of building a sense of collective belonging that allows them to 'survive' the resistance they will have to endure. If you are going to start pushing back – start with finding a friend, a significant other or like-minded others who will serve as a means of psychological support for when the resistance comes your way.

In the next chapter we confront the inevitable and generative challenge that follows when you break the rules and abandon convention, and that is: how do you know what you have in mind instead will work? The honest answer to that challenge is, you don't know whether what you have in mind instead will work, therefore you need to experiment. As the Austrian-born philosopher Karl Popper put it, 'all life is problem-solving' (1999). And to solve problems we need to constantly identify them, hypothesize solutions and test them – in other words to experiment. This is the next differentiating characteristic of the Maverick leader: the willingness to experiment, to learn by trial and error to find new and better ways to create better outcomes for more people.

CHAPTER FIVE

Experimental

Learning through trial and error

We don't put things into practice. We create theories out of practice.
NASSIM NICHOLAS TALEB

In Chapter 1, we introduced Oscar Corona Lopez. Oscar started his own company, an agency for a large Mexican insurance company. Oscar quickly recognized that in order to succeed in a business in which 90 per cent of start-ups failed, he had to experiment. He had to be open to changing his mind in the light of results, if he was to avoid a model causing financial ruin and heartache for his compatriots:

> I learnt quickly there is no one predetermined guaranteed path to a new
> business model for agencies, there is only a series of business experiments from
> which you learn, construct your next experiment and in so doing move closer
> to your desired outcome and further away from the failing model you left
> behind.

Question, hypothesize, experiment and learn

One of the areas in which Oscar challenged convention and experimented with new approaches was in recruitment. His competitors recruited people in the traditional manner: putting out an advert with a job description;

defining applicant requirements; selecting on the basis of CVs; interviewing the selected candidates and then making a recruitment decision.

Instead, Oscar asked himself a question – all good experiments start with a question. He asked himself the question: 'Where do you find large numbers of people queueing up to take part in something?' Think about that question for a minute. Notice that the question itself indicates a different mindset about what it is to join a business. At the heart of the question is the phrase '*to take part*'. Some of the synonyms for the phrase 'to take part' include 'throw in with', 'come on board', 'sign up with' and 'be in'. In contrast, the more conventional question, 'How do I persuade people who have the required pre-existing competencies to apply for a predefined role?', has at its heart the phrase '*to apply for*', the synonyms for which include 'to bid for', 'to appeal to', 'to seek to' and 'to claim'.

A good question not only challenges the status quo but reframes the problem one is trying to solve. By asking this question as he did, Oscar not only asked a good question; he also reframed the problem. Instead of trying to find the best people from among those looking for a job in sales, he defined the problem as trying to find the best people from those wanting to take part in something exciting.

One of the answers that Oscar came up with to his question was to take part in a reality television programme, such as *The Voice*. For those of you who don't know, *The Voice* is a television programme, franchised in many countries, in which 'hopefuls' line up in order to take part in the show to get the opportunity to display their singing talents in front of a live audience and panel of established singing stars.

Oscar then turned his question and his answer into a hypothesis. This is the second stage of a good business experiment, converting your question and your most compelling answer into a hypothesis that can be tested. Oscar's hypothesis was:

> **IF** I think of my business as an exciting experience, present that experience to the outside world and design an audition process rather than a recruitment process, **THEN** I will have the opportunity to select people who want to take part in and contribute to an experience rather than those who want a job to match their existing expertise, and this will create a more successful team.

We have highlighted the IF and the THEN to illuminate the form of a hypothesis: **IF** X **THEN** Y, where X is doing something different (in this case, thinking of the business as an experience) and Y is a new benefit (in this case, people wanting to contribute).

With this hypothesis in mind, Oscar scoped his experiment as follows. First he created a short video which he posted on social media outlets trying to capture the atmosphere, experience and the journey they were embarking upon. It was exciting, it was fun, it was playful, it was about joining and taking part in an adventure. Those interested in taking part were invited to make a short one-minute video introducing themselves. From reviewing the videos, Oscar and his team then selected 20 people to take part in a three-day exercise to raise as much money as they could for a children's cancer charity that Oscar and his business support. On the basis of what each of them achieved and how they achieved it, a smaller number were selected to take part in a casting exercise where they presented their case to take part in the journey ahead. The 'winners' were invited to join the team.

The final part of Oscar's business experiment was to measure the performance of the winning candidates compared to those selected in the past by traditional methods. This, in the language of experiments, is known as the 'control'. And in a business experiment the control is usually one of two approaches: comparing performance in one part of the organization, a part that is following the conventional approach, with a part where the experimental approach is being applied; or comparing performance before the experiment with performance after the experiment. The result in either case is an opportunity for learning what worked and what did not, scaling what worked and designing the next experiment to address what did not work.

What Oscar learnt was that by taking this approach he was able to select candidates from a much wider range of talents, attitudes and experiences, and learn more about the characteristics that make for a successful sales ambassador, the term he uses for his team members. As a result, he was able to further refine (to continue to experiment) the process to increase the percentage of high performers in his team.

But this is not the only area in which Oscar experimented. The experimental mindset is wired to challenge everything: how we do business, how we organize, how we treat people, how we lead, how we treat customers, how we treat citizens, how we look after people. It means continually asking questions, creating hypotheses and developing experiments to learn and make things better.

> The experimental framework: ask good questions; create a compelling hypothesis; scope structured experiments and learn from the degree of success against the hypothesized benefits.

The experimental mindset also recognizes that experimentation is not a free for all. As Oscar put it to us: 'There are areas of the business I cannot experiment with, at least for the time being.' He could not experiment with certain government regulations; he could not experiment with certain laid-down procedures insisted upon by, as he put it, the mothership, the big insurance companies providing the policies. And this, of course, is the reality for all of us: there are constraints that we have to work within. *The art of choosing what to experiment with is recognizing the difference between a constraint that has to be complied with, a regulation or a legal requirement, and a convention, tradition, or so-called 'best practice' that may no longer be the best way of doing things.*

It is popular these days to talk about creating a sandpit in organizations, a place where people can play and experiment. What is rarely mentioned is that sandpits have edges, they have boundaries. A sandpit without edges is as an invitation to wreak havoc. Without constraints – boundaries – experimentation has no meaning; without experimentation, falsehoods masquerade as constraints. Take learning to ride a bike, for example, without stabilizers.

We discover by doing

How do we learn to ride a bike? Do we buy a book on the theory of balance in motion? Or do we get on a bike and give it a go? We get on a bike and give it a go. But thankfully, our parents, with a bit of luck, have bolted stabilizers onto the bike, or, having failed to secure said stabilizers, run along behind us, holding on to the saddle to make sure that we don't topple too often, while we experiment within the constraints of stabilizers or the parental grip on the saddle. You don't learn to ride a bike without trying to ride a bike. 'To seek to know before we know is as absurd as the wise resolution of Scholasticus, not to venture into the water until he had learnt to swim.' A point made by the early 19th-century German philosopher Frederick Hegel in arguing that the journey towards truth progresses from what we thought we knew, that then fails to explain what happens, to what seems to better explain what actually works (Scruton et al, 2001).

Mavericks find it more natural to jump into action, knowing full well that they may fail, than to suffer analysis paralysis. As Nassim Nicholas Taleb has observed, 'We are largely better at doing than we are at thinking.' For example, he has shown how most of the developments in medicine arose not from 'top-down theorizing' but from 'experience-driven heuristics' (Taleb, 2012). Medicine is a craft. Knowledge advances by trial and error. But just as the child learning to ride a bike works within the constraints of stabilizers, or parental saddle holding, medical researchers hypothesize and experiment within the constraints of the structure of an experiment and the experience that has been accrued through previous experiments.

Mavericks instinctively understand the truth of this observation. They resist the popular notion that effective practice is essentially the application of proven knowledge or the adoption of best practice. In a sense, Mavericks reverse the standard model of the growth of knowledge by cleaving to the belief that most theory is the post-rationalization of the discoveries first made by those solving practical problems, and that therefore *progress is best accelerated by focusing on those problems that most matter to people and trying something different in the full knowledge that at first we may fail before we succeed.* Failure is essential to progress.

Failure is hard but necessary

So, wouldn't it be nice if we were all OK with failing? If we looked down the barrel of a challenge and thought, 'If I fail then that's great!' We often hear messages similar to this – embrace failure, welcome failure, and they sound motivational, inspiring even. But in reality, when the rubber hits the road, they are nothing but bumper stickers that do little more than momentarily give us courage. Why? Because the reality is they are simply not true. No one likes failure. No one wants to embrace failure because no one wants to fail. Not intentionally anyway.

Failure is hard, it is emotionally draining. It is disappointing, disheartening and can even feel embarrassing at times. It generally comes with a cost: time, effort, energy, resources. So let's get one thing straight before we go any further: no one wants to fail, not even our Maverick leaders. *However, what differentiates Maverick leaders is that when they do fail, they don't let it hold them back.* They don't give up and they don't dwell on the failure itself. Instead, they pull themselves up by the bootstraps and try again. They remain undeterred, because failure, as uncomfortable and frustrating as it is, is a part of the process of experimentation. It is not the end of the process, it is the process, and that perspective makes all the difference. As Churchill put it, 'No boy or girl should ever be disheartened by lack of success in their youth but should diligently and faithfully continue to persevere' (1946).

In the Introduction to this book we said that key to what makes a Maverick leader is their mindset. Research showed us that how we perceive a challenge influences how we approach the challenge (Dweck and Leggett, 1988). If we see the challenge as a performance-driven task we are more likely to feel the weight of its potential failure and possibly back away from it to avoid failure. If we perceive the task to be a learning opportunity we are more inclined to experience failures or setbacks as separate from ourselves and in so doing, preserve our view of our abilities and capabilities. We avoid getting caught in negative self-talk that would leave us feeling too discouraged to continue with the task. So how you view the task and how you view yourself matters, but there is more.

In Dweck and Leggett's seminal research they also found that children who adopted the learning response were more likely to be creative and persistent in their problem solving. They seemed to integrate their learning into their next attempt. They built on their failures in a way that propelled them forward into another attempt. In Chapter 6 we will see the ways in which Maverick leaders are undeterred, but in the rest of this chapter we explore how their ability to remain undeterred, coupled with their mindset of experimentation, creates a powerful momentum, fuelled by trial and error, towards their goals.

Trial and error

Tim Harford, the self-styled 'underground economist', has made the argument that the part played by 'eureka ideas' in the development of knowledge, what he calls 'lightbulb moments', is modest. It is the painstaking work of experimentation, bringing ideas to life, testing and improving them through trial and error, and turning them into viable products and practices that contributes most to human flourishing and prosperity. Harford's argument finds an echo in Matt Ridley's observation that:

> Innovation is the parent of prosperity but it is the child of freedom. History shows that innovation happened where people were free to experiment, fail, try again, change their minds and back themselves (Ridley, 2020).

Historically, mankind could not conceive how the world came into being without a supreme designer. This is because we overestimate the role of design in the creation of an ordered world and underplay the role of chance or, more precisely, the role of a random process with a selective criterion. The great lesson of evolutionary theory is that a blind process can get to better outcomes than a purposeful plan: 'Human institutions are often the outcome of human actions but not human design' (Ferguson, 1767).

This idea, though simple to state, is profoundly counter-intuitive, but it is one that Mavericks instinctively understand. The heuristic is as follows:

1 Come up with any number of tentative solutions to the problem at hand.
2 Invent variants on the currently inadequate solution to the problem.
3 Ruthlessly cull the failures and cultivate the successes.
4 Repeat ad infinitum.

From our interviews with Mavericks, we see that once you recognize that there is no proven path to a better future and you take the first step towards creating one, you embark on a journey of trial and error. Usually this first step is a stab in the dark. In our conversation with Akin, the Maverick leader who decided to change the narrative of what it means to be black and started his own consulting organization, he reflected on his beliefs of leadership, commenting:

> Leadership is about creating something special, and you can't do that following the rules... I'm not saying we shouldn't have any structure, but actually there is an excitement about doing something and not knowing if it's going to work.

Maverick leaders learn and work out how to navigate their path along the way, through trial and error.

In joining a struggling and polluting carpet business, Rik Vera decided very quickly not to attend the annual 'must be seen at' showcase Expos which cost money and waste time, but rather to find inspiration from somewhere else and transition it to his industry. He capitalized on the introduction of the internet at the end of the '90s, and followed ideas from Amazon, Dell and tobacco companies, organizations in sectors that found a new form of connecting and communicating with their customers, away from mass communication models. He realized he could adopt their models, dismantle them, and through trial and error, rebuild them into something new and better for his business in the carpet industry:

> You get those people who get the Lego box and go 'wow, this is amazing' and make something by following the plan, and you get those people who take those blocks and build something new and feel 'wow, that was not designed by the plan'.

Experimentation itself is the action or process of trying out new ideas. It is the ability to harness curiosity, creativity and persistence in the pursuit of creating something new. Creativity is the ability to establish new ideas, to link two previously unrelated concepts together and establish something different. Creativity requires a level of playful 'wondering' and we all have the ability to do this. Some of us have just forgotten how.

Curiosity and playfulness

The work of renowned Swiss developmental psychologist Jean Piaget highlighted the importance of play. He showed how play was integral to the cognitive and emotional development of the child (Piaget, 1951). Piaget, Vygotsky and several other developmental psychologists have shown us that it is through play that children curiously engage with the world around them, absorbing information at a rapid rate through all five of their senses. One of the authors has a three-month-old and, like any other parent of an infant, he can attest to the frequency at which babies put items into their mouths at any given opportunity! This is the sensory-seeking play of infants. It is the start of curiosity and it is also the basis for our cognitive development. We saw in Chapter 1 how far children can take playful curiosity in the overfilled bath and living room flood incident.

The motivation to be curious is especially evident in children. Children use play as a means of making sense of the world around them. Like mini-Mavericks, they constantly bend the rules of convention. They use their imagination of how the world could be to shape their play: humans can fly, people can live under water, we can fight invisible pirates and create an entire home (or army fort) under a pegged-up blanket. When it comes to experimental learning children are the gold standard because they move through the world with an insatiable curiosity free from the boundaries of 'reality'. Maverick leaders use their vision (imagination) of how the world could be better, to shape their experiments free from the boundaries of convention.

So what happens to that zest for creative learning? As we saw in Chapter 1, evidenced by the research of George Land and Beth Jarman, our motivation to be creative gradually diminishes as we engage in a world with forced structure. A world which is less tolerant of curiosity and heavily oriented around external motivation; at school and later at work, reward/

punishment systems are used to direct us. A world which is 'performance' rather than 'learning' oriented. When asked what limits Mavericks from flourishing, Akin suggested that organizational structures can be the limiting barrier that shuts down the Maverick spirit. The need to err on the side of safety, or the desire to 'be the best in the industry' can lead to a performance-driven culture which can make it, as Akin put it, 'really hard for Mavericks to be given permission to actually do what they do. In organizations that are management driven, Mavericks die.' They are too structural, too bureaucratic and too focused on performance and efficiency, so that they inevitably cripple creative potential. When discussing the importance of organizational context in harnessing creative learning, Maverick leader Christine Apiot Okudi from Uganda emphasized how toxic a harmful rigid culture can be for the Maverick spirit. She commented, 'Driving people harder doesn't work.' There is a need to look after people and look after the culture. People need to know the objectives and have the opportunity to contribute. There needs to be true collaboration, they need to be part of the goal. When people make mistakes, it is a question of how to use that mistake for growth.

Jens Meyer, former Dean of Programmes at CEDEP and Adjunct Professor at INSEAD, is intrigued by how people learn. He described to us how his passion was fuelled by frustration with existing business school pedagogy. He had witnessed so many management development programmes that got tied up in bureaucracy, cost a fortune, made the teacher the master and didn't deliver transformative learning.

'We can do better pedagogy!... but we need to think beyond ourselves and our own organizations', he said. Jens believed that to inspire a change of culture within the client organization it was necessary to create a context in which 'you can actually get people to see and think differently'. To this end, he designed 'flat floor' spaces that activate curiosity, movement and engagement; he insisted on learner-centric teaching; and he emphasized two crucial concepts that encapsulate his Maverick leadership mindset.

First, recognize that 'We each have to make an effort.' For Jens, being a Maverick leader and making a difference demands an overpowering sense of responsibility. He explains:

> There are moments when I hope for luck. But I don't think I'm a person who is happy with a lucky situation. You've got to do it. You've got to earn it. You have to make an effort. You do what needs to be done. Freedom comes from 'what did I put in?... and do I have the right to take it out?'

Second, 'We have to change our mindsets. We have to learn to see things (sometimes even the same things) differently.' What he most wants to see is people becoming curious and making more of an intellectual effort to think about 'What can I contribute to making this world better? What could be my contribution?'.

For Jens, getting people to ask these questions brings about a contagious energy. He cherishes those moments when his clients think differently about their existing challenges. He uses the metaphor of 'getting off your chair' and 'looking at your desk from the other side' and 'seeing something else'. He feels that this is his duty as a teacher. It is his life philosophy, one which he has poured into every business school and executive classroom he finds himself working in. Consequently, he has enriched the lives of countless individuals (and organizations) in the process.

If we want to develop our inner Maverick, we need to develop our capacity for experimentation. This means we need to re-engage with our ability to be curious, to be playful, to be creative and to be open to learning. These are core ingredients in developing an experimental mindset. Underpinning all these attributes is the willingness and our courage to think for ourselves.

An experiment by Chase and Simon provides a simple demonstration of the need to think for ourselves in a changing world (Chase and Simon, 1973). In the experiment, chess masters were shown a game in progress for five seconds. Asked to recreate the board layout in another room they achieved 99 per cent accuracy. This compares to 16 per cent accuracy when the same task was given to non-chess players. The interesting part is what happened when the chess masters were shown chessboards with the pieces placed randomly. On these occasions, their ability to recreate the board was no better than non-chess players. Their expertise, pattern recognition relating chess-playing strategies, was of no use. The rules of the game had changed. Deploying expertise from one context in a different context is a high-risk approach. It is the practice of 'thoughting' over thinking.

Think for yourself

The Philip Tetlock research on the efficacy of expertise has contributed significantly to our understanding of the limits and fallibility of human expertise (Tetlock, 2017). In one of his more famous studies, he invited a sample of 300 recognized experts to make specific forecasts on a variety of phenomena in their area of expertise and then track their accuracy. Very few of these forecasts came true. The experts outperformed a control group of undergraduates – but only by a slim margin. On any objective criterion, they performed poorly. In other studies, experts on Russia did no better than experts on China at predicting Russian phenomena, and vice versa. Tim Harford drew from Tetlock's research the following maxim: 'Think for yourself'.

Maverick leaders know exactly what Frank Lloyd Wright meant when he allegedly said that 'an expert is a man who has stopped thinking because "he knows"'. This is not to deprecate the effort that goes into the mastery of any discipline but simply to recognize the dangers of hubris. When facing novel problems, a mind less constrained by the reigning paradigm or the 'current state of knowledge' can provide the necessary latitude of imagination. A Zen proverb observes that 'In the mind of the expert there are few possibilities, but in the mind of the beginner there are many.' The Maverick is not embarrassed to act sometimes as though a novice.

Paul Ormerod's research on the scale and frequency of corporate failures illuminates the shortcomings of planning. He showed that the relationship between the size and frequency of corporate bankruptcies accurately mirrors the pattern of extinctions in the fossil record. In other words, the enormous effort that goes into analysis, forecasting and planning would seem to be largely ineffectual. We are blinder than we think (Ormerod, 2005).

Not having a plan or an itinerary does not rule out the possibility of making progress. Being suspicious of theory and ideology, the Maverick leader invests his energy instead into keeping his eyes open, feeding off random occurrences and grabbing opportunities as they arise.

Studies of how the brain naturally thinks about the future confirm Ormerod's thesis that the virtues of planning are exaggerated. The brain spends very little energy forecasting the future. What it does instead is to imagine various possible scenarios and then, irrespective of their likelihood, devotes effort to working out practical responses to each of these eventualities.

If we combine the findings of Tetlock on expertise and Ormerod on planning, we come to the conclusion that we are a hubristic species: we know far less than we think we know. Maverick leaders would seem to have an instinctive grasp of these truths. Their natural approach to problems mimics the evolutionary approach of variation and selection, or what John Kay, an economist, has called 'disciplined pluralism':

- They bring their creativity to every problem, both big and small, coming up with fresh ideas, both rational and irrational, knowing full well that most of them are destined to fail.
- They refrain from pre-judgement of these ideas; and they banish any aversion to loss that they might feel.
- They apply the ideas to the real world but in a contained manner; they bet the field, never the farm.
- They pay careful attention to the results of these trials; they seek out whatever feedback they can; and they let reality, not human prejudice, be the ultimate judge of the outcome.

For the Maverick leader, the enemy is dogmatism, arrogance and the pretence to omniscience; their ally is their own curiosity, humility and sense of personal fallibility, their ability to think for themselves – to be able to think new thoughts – to be creative.

Bending, breaking and blending

The Creative Brain is a documentary starring neuroscientist Dr David Eagleman, who sets out to unpack what exactly creativity is (Beamish and Trackman, 2019). He highlights how creativity is not limited to one portion of the brain (although the prefrontal cortex does play a significant role in imagination), and argues that creativity is the culmination of multiple neural connections. Neither is creativity having a brilliant original idea, but rather it is the coming together of two or more previously unrelated concepts, merging ideas from different and even contrasting resources, which in doing so creates something new. He refers to the act of creativity as 'bending, breaking and blending'. It is the ability to refashion something old in a different way, or integrating it with a completely different concept. The partner of one author of this book recently fashioned an illuminated long-arm paint pole, by connecting a handheld paint brush to a broom stick and taping on a torch, in order to paint a high wall accurately at night! It is this form of bending convention, breaking norms and blending of ideas, thoughts and objects that encapsulates the essence of creativity.

What was fascinating about Eagleman's work was not only that it reinforced the idea that there is no single part of the brain 'responsible' for creativity, but that all of our creative contributions are inherently unique. This is because each new idea is a combination of older ideas, mixed with a new stimulus and your own emotions and memories. *In this way, we all have the capacity to be creative because our personal life experiences form part of the ingredients that make our ideas novel to begin with.*

One statement stands out from Dr Eagleman's interviews. One of his interviewees commented, 'Creativity is the power to imagine the world that isn't in existence yet.' This is a crucial component of the experimental mind-set evident in Maverick leaders. Mavericks are looking at the world in creative ways because they see a world where things can be better. They don't necessarily have the solutions immediately, but they can imagine something different and then they start curiously experimenting with ideas that will help pull that world into existence.

At Fluxx, for example, the place of work for Maverick leader Hannah Silverstein, asking 'why' is at the heart of the projects she works on.

To be experimental is not just about being creative and curious. It also requires an openness to learning. With each failed attempt, Mavericks learn something new. Rather than stagnating in disappointment, they integrate their learning and try again, differently this time. The difficulty about experimentation is that this form of learning is hard work! In fact, all learning is hard work. *This is why being a Maverick leader, someone who is open to experimental learning, is not simply a job: it is a dedication, a dedication to learning.*

Learning

The idea of learning conjures up memories of school days where we all struggled through something: algebra, accounting, a language – you'll have your own memories here. However, experimental learning is not confined to institutional or academic modules. It refers to our openness to trying new things, *our willingness to part with old methodologies or orthodoxies and replace them with new ones, and our ability to break away from habits and routines that are effortless in return for engaging with something effortful.* Learning requires us to step out of our zone of comfort and live on the brink of our own competence, constantly straddling between 'I know what's going on' and 'I'm feeling so lost'. Interestingly, it's often at the point of despair in the learning process that the solution begins to become apparent. Noel Burch's model of developing conscious competence helps us understand how learning occurs and why it is so psychologically difficult to do (Adams, 2015).

We start at the bottom in a position of **unconscious incompetence**. We are not even aware of how much we don't know. We have no insight into the skills deficit we have and are essentially in a state of ignorance. With a desire, motivation or curiosity to learn (or because someone or something highlights our ignorance) we then move to step two, conscious incompetence.

Conscious incompetence is perhaps the toughest stage. We become consciously aware of our shortfalls. The challenge ahead of us is evident and the depth of learning or upskilling required becomes (painfully) apparent. This is often when we feel most deflated and wanting to give up. It is also the stage of the most experimental learning as we try new ways to upskill ourselves to meet the task at hand. However, because we are not yet competent, our experimental attempts usually yield the most setbacks and failures. Therefore, psychologically, the stage of conscious incompetence is the most gruelling, because it is where we become most self-conscious of our inability.

This was echoed in the research by Dweck and Leggett as they observed the participants who at this stage of the learning process adopted the helpless response. Those who did so would not only attribute their failure to their own personal inaptitude, but they would also try to avoid the task by commenting that they were bored or by trying to distract (and impress) the observer through commenting on past successes they had accomplished or skills they had which were irrelevant to the task at hand. These participants showed higher levels of negative emotion such as anxiety or despondency, despite having made some progress previously. They viewed challenging tasks as a threat to their self-esteem and quickly became overwhelmed by the task. They seemed to spiral into a negative emotional cycle of self-doubt and inadequacy that then impaired or reduced their ability to complete the tasks successfully.

For those of us in corporate and organizational settings, being at this stage can feel embarrassing and even shameful, especially if you adopt a performance mindset to the challenge at hand. In our interview with Hannah (the creative consultant Maverick), she highlighted that one of the biggest limiting factors to being experimental is fear or self-doubt. Experimentation and venturing into the unknown inevitably elicits these fears, which is why, when things are not working out, most look to find an easier way, a less cognitively and less emotionally taxing alternative. It takes self-belief, a moral compass and some affirming self-talk to move you from this stage to the next one. Thus it is at this critical juncture between conscious incompetence and conscious competence that the spirit of being undeterred and the spirit of experimentation are witnessed in Maverick leaders.

Gradually, and painstakingly, we move from this position into **conscious competence**, in which we begin to see signs of progress. We start to regain a sense of mild confidence that we can understand and address the challenges before us. As a Maverick, you start to see a sliver of the imagined world you hoped for. However, our actions and thoughts in this stage of learning still require immense cognitive effort and concentration for the learning trajectory to continue. This is wonderfully illustrated in Destin Sandlin's experiment of learning how to ride his mechanically re-engineered backward bicycle. A bike which operates in reverse – when he turns the handlebars left it will force the wheels to go right and vice versa. Sandlin refers to a 'clicking point' – a moment, after extensive practice and several failed attempts, in which his brain seems to 'just get it' and the neural pathways to make sense of this activity are embedded. This is the moment in which he becomes consciously competent at riding the backward bicycle, but that doesn't mean it is easy or automatic. As he reminds us in his experiment, it still took tremendous concentration and effort, so much so that a single distraction such as a ringing mobile phone quickly resulted in him falling off the bike again (Sandlin, 2015).

As we begin to become more and more proficient in the skills required, we move into the stage of **unconscious competence**, where less cognitive effort is required to complete the task at hand. At this point, you are more likely to feel confident enough to teach this skill to others. In many ways this stage is the development of mastery. The point at which you can say, I've got it! The solution is known and acted upon by yourself with relative ease. We can all relate to this stage. If you learnt to drive a car you can remember the amount of focus and effort that it required as you were learning, frantically checking all the blind spots with your head spinning around in every direction, until one day you realize, it just got easier than it was (you could even start thinking about other things, like dinner, while you drove).

Developing unconscious competence is gradual and often not even noticeable. Once you are there you are essentially at a point of 'non-learning', and what was once unknown has become so familiar it can now form a habit. Hence it is also a stage at which people risk stagnation. Mastery is a comfortable position, it boosts our ego and makes us feel most in control. It is our highest point of competence. Therefore being experimental is hardest for those in the position of unconscious competence because it requires them to move back to the start of this stepped learning process. To risk ego, reputation and status by reverting back to the position of least competence and begin learning something new once again.

Maverick leaders are Mavericks not necessarily because they love learning; they, like all of us, see learning as a hard, painstaking journey. They are Mavericks because they are curious about and determined to realize the possibility of a world that looks and works differently – better. A world which doesn't yet exist. And in order to achieve this, they have to be open to trying new ways, adopting new possible solutions and engaging in the learning journey. A journey that starts with the first step being in the dark, an unknown 'wondering' of whether or not an imagined solution might work. A journey fraught with countless failures and setbacks that challenge their sense of self-competence and force them to ask how committed they are to finding a better way. A journey that might force them to part with a previously 'known' way of doing things, old habits, status or existing orthodoxies.

Mavericks understand that to change the world means you have to give up something too. To be experimental is to risk failure. To lead is to risk your reputation. The more entrenched we are in preserving our unconscious competence, the less likely we are to risk being experimental and the less likely we are to be Maverick leaders.

In the next chapter, we explore the most important question for the Maverick leader, which is: How do I persist and sustain my energy and confidence in the face of resistance, politicking and occasionally outright hostility? The answer, we discover, lies in asking ourselves fundamental questions and providing ourselves with answers. What is my life philosophy? How do I need to define my higher-order goals, the things that should inform the decisions I make and the actions I take, in order to live my life true to my life philosophy?

CHAPTER SIX

Undeterred

Resisting opposition

In Chapter 1 we saw how so many of us wish things could be better and how this motivates some people to strive for change. In Chapter 2 we saw how at any point in life the collision of our awareness of wrongs, our belief that things should be better and our life experience give birth to a Maverick leader. In this chapter we explore the challenge of pursuing an alternative path, a path that challenges the status quo and meets with resistance and opposition. We explore what it is that we can learn from those that persist and succeed, those that remain undeterred, able to overcome resistance, hostility and even direct attack to create something better.

Still striving

Khadim Hussain, whom we met in Chapter 1, lost the use of his legs through polio. When faced with insult and attempts to stop him going to school, he determined that he 'would change their [his opponents] mindset'. Khadim belongs to and represents a community which is unheard, politically marginalized, economically disadvantaged and geographically excluded, isolated near K2, the second-highest peak in the world. His community is both culturally sophisticated and very conservative. For two decades Khadim has been combating the conservative mindset and cultural beliefs that impede girls' education in his community.

Khadim started promoting girls' education by going door to door in a wheelbarrow, pushed by his friends, to raise awareness and convince parents to send their daughters to school. During this endeavour, the feudal-like system of local lords in rural villages tried to pressurize him to stop. Even his own father was against him and didn't like what he was doing for the village. The villagers didn't believe in girls' education. So they didn't send their daughters to school, believing it to be a sin. But they all failed to stop him. It took consistent, passionate effort and determination to change the mindset of parents and the community at large. Now, the first school is a secondary girls' school teaching hundreds of girls. Thousands of girls have graduated from the school. More and more parents are demanding higher education for their daughters.

Today, Khadim is given high respect and is no longer seen in his community as a disabled person. He is seen as a leader, as an instigator of positive social change. His father feels proud of him. Khadim remains as determined as ever to keep striving to make things better. Since 2007, he has led a non-profit organization, the GRACE Association Pakistan, where he works in partnerships with supporting organizations, embassies in Pakistan and the target communities to provide learning opportunities to children from economically disadvantaged families. Khadim has established several schools, community-based organizations, non-governmental organizational networks, women's organizations and volunteer groups. These programmes are creating significant changes on the ground, securing a lasting positive impact on the socioeconomic situation of the people he serves.

However, there are still many dissenting voices in the society. People who don't want change in the lives of poor people. People who want to protect the status quo in which they are privileged. Khadim remains determined to keep working voluntarily for change, developing synergies with the young people trained through the programmes and projects of his non-profit organizations. And his motivation, his higher goal, remains 'to contribute to promote peace and prosperity for all in Pakistan', where such endeavours are more important and more needed than ever.

Higher-order goals

For decades, psychologists have been researching what makes certain people more successful, more able or more tenacious than others. Early theories that cognitive ability or IQ alone determine success were quickly refuted as several studies have highlighted that these attributes in isolation are not sufficient. Even when people are matched with others of equal intellectual ability and education, their ability to perform will differ. Where does this hidden capacity come from? This was a question that psychologist Angela Duckworth explored in the development of her concept of 'grit'. Grit, she argues, is the 'perseverance and passion for long-term goals', in which individuals work 'strenuously towards challenges, maintaining effort and interest over years despite failure, adversity and plateaus in progress' (Duckworth and Peterson, 2007).

There are several key components in this definition. The emphasis on the interplay between passion and perseverance – the importance of goals. The suggestion that gritty individuals are able to sustain their momentum over a longer period of time. That gritty people manage to maintain their stamina, their ability to persevere despite boredom, distraction or disappointment. These are the hallmarks of the gritty trait. Grit is the key to understanding the Maverick characteristic of being undeterred. This is not unsurprising, as grit, Duckworth suggests, is thought to be the one personal characteristic that most, if not all leaders possess, regardless of the field of their leadership.

Higher-order goals, also referred to as superordinate goals, are embedded in our belief system. Having a clear perception of what these goals are serves as a source of endurance in sustaining attention and stamina when faced with challenges.

One of the important constructs in the concept of grit is the idea of hierarchal goal formation. We all have goals. Some of us have goals for the day or for the month. On New Year's Eve, many of us set goals which few of us keep – or maybe it is just us authors. However, the idea behind grit goals is that they are conceptualized in a different way. They are hierarchal, descending from a highest-order goal towards lower-level goals that produce our actions. Khadim Hussain faced and still faces considerable resistance as he strives to increase access to education for young people. It is not his focus on day-to-day actions, the things that just need doing, that sustains him in the face of such hostility; it is the higher-order purpose of his actions – to continually widen access to education to enhance the life opportunities of those historically denied access to education – that sustains him and provides the foundation for his ability to be undeterred.

Higher-order goals are long-term-oriented, sometimes life-long and often abstract in nature. There may be just a few of them. They are highly valued by the individual. Subordinate to these higher-order, long-term goals are more immediate, more practical, less abstract, context-specific, short-term goals. These are referred to as lower-order goals which give rise to actions that ultimately support the higher-order superordinate goals.

Lower-level goals require self-control in order to be achieved. For example, not staying up all night watching episode after episode of *Suits* (a series on Netflix) when you have a work deadline for the next day and need a good and full night's sleep, requires a conscious effort. It requires the self-control to forego the chill-out, therapeutic, six-hour experience of the intrigue between the compelling characters of Louis, Donna, Rachel, Mike and Harvey, and instead go to bed! Superordinate goals, on the other hand, require more than just self-control. They need to be sustained in the long term; they require grit. This is the distinction between grit and self-control, but it also highlights how these two concepts work in tandem:

> Understanding how goals are hierarchically organized clarifies how self-control and grit are related but distinct. Self-control entails aligning actions with any valued goal despite momentarily more alluring alternatives; grit, in contrast, entails having and working assiduously towards a single challenging superordinate goal through thick and thin, on a timescale of years or even decades (Duckworth and Gross, 2014).

Life philosophy

The power of higher-order goals was very striking in our Maverick leaders. We noticed a common trend among those we interviewed. They all, like Khadim Hussain, seemed to have a very clear sense of why they were doing what they were doing. Some called it a life goal, or a sense of vocation. The theory of grit refers to higher-order goals as being embedded in an individual's belief system, and requires one to have a clear perception of one's higher-order goals. It is this that serves as a source of endurance.

While our Maverick leaders may not use the language of higher-order and superordinate goals, there was a definite sense of intrinsic purpose that emerged in our discussions with them. These 'life philosophies', as one could call them, were not always explicitly stated. In fact, we found them through analysing the interviews and looking for key repeated terms or phrases... and without fail, in almost all the interviews, they were present.

Here are just a few examples:

I just want to help people feel better, and wanting people to know that they are cared for and loved...I always had a sense of fighting for the underdog, the importance of justice (Annmarie Lewis).

I want to create an impact, challenge and push the limits to a higher standard (Janna El-Hadad).

Every human being has the capacity to be great (Andre Norman).

Giving back to my country, [Mexico] my people, all the wonderful things that I have received. It is my responsibility, my duty, to make a positive impact (Oscar Corona Lopez).

I have a real burning passion to stimulate brilliance in people, it's as simple as that (Akin Thomas).

This is my belief that we should be like the drop of rain which falls on the soil and then disappears, and as a result, there is a rose, a flower and people see and smell and enjoy the flower, not the drop of rain. This is my belief and work... I personally and critically believe in (Khadim Hussain).

These philosophies serve as a sort of North Star for the Maverick leaders in this book. They continuously circled back to them (sometimes unknowingly) in their interviews. They used them in their stories as justification for why they did a certain act or behaved in a specific way. The manner in which these guiding philosophies seemed to echo throughout the interview narratives, both individually and collectively, has led us to believe they serve as core values for these Maverick leaders. They are the single, conscious and unconscious reference points in the minds and lives of Mavericks that orientate them and their work.

It is this shared attribute that also led us to believe that for Maverick leaders, *the professional is personal*. What they do is not just a job or a means to an end. It may not have started like that in some of their stories – for example, remember Rik Vera who went into sales due to need not desire – but ultimately each of our Mavericks found a sense of deep value and personal self-expression in or through their work. In Rik's case this was 'doing good for people and planet'. This has resulted in what they do being intimately woven into who they are... or vice versa. Khadim highlighted this point most saliently when he jokingly referred to a situation in which he explained to his partner early in marriage, 'I told my wife that I'm already married to the organization, the community organization.'

The professional is personal

In some instances that passion which fuels those guiding philosophies results in Maverick leaders highlighting instances or experiences where their emotions felt uncontained. The types of behaviours that in corporate organizations may be frowned upon or even disciplined. What we have come to understand from interviewing Maverick leaders is that their passion is their driving force. Hence, in Maverick leadership your emotions are an asset and should be utilized, rather than something that needs to be overly regulated or 'tucked away' at work.

The word emotion comes from the Middle French word *émotion*, which means 'a (social) moving, stirring, agitation'. We are emotional first, rational second. Our emotions move us to act. Some of our emotions motivate defensive, protective action; others motivate expansive, exploratory action. As part of our research into Maverick leadership we ask people to describe their emotional environment at work. We ask them to select 5 words from a list of 30 that most reflect the dominant emotions they experience around them. We also ask them to rate the extent to which they see their organization as innovative, agile and able to respond to threats and opportunities, and generate value for their customers. We call this the organization's 'generative factor' (GF).

This allows us to look at any differences between those environments with a high GF and those with a low GF. Figure 6.1 presents data from one of the organizations in our study, and shows the extent to which people in different departments or divisions of the organization have different perceptions of its generative factor and Maverick behaviour. The dotted line represents the responses of those people who regarded the organization as having a high GF and shows that they see similarly high levels of Maverick behaviour. Conversely, those who perceived low organizational GF perceived limited Maverick behaviour (dashed line). This clearly reveals a positive relationship between Maverick leadership characteristics and the organization's ability to innovate and respond to threats and opportunities – to generate value for their customers. This is not surprising when you think about the importance of these characteristics to being innovative and able to respond to threats and opportunities.

In our study, we also compared the extent to which people saw Maverick leadership behaviour around them with the way in which people described their emotional environment. Table 6.1 shows how much more frequently

FIGURE 6.1   Maverick leader characteristics drive innovation

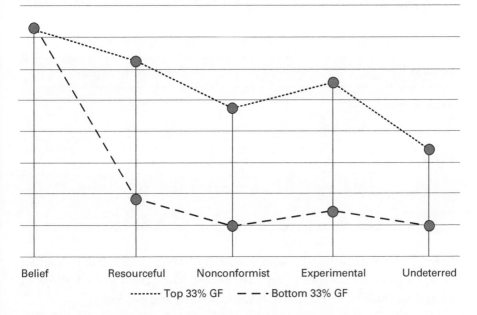

certain words were used to describe the emotional environment in which the Maverick leadership characteristics were most present, compared to when they were least present.

TABLE 6.1   Maverick leadership fosters positive emotions

Emotion	Times more frequent
connected	3
excited	4
valued	3
respected	3
appreciated	9

If we want people to bring their whole person to work, to make the professional personal, how much more likely is this going to happen if people feel connected, excited, valued, respected and appreciated?

In contrast, Table 6.2 shows how much more frequently the words were used to describe the emotional environment in which the Maverick leadership characteristics were least present, compared to when they were most present.

TABLE 6.2   The absence of Maverick leadership increases negative emotions

Emotion	Times more frequent
disenfranchised	6
excluded	6
fearful	7
isolated	6
powerless	6

Again, is this surprising? To what extent are Maverick leadership qualities going to come to the fore in an environment characterized by feelings of being disenfranchised, excluded, fearful, isolated and powerless?

As emotional beings, we connect emotionally, not just to each other but to what we do. The more we are told to, or feel that we need to, contain, constrain, deny or subdue our emotions, the less we are bringing our whole person to what we do and how we connect with others.

An exercise we often use with executive classes involves groups of 10 to 15 people tackling a problem that at first seems straightforward but turns out to be much more challenging.

We set three success criteria: to solve the problem, to execute the solution as fast and effectively as possible, and to maximize the learning across the group. The most successful groups are the most noisy and excited. Everyone is contributing. They're shouting, even manhandling colleagues in pursuit of finding and executing a solution. This is behaviour not normally accepted within the 'civilized' and emotionally controlled workplace. Observing from the outside it looks ill-disciplined and certainly impolite. Yet when you ask the participants at the end of the exercise what it felt like, no one uses the words ill-disciplined or impolite. The words used to describe what people felt like are typically appreciated, engaged and included. To succeed in this exercise requires people to experiment, break conventions and persist undeterred in the face of repeated failure. This is not going to happen unless people throw their whole selves into the exercise, and that means engaging emotionally.

The groups that perform least well are those that attempt to plan and control activity, to work it out theoretically rather than through trial and error. These groups tend to break up, with people becoming increasingly uninterested. There is little noise, very little activity and zero excitement. The conversation becomes concentrated in a small group while others are left isolated and excluded, feeling powerless. Many such groups simply give up. Far from the professional being personal, the professional has become transactional. Tell me what to do and I'll do it, don't tell me what to do and I'll wait for further instructions.

A blank canvas

Guatam Duggal is Managing Director and Global Head of Bancassurance at Standard Chartered Bank. Guatam's request of his team is, 'I want you to imagine you have a blank canvas. Write or draw on it your vision, your dreams for the best future you can imagine for our customers and for our colleagues.' This simple request is an invitation to express and act upon:

- what we all know and experience, which is that things are simply not good enough
- the desire we all have to contribute to making a positive difference
- the capability we all have to shape what better looks like

What Guatam is trying to instil in his team is not 'you can have whatever you want' but 'if you don't know what you want you're never going to get it'. But if they do know what they want, he is interested and will work with them and support them to try and make that happen. This is the role that others can play in strengthening people's resilience, their determination and ability to be undeterred and actively pursue their vision of what better looks like.

The Maverick leader characteristic of being undeterred is distinct and unique among the other characteristics of resourcefulness, nonconformist and experimental. Why? Because, more than any of the others, it is a function of relationships. All our Maverick leaders told us of how they got strong positive emotional support from somewhere: some from their church, some from their family members, and some from supporters in their organization. No one goes it alone. Many of you will be familiar with the African proverb, 'If you want to go fast, go alone, if you want to go far, go together.'

Maverick leaders want to go far and understand that at least initially that may mean they cannot go fast because they need the support, the encouragement and the wisdom of others to sustain them, to enable them to be undeterred in the face of opposition and hostility.

Go together

Mmusi Aloysias Maimane is a black South African politician, the leader of South Africa's opposition Democratic Alliance (DA) political party from 10 May 2015 to 23 October 2019. In sharing his story with us, Mmusi said, reflecting on his youth:

> I can remember most as a young teenager running programmes where it became [so obvious] that black kids and white kids needed to be in the same place, in the same dormitories, because it was important for us to figure out that space [to figure each other out].

The Democratic Alliance is predominantly a white political party, and for Mmusi to join it was perceived by many black South Africans as a kind of betrayal. When asked about his rationale for joining the DA, Mmusi explained his driving principle:

> To govern in a way that the oppressed and the oppressor end up in the same place such that both are liberated from the mindset of inferiority and the mindset of superiority – we need to achieve both if we are going to build a reconciled society and work together as one people, able to prosper together – that's what one South Africa is about.

When Luciano Cirinà interviewed for a job at Generali, one of the largest global insurance companies, he immediately told the HR recruiters that he wanted to work abroad. During the interview, his potential boss, the head of the R&D department, promised to send him overseas, but just for occasional business trips and only after proving his skills for three or four years at least. Not satisfied with the proposal, Luciano stood up and said, 'Your offer is attractive, but it looks too domestic. I acknowledge your seniority; however, I have to look inside myself and follow my ambitions. I want to go abroad from day one; therefore I have to decline your offer.'

Luckily for Generali, another person got hold of Luciano and offered him an alternative job: a one-way ticket to Germany with no chance of returning to the company's Italian headquarters. Luciano was undeterred by the frightening proposal; he was thrilled at the chance to fulfil his goal. No one was there to mentor him. He alone would be responsible for his mistakes. Luciano's Maverick spirit turned out to be the beginning of a fortunate journey for him and for Generali, where he has worked for 32 years. Fortunate, because today Luciano is a member of the Group Management Committee, and is running the most profitable market across the entire Generali Group.

It is not by accident that under Luciano's management in the Austria, Central and Eastern Europe and Russia region, Generali is overachieving results and beating competitors. His love affair with this multifaceted region dates back to when Generali asked Luciano to take over the Austrian business. At the time the company was failing badly. The previous CEO had engaged consultants to advise on restructuring and 'to tell him what to do'. The consultancy's fees were pricey, and the restructuring proposals and consequent redundancies had the staff and union reps 'up in arms'.

Before taking on the role as CEO of Generali Austria, Luciano asked for two things: the company's commitment to relocate his family to Vienna and the replacement of the entire Austrian management team. His superiors agreed. Once in position, Luciano found himself in the middle of a legal court battle with the unions over whether the restructuring was legal. Luciano knew he was almost certain to win in the courts, and the restructuring would proceed. Generali Group thought the path to follow was clear: take on the union and win in court. But for Luciano, this would have been a Pyrrhic victory.

Therefore, Luciano, moved by his Maverick spirit, surprised all by inviting the union representatives for beer and sausages at a local pub. Not a conventional approach for Generali Group at that time (or now for that matter). Why did Luciano opt for beer and sausages rather than a court battle that he could easily win? Because, apart from being sociable and investing in building solid and long-lasting relationships, Luciano followed his 'life philosophy' forged in his experience in a local rugby team as a young man. A team drawn from all walks of life, including, as he put it, 'steel workers fighting for greater safety to protect their lives'.

Unlike many conventional managers who see industrial relations as management against unions or shareholders over employees, Luciano is prepared to get behind the polarized positions and find common ground through deep respect for others. And so it was, without any formal written agreement with the national union or the local union representatives, Luciano made an agreement, based on trust, to reduce the staff by meeting individual needs and circumstances. Then, finally, the unions' representatives agreed to let the court case fade away.

Being a Maverick leader is neither about putting yourself above others nor outside and beyond your community or family. When you need to challenge your community's norms, conventions and practices, it is about connecting with and going together with others, even your oppressors or opponents. The alternative? To go it alone, bosses against unions, blacks against whites, a recipe for disaster. Luciano's mantra is clear: 'If I can make a positive difference by being me, by doing it my way, I will. If I can't, I go where I can.'

Mmusi told us the story of when he and his colleagues were trying to set up a structure to help a township get organized. The idea was to help move the township on from its origins within the apartheid system. He told us of a young man who lived all his life in the township, no white people around at all, who refused to stand for the executive of the structure, because he said, 'I will not until there are white people in the structure itself.' Mmusi's reaction, 'I thought wow, here is a kid who comes from the townships who gets that the project is always about diversity, not about one race dominating.'

Nonetheless, even attempts to go together will meet with strong opposition and hostility from some and possibly many, at least at first. We asked Mmusi where he gets his ability to persist, to be undeterred in the face of opposition: opposition from white people who see their policies and actions as a threat to their position; opposition manifest in attacks on Twitter, from the press and at times threats to his security and the security of his family. Mmusi's response was, 'I have a steel conviction that says, we were placed on this planet to bring about significant change, and… in that instance the opposition becomes miniscule, in contrast to the goal.' His response echoes the words of the philosopher Immanuel Kant: 'God has set us on the stage where we can make each other happy, it rests with us, and us alone to do so' (Kant, 1997). This a life philosophy.

Life philosophy and higher-order goals

Returning to grit, Angela Duckworth highlights the value and influence of a well-developed life philosophy. This philosophy aids and aligns your higher-order goals. It is often an existential 'why' that creates a deep-seated sense of purpose and serves as something of a compass or guidepost throughout your adult life. People who display higher levels of self-control and grit are able to remain focused on their lower-level goals (by using self-control) despite competing distractions which may arise. When these goals are challenged or not met, gritty people are able to quickly redirect their energy into pursuing a new goal that still aligns with their higher-level/superordinate goals. This is often because these individuals have a coherent sense of the value of their ultimate goals. They are grounded by their life philosophy or value system.

Urvashi Sahni recalls being an independent and resourceful young mind right from the age of nine when she coordinated her classmates into putting on a play from their textbooks and used it as a local fundraiser. As a young married woman, she was prevented from attending university classes. However, she explained that she 'was never willing to accept boundaries' so got her Bachelor's degree in political science, sociology and economics through home-based self-learning. 'I found professors to help me, and when I needed to get extra reading, I went to the library in town. In that way I got my Bachelor's degree.' Fast forward a few years and Urvashi felt the available courses did not sufficiently answer the questions she had about life, gender equality and meaning. So instead of following a set curriculum, Urvashi asked girls to write down their questions and, combined with her own experiences, at the age of 26 Urvashi designed a course in philosophy and education, to equip girls with philosophical training, critical thinking skills, social skills and, perhaps most important of all, agency – to imagine a life different to the one society had carved out for them.

This was the start of her career in education, a career which has expanded into education activism, the establishment of Study Hall Foundation, and given Urvashi international platforms, such as the World Economic Forum, to share her insights on global education reform. When asked about her incredible ability to authentically connect with people regardless of their background, whether they are heads of state, Nobel Prize winners or men and women in the rural villages, Urvashi reminded us of the value of purposeful belief:

> When you believe that you are engaged in something important and you
> believe that what you're doing is really going to make a difference, because you
> want to make that difference and you're trying to make that difference and

you're moving heaven and earth to do it, and you will give anything, anything, anything to make that difference, I think that it's not a job and it's not a career for its own sake. No... it is a cause... and it's much larger than you, which is why I think you forget who you are.

Her advice on what it takes to be a Maverick leader? Give yourself permission to be confident. Don't overthink things. Act from the 'inside'. Know what propels you. Care deeply about what you are doing. Say something – say it often, say it to everyone:

I care so much about what I do and what I talk about that I don't think about who I'm talking to, it doesn't matter. It's more about getting the message (out) there and making them listen and having them help. I think I've learnt that I have something important to say and I'm going to say it to whoever will listen and I think it needs to be said.

The good news is that grit seems to grow with age. So, if you feel as though you are not quite as unrelenting as some of the Maverick leaders in this book, there is still capacity to develop this attribute. Furthermore, there is a probability that you can develop this more easily as you get older. This is because, with the added advantage of age, you can draw on previous experiences as a reminder that 'sticking the course' is often better in the long run for the achievement of higher-level goals rather than getting distracted. An important feature in the development of your own unrelenting inner Maverick is to consider the emphasis put on the value of having a life philosophy.

Resilience

Beyond our own ability and grit, our capacity to persevere is shaped and bolstered by our internal resilience. Resilience, in its simplest form, can be understood to be a 'process of successful adaptation despite challenging circumstances' (Masten et al, 1990). There are two important aspects to note when it comes to building resilience: 1) it is developed in context of others and our environment; and 2) it is not a fixed characteristic: resilience can change (grow or diminish) over time.

Many researchers have focused on individual traits that contribute towards resilience; however, it is perhaps more helpful to understand how resilience is developed in the context of our broader social systems and relationships. In order to do this, we can use psychologist Bronfenbrenner's social ecological systems theory (Bronfenbrenner, 1977). It highlights how we are embedded within a broader social environmental structure that shapes us as individuals and is simultaneously shaped by us. We are both a by-product of our environment and have the ability to influence and change our environment. Bronfenbrenner argued that there are five 'layers' of social structure in which a person is embedded. Maverick leaders get this. They can see society operating in (and often oppressing through) these social systemic layers and, as we will see later, Mavericks work across these layers when advocating for a better society.

The first (and often most significant) layer is the **microsystem**. The microsystem includes relationships with others with whom we have direct and frequent contact. For example, our family, friends and co-workers. These relationships correlate to Erikson's theory of psychosocial development, discussed in Chapter 2, which highlights how relationships with others in early childhood enable the development of trust, autonomy, confidence and industriousness, all of which are understood to be traits of resilient individuals.

The second structural layer is the **mesosystem** and it refers to the type of engagement between our microsystems. For example, the kind of relationships that exist between our family and friends, or our family and work colleagues. If there is a positive relationship between these microsystems then the mesosystem will be positive too. We can think of the mesosystem almost as a commentary on the quality of our microsystems. It reflects how healthy or unhealthy our close relationship networks are.

The third structural layer is the **exosystem**. The exosystem includes relationships in which we have less direct, more removed contact, yet these relationships still form a significant part of shaping our daily experiences. For example, the community to which you belong, the institution or organization you work for.

The fourth structural layer is called the **macrosystem**. This is the most removed system, made up of values, beliefs, political ideologies, socioeconomic status, geographical location and social norms which shape and influence all the embedded systems within it. For example, the macrosystemic influence of personal wealth, nationality or social rights within your country of residence will influence the kind of work you do, the extent of the networks you can form and the ways in which you view relationships and yourself.

The fifth layer is called the **chronosystem** and simply refers to how the system changes and is influenced over time by external factors. The context in which you live. This includes significant moments or transitions that happen 'to you' by virtue of being alive at that particular point in time. These can be personal or social. For example, navigating a significant medical diagnosis at a particular age or, more broadly, how growing up during World War Two impacted a generation or how the implications of climate change are influencing the micro-, meso-, exo- and macrosystems for children growing up in today's context.

As you can tell, these social structural layers are distinct but interconnected. When researching factors that bolster resilience, thinking about individual personality traits alone is insufficient. In order to understand someone's capacity for resilience, you cannot ignore the external environmental factors, the social structures around that individual, that aid and develop, or reduce their personal capacity to cope.

Invest in yourself

Damaris Seleina Parsitau has been told she is a 'too much' woman for standing up for and setting about delivering girls' education in Maasailand. She has been fought by religious leaders for stepping on 'their business', by men in her culture for challenging the patriarchy, and by political leaders who feel she is looking over their shoulders, seeking a political role for herself. Despite opposition from all quarters, today Damaris is a thought leader in girls' education in Kenya, and the founder of Let Maasai Girls Learn, an initiative that seeks to rally global, regional and local action for girls. She holds a PhD from Kenyatta University on religion, gender and public life in Kenya, as well as an MA from the University of Nairobi and a BA from Egerton University.

Damaris does not give up easily. Where she came from, she had to overcome much to achieve what she has achieved. We asked Damaris where she got her spirit from, her ability to be undeterred by obstacles, by resistance, by people who want to stop her. Her answer: 'I draw on myself, strategizing, rethinking, how do I overcome this challenge, how do I renegotiate, how do I speak to people better?' This is not a blind act of faith that somehow, she will find a way. Damaris invests in herself; as she put it: 'I invest in learning, in educating myself, in speaking to people, in engaging in conversations with people that inspire me and trying to read about them, how they have overcome challenges.' And she added, 'But I also rely on the people around me, the resourceful people around me.'

In the words of Luciano Cirinà, 'This enthusiastic journey could not have been possible without the endless support of my family, the commitment of the many colleagues I met along the way and the trust of Assicurazioni Generali. My heartfelt thanks to all of you.'

We all have it within us

Maverick leaders are *obsessive*. They feel they bear a debt of obligation to the world; furthermore, they have a strong sense of what they want to achieve by way of change; they won't let go or let up easily; they understand that success will almost certainly come only with hard work and perseverance; and, to this extent, their behaviour may come across as compulsive. But they are also collaborative, resourceful and experimental. They have a higher-order purpose, a high-level goal that directs and informs their day-to-day decisions and provides the grit required to persist in the face of setbacks and opposition.

These are characteristics we can all develop and practise if we are inspired to make our world a better place.

In the next chapter we explore how the dominant thinking around what leadership and followership are runs counter to the Maverick leader's mind- and skillset. The Maverick leader does not seek followers, she seeks co-creators. The Maverick leader does not seek authority or indeed use authority above influence, he works with purpose and betterment. The Maverick leader, whatever his or her hierarchical position, does not use hierarchy to get things done, but uses questioning and learning to move things forward.

Maverick styles of leadership

We have described five attributes associated with Mavericks who make a positive difference to the world. We have emphasized the importance of personal agency in the formation of the Maverick mind and character. But what are the external forces that shape Maverick behaviour? From what models of leadership do they draw inspiration? Within what kinds of organization do they most naturally thrive? In what forms of societies do they give of their best and flourish?

Mavericks, of course, are not simply the beneficiaries of certain types of organization, community and society. They are also the shapers of institutions. In fact, the history of mind and culture is largely a history of the extraordinary individuals, many of them Mavericks, who brought new ideas and practices to the way in which the collective life is lived.

Civilization could be said to be the setting in which the human spirit was able to find its fullest expression. It is the state of society that is most favourable – *and receptive* – to the moral aspirations, nonconformity, resourcefulness, experimental spirit and resilience of Mavericks.

History moves at a variable pace. At certain moments, there is a quickening of the pulse. The Renaissance, the Enlightenment, the Industrial Revolution, for example, are moments characterized by a critical mass of highly original thinkers whose combined talents took history in a new direction. Among these individuals there will have been a disproportionate number of Mavericks, as we have described them in earlier chapters. In this and the next two chapters, we describe the contextual factors that are both the cause and effect of their ability to reshape history.

Leadership is in our DNA

To lead and to be led is natural. We are a species that would seem to expect – and require – leadership, even if sometimes we regret the fact, and disparage those whom we trust with the task. Human societies have never been entirely egalitarian. We find it difficult to imagine any form of collective activity without some degree of hierarchy. We look to leaders to show the way, set an example and inspire action.

However natural leadership might be, we do not have to put up with the model of leadership to which we have become accustomed or the leadership behaviour that we see all around us. We should be asking more insistently what kind of leadership is best fitted to the particular challenges facing the world. And from personal experience, we should be reflecting on what attributes we most want to find in our leaders. Just as important, what attributes do we *not* want, and *not* need?

We would benefit from more leaders who exhibited the idealism, resourcefulness, resilience, playfulness and originality of the Mavericks that we have featured in earlier chapters. The truth, however, is that most organizational cultures are wired to elicit far less ambitious forms of behaviour. In place of courage and creativity, we find a debilitating aversion to risk and a reluctance to test heterodox ideas. The workplace can so easily become overly compliant and complacent.

So, what in particular is inhibiting the Maverick spirit that we would like to believe lurks in every manager?

Organizational distortions of leadership

Every leader is, at least partly, a creature of the organization he or she leads. For example, highly bureaucratic organizations will favour leaders who regard their role primarily as one of control and coordination. Hierarchical organizations will equate leadership with seniority. The fact is that very few organizations are natural settings for Maverick leaders. Three particular practices perpetuate the preponderance of non-Maverick leaders.

First, the leaders who earn promotion are likely to be those who are admired for being a safe pair of hands.

They knuckle down to the daily task of doing a good job. They don't rock the boat. They are loyal citizens of the organizational culture. And they surround themselves with like-minded, equally dutiful staff.

In short, their behaviour is entirely rational, if by this we mean behaviour that is self-promoting within the culture they inhabit. In his theory of organizational action, Chris Argyris has described this as 'model 1 behaviour' (Argyris, 1977). The core values are to succeed, not fail; to suppress negative feelings, such as disloyalty or personal frustration; and only to make decisions that can be defended rationally. Such leaders betray a very distinctive style: they want, above all, to be seen to be in control; they go to great lengths to protect their reputation; they discourage enquiry, regarding it as a form of disloyalty; they treat their views as self-evidently sensible and correct; they abhor open debate or meetings that confront difficult issues; in short, their behaviour is primarily defensive.

Second, the leaders are appointed by those above them and are therefore nothing like as diverse as those they are appointed to lead.

They are the kind of people that those already in power believe will make great future leaders. In other words, they resemble those who select them. No wonder that each generation of leader is a chip off the same block. However, there is no evidence that this is a good way for leaders to find their successors. If anything, evidence points to diversity rather than uniformity as a critical ingredient in a leadership team, especially in turbulent times calling for innovation. The fact is that our leaders are chosen from far too narrow a sample of applicants, mainly because the process of selection itself is controlled by far too narrow a sample of selectors.

In some organizations, leaders are now being chosen 'from below', rather than above. Perhaps the best judge of a leader is someone who has experience of being led by them, knows what it feels like, and has seen the results. Leadership skill is very difficult to assess from above. Because leaders derive their ability to influence events by attracting a following, it stands to reason that those in the best position to recognize the leaders of the future will be some of the youngest and most junior people in the organization. They will be those wanting to be inspired. In particular, they will be looking for creativity, emotional intelligence, empathic skills and humility in their leaders, a rather different set of attributes, but ones associated with Maverick styles of leadership.

Third, the leaders owe their authority to their position in a hierarchy and therefore tend to exhibit authoritarian behaviour.

Many organizations continue to confuse leadership with management, and leaders with bosses. True leaders don't give instructions. They do not deal in the currency of orders and obedience. They don't need to. The power they exercise is at the discretion of their followers. Theirs is an invitational model of leadership. If your power resides mainly in the position you hold, then you're a manager, not a leader. Great leaders hold sway by permission, not by coercion. Increasingly in business, we have noticed a healthy trend among our corporate clients to allow leaders to emerge through the force of their character rather than the authority vested in their position.

In short, the market in leadership must never become a closed shop. We need to find more ways to open up the market in leadership, design a more inclusive process of selection, imagine a more distributed model of how power is best exercised, and introduce a greater variety of leadership styles.

Non-hierarchical forms of leadership

Madalo Samati is the current Executive Director of the Creative Centre for Community Mobilization (CRECCOM), Malawi. She is the Chairperson of the government-commissioned National Girls Education Trust, advises the Ministry of Education, as well as the Malawian First Lady, and was described as a leadership inspiration in a tweet by Michelle Obama. If you met her you might describe Madalo as a down-to-earth, intellectually humble, warm person with a very contagious laugh. But she told us proudly that there is a stubbornness and feistiness in her. At the age of nine, while visiting her grandmother, she broke all social and traditional norms by single-handedly killing and preparing a chicken. Refusing to see why she had to wait for her brother or uncle (or any male) to return home to get the job done, she decided she could do the task and was hungry, so she took action. Consequently this caused some upset and quite a lot of shock as this was not a 'role or work' for a girl, but Madalo has never been one to let social expectations hold her back. Rooted in her spiritual faith, Madalo is self-confident, doesn't get bothered by what critics have to say, is fearless and a strong-sense-of-purpose kind of person. Empowering others is her calling: 'I believe I was born to do this and I'm living it out.'

Growing up, she and her seven siblings were abandoned by their father. Their mother worked tirelessly to keep them in school. For Madalo, education was the only hope of getting out of poverty. Described by her mother as a 'stubborn' child, Madalo realized quickly that her stubbornness was an internal strength that she could harness for her (and others') greater good. She explained how witnessing the struggles of her mother, and watching countless girls in her community drop out of school due to teenage pregnancy (her sister included) was motivation to never become dependent on someone else, especially a man, and never blame someone else for her failures. Right from the age of nine, Madalo realized the ways in which social structures placed less value and expectation on girls and that she needed to make her own way in the world – and with a bold tenacity, she did just that.

It was in university where a passion for social change emerged, being able to see the power that information had in changing people's lives and transforming communities. She reflected on her early career and how her Maverick spirit was evident from the start: 'I grew a passion. To tell the girls (in village communities) that it is possible for you to change the world.' In 1999 Madalo began working at one of the first NGOs in Malawi with the mission to mobilize and empower rural communities to find local solutions to challenges they faced. Currently CRECCOM is nationwide, and under Madalo's leadership the organization has trained over 500 interns, launched its first social enterprise and redesigned its 20-year plan (almost overnight) when Covid-19 struck. Madalo gets what it means to be adaptive, especially when organizational survival depends on it. When Covid emerged in Malawi, Madalo was one of the first to recognize its severity and without waiting for permission began an urgent re-visioning of 'how' CRECCOM works. Her focus across the seven pillars within the organization shifted to just one single question: 'How do we remain relevant in a Covid world?' With that single focus in mind, Madalo has led her team, organization and community through the pandemic.

She doesn't view her role as a position or status to cling to; in fact, Madalo flattens hierarchy and invites succession planning, insisting that her job is make the organization less dependent on her, and therefore able to reach new heights one day in her absence.

There is a widespread feeling that leadership, particularly in its hierarchical form, is not delivering value. The trust that followers place in their leaders, whether at work or in society generally, is low, and falling (Edelman,

2021). Leaders are increasingly seen as remote, dishonest and untrustworthy. They are believed to be motivated primarily by self-interest. The notion of service to the community would seem to belong to the past.

This is where Mavericks come in. Perhaps they are the ones to show us a way out of this quandary. Instead of waiting to be appointed to a position of power on the basis of their credentials, they give themselves the right, even the duty, to 'be the change they want to see in the world'. In other words, they *appoint themselves* to make a difference, at whatever level they find themselves in the organization. They don't need anyone else's consent to act as a responsible human being. And they are not prepared to wait to be given permission by the powers that be.

We could say that one of the problems in a modern economy is that too many jobholders choose **not** to exercise the authority already vested in the job they hold, with the result that many workplaces are rather passive. Too many people are waiting for instructions they do not need – *and should not want*.

Mavericks are tempted to dismiss 'learnt helplessness' as an excuse for inaction. They disapprove of a state of affairs in which even the authority of the job is not being fully exploited by its holder. The danger of such passivity is that it creates greater opportunities for power seekers to take up the slack and exert disproportionate authority. Some organizations are little more than a few 'actives' commanding a multitude of 'passives'.

The crisis of authority in the world is that we have a system of incentives, rewards and mechanisms that brings the wrong people to the top, or rather, it brings an unrepresentative or insufficiently diverse group of people into positions of power.

Even democracies are failing in this task. Gaining any kind of power has become an obstacle race that only those psychotic enough to want to exercise power over others have the patience to handle.

The Maverick leader is representative of a class of people who have the potential to change the world for the better but are unprepared to comply with the processes – and jump the hurdles – that have formed the traditional route to leadership. They see these processes as biased and unduly restrictive.

The liberating benefits that Mavericks can bring to the world are readily apparent in those organizations that are less hierarchical, less bureaucratic and more open to experimentation. In new ventures, entrepreneurial start-ups, innovation labs and hackathons, the ability of Mavericks to contribute and make a difference is all too evident. It is at a certain stage in the growth of a firm that these opportunities tend to be closed down and a mix of fear and deference takes hold. And yet, it is often the large organization that stands to benefit most from an injection of the Maverick spirit.

The emergence of the Maverick leader

Wherever organizations are loosening up, dismantling hierarchy, flattening their structures, encouraging communities of practice, or using hackathons to tap into the wisdom of the collective, we witness a new style of leadership emerge, one that is more purposeful, person-centred, creative and resourceful. The power of these emergent leaders to effect change does not reside in their position, or their followership, or their authority, but in their actions, their way of being and their outward focus.

They are noticed for *what they do* rather than *who they are.*

Their legitimacy as agents of influence is vested not in their title but in their talent, particularly their independence of thought and commitment to action. In the way they behave they are setting a style and providing compelling answers to the three big questions asked of any leader, however that term is defined:

- What cause are you serving, or what truly matters to you?
- What kind of person are you and whom do you aspire to become?
- What values guide your will, and how would you like to be judged?

When these questions are well answered, Maverick leaders will discover that they instigate – and in turn become part of – a movement of fellow Mavericks. This is the network effect that often renders Maverick leadership so effective.

Andre Norman

My belief is that every human being has the capacity to be great. I've met people who've lived their entire lives in wheelchairs. I've met people born without limbs. I've met people who are blind. I've met people who have been given the worst hand you could ever imagine. And they've raised themselves up to be great.

129

This is the conviction of Andre Norman, the 'justice warrior' whom we met in Chapter 1. Yet his optimism is tempered by the knowledge that society does not give everyone an equal chance. Communities differ in the opportunities they create for their members:

> We are 400 years into this experiment called America. And our communities don't look much different than when we first got here. So, when I watched George Floyd die, that looked a lot like slavery to me.

Andre is determined to bring about change:

> I've been told that the environment will change the person before the person changes their environment. That has been the standard. I can't accept that. We must change the environment if we are to change the person.

Pitting himself against the status quo, he sees himself as a change agent and an outlier:

> I will change the environment. That is my goal. If something is working for everybody, not just a few, then it doesn't need to be changed. But if something is not working for everybody, then it needs to be challenged and changed.

He believes that many people in all walks of life can feel constrained – not only those in prison, but also many people in corporations, agencies and communities. 'There are so many people trapped in businesses, including CEOs.'

He knows full well that there will be pushback, resistance and resentment, but insists that he is built to withstand it: 'My father came at me hard. Society came at me hard. So, I've been conditioned to withstand whatever it is that's coming at me. I don't yield. I only go forward.'

Not quitting has become part of his character:

> I say to people, I don't have setbacks. I just have learning lessons. When I was a child, my father walked out of the house. He taught me it was OK to quit on his family. And the lesson I internalized is, it's OK to quit. And I became a professional quitter. I quit on school, I quit on band, I quit on sports, I quit on leadership, I quit on church, I quit on choir, I quit on everything. So I learnt how to quit anytime it got tough. I walked away because that's what my dad taught me. I became a professional quitter. And it wasn't until I confronted this and dealt with it that I learnt the big lesson. Quitting is not the way. Regardless of how huge or insurmountable the problems in front of me, quitting is not the

solution. Therefore, I can only win. Even if I don't get there, I'm going to win because I never quit.

Andre wants to give a voice to those with first-hand experience of the inequalities that most need to be addressed in society. He reflects on his own early life and how the attempt by the authorities to fix the school system involved 'decisions from on high' affecting 'somebody down low'. He says, 'I see that person as myself.' Nowadays, working closely with powerful people, he says, 'My first thought is the person at the bottom of the totem pole.'

He observes that, in the United States today, there are a whole range of people who have appointed themselves to be spokespeople for minority groups. For example, there's a lot of conversation around prison re-entry, prison reform, criminal justice reform, but none of the people who've been in the system are at the table. So you have people who don't understand the nuances and intricacies of what they're talking about.

He points to various troubling issues: 'What is the impact of changing an entry process into a prison? What is the impact of using an extra blanket or pair of socks? What is the impact of solitary confinement? What is the impact of any of this stuff?' But he goes on to suggest that the approach to these issues is utterly ineffectual: 'We all know – and the government knows – that the people sitting at the table have no clue. So you have people who don't understand speaking for those who are going through something, and it just makes it worse.' He adds, 'The people that we currently have at the table can't impact change. They have great narratives, they have great sound articulation, they dress up well, but they can't, and won't, bring about change.'

Who *does* understand? Whose voice *should* be heard? How is the truth *best* articulated? Andre gives the example of Ferguson, Missouri, where Michael Brown Jr died in 2014. His death sparked the Black Lives Matter movement. This is how Andre tells the tale:

I've gone and I've worked in Ferguson. And I met Michael Brown Sr, the father of the murdered man. And I spent the last five years mentoring him. I now put him at the table, and I show him how to navigate. He made some mistakes along the way. He's not a spokesperson. He's a real speaker. He's a hurt father. So, we're putting him at the table. We're not worried about him saying the wrong thing. We're not worried about him being offensive. We put him at the table and let him speak from his heart, because, when people die in the street, it's not a concept, it's a passion. When you suffer passionate losses, you need to have people speaking for those losses. And it's not always going to be politically correct. It's not going to be accurate all the time. So, we have to be OK with the inaccuracy.

This is where we find Andre today – with, for example, a young guy just out of prison, with immense talent, trying to find his way, but without anybody to give him a real opportunity:

> I go back, and I find these people. I work in prisons, detention centres, inner city spaces, treatment centres. I challenge – and I train – these people to be advocates. They think they can't be advocates. They don't dress right. They don't look right. They don't talk right. But what they do have is the experience from which to tell it as it is.
>
> I want to humanize the cause and humanize the people in the cause.

Andre recognizes the Maverick within himself in so far as his motivation is not money. 'Sure, I want to make more money, but that's not my driving force. What drives me is: How do I help people? How do I connect to people?' And the way he does so is powerful:

> I experiment with the concept that prisoners, felons and gang leaders can be world leaders. And they can impact change globally. That was my experiment – and I was the first test case. We're now 21 years into the experiment. And it's still going. I go inside prisons across the country and around the world. And I get these people – the downtrodden and the forgotten – to stand up.

He sees leadership potential all around him. 'I believe that former felons, criminals, addicts and people who've been cast aside can lead.' And this is what he wants to achieve:

> For those who are biblical, I'm looking for Davids. I want an army of Davids – an army of those who've been overlooked, overshadowed, cast aside and forgotten. I'm saying, 'You're the true kings, you're the true power, not the people who sit at the top of the hill.' So, I go into prisons, and I convince prisoners who used to kill each other that now they need to save people. They need to think deeply. They need to do differently.

What are the leadership lessons of Andre's journey?

He is a wonderful advocate of self-leadership: finding your own voice; operating from your own first-hand experience; earning influence by drawing upon something that you know better than anyone else.

We are all potential leaders if we lead from what we know. Authenticity in a leader comes from speaking from lived experience and direct know-ledge. Too often, power is given to those who feel entitled to it rather than to those whose experience merits it. Too many leaders are spokespeople for the concerns of others, concerns that were never part of their own life.

The Maverick leader looks to find the leadership potential in others. In Andre's case, it is among those who have suffered various forms of injustice. The Maverick leader tries not to usurp the voice of others with greater experience of the issue at hand. The Maverick leader is acutely aware of territory where the voice of others would be more authentic and therefore more effective than his own.

The Maverick leader's relationship to the concept of leadership itself

Mavericks are, in a sense, natural leaders: they like going first, they don't wait for permission or 'the right moment', they are impatient, they are happy to force the issue, they pre-empt excuses for inaction, and they repress their own doubts. They make things happen.

They live the sentiment that inspired Robert F Kennedy to say that:

> Few will have the greatness to bend history itself, but each of us can work to change a small portion of events. It is from numberless diverse acts of courage and belief that human history is shaped. Each time a man stands up for an ideal, or acts to improve the lot of others, or strikes out against injustice, he sends forth a tiny ripple of hope, and crossing each other from a million different centres of energy and daring those ripples build a current which can sweep down the mightiest walls of oppression and resistance.

Mavericks possess a strong sense of their own identity as free spirits and self-confident actors on the stage of life, albeit sometimes over-confident in their own ability to shape the world in line with their vision. They are not in the least fatalistic. They hold fast to a belief in human agency and the power of will. Their view of history is that it is the record of those who 'showed up', found their voice, refused to be cowed, either by events or by bullies, and resisted the temptation to plead helplessness.

But 'leadership' as a concept is not part of their vocabulary, or their identity, mainly because it implies some notion of followership. Just as they themselves would hate to be led, so they are loath to lead, given its traditional associations with hierarchy, inequality and the prerogatives of the powerful. In this respect Maverick leaders are unusual leaders. Not only would they run a mile from following anyone else, they're also somewhat dismissive of those who choose to do so. For example, they would be uncomfortable in the presence of acolytes. For the same reason, they regard leadership as almost irreparably contaminated by its associations with 'great leaders', 'charismatics' and 'men of history', all of which tend to be associated with notions of loyalty, solidarity and alignment among 'followers', 'fans' and other assorted adherents.

It is tempting to fall for the belief that history is the creation of a rather small number of very special individuals. In *War and Peace*, Tolstoy famously challenged this concept. Why did France invade Russia? Was it the ambition of Napoleon? Was it Czar Alexander's stubbornness? Were the decisions of senior diplomats to blame? Tolstoy argued that we should not pay too much heed to the 'great men' theories of historians. In fact, he preferred to cast these 'heroes' in the role of 'history's slave'. We should, he suggested, blame 'the millions of men' who so easily succumbed to the will of 'these weak individuals' (Mouton, 2017). It is perhaps a handy falsehood, generously offered by historians, for the mass of people to have someone to blame for their lot. When things go wrong, it is the fault of our leaders.

In *Doom: The politics of catastrophe*, Niall Ferguson makes the case that leaders are less responsible for the events of history than the networks over which they preside or within which they live (Ferguson, 2021). And this is truer today than ever before, because the world is so much more complex. Ferguson draws upon the Covid-19 pandemic – and the responses of our political leaders to the gathering crisis – to challenge the simplistic view that individuals make history. 'The problem is systemic', he counters, making the point that bureaucracy bore as much of the responsibility as governments for the decisions that were made.

One way in which individuals working for domineering leaders choose to handle them is by 'asking for forgiveness, not permission' whenever they take a risk by acting autonomously. Maverick leaders are uncomfortable with this tactic. They see it as giving such leaders another reason to act as gods. To a Maverick, there is nothing to forgive when someone tries in good faith, but fails, to make the world a better place. The very notion that one of the roles of the leader is to atone for the sins of the brave souls who go out on a limb to try something bold and creative is absurd and demeaning.

If anything, leaders should be there to encourage a greater number of 'bold failures', not fewer.

The art of leadership, for the Maverick leader, is to build a coalition of change without the need for a hierarchy or the exercise of authority.

What sets the Maverick leader apart?

There are three relationships that define the Maverick leader's role and style of leadership.

First, there is their **relationship with the world**, the object of their strategic intent. This is their prime focus. There is a cause to be served, a reality 'out there' to be altered in some way for the better. But how exactly?

Second, there is their **relationship with their sense of self**. This is important, in so far as they tend to load onto themselves, rather than others, a disproportionate duty of care to the world they find themselves in. Who do they need to be – or become – to fulfil this obligation?

Third, there is their **relationship to others**, particularly those who have the potential to add huge value to the enterprise. To the extent that the cause can only be served if large numbers of fellow enthusiasts are brought on board, what needs to be done to build a movement of equals? How do you catalyse such a network?

Leading with intent

The existential nature of some of the challenges facing the world is daunting:

- the human impairment of the planet's ecosystem
- the declining trust in shareholder capitalism
- the emergence of artificial intelligence (AI)

For the Maverick leader, a strategy that measures up to these problems cannot be simply a plan of attack, with targets and milestones. It is more likely to be a range of speculative ideas. The ends and means still have to be discovered. Trial and error is the only possible method. Pretending that it can be cast in the form of a traditional plan, as though it were a budgeting exercise with predictable outcomes and key performance indicators, is to misconceive the scale and complexity of the issue. The very unpredictability of the ways in which success will be found means that the conventional use of promises and commitments to bring people into line becomes irrelevant. The adaptive capabilities of Maverick leaders make them more suited to challenges whose achievement requires an openness to experimentation, surprise and discovery.

Suman Sachdeva is an Education Specialist in UNICEF and a woman who leads with intent. She reminds us that for impactful change you need sustainable collaboration. After working on a government education reform project in the mid-'90s, Suman realized that if they were really going to have an impact on the lives of marginalized communities, education needed to be understood more holistically; it needed to incorporate social inclusion and most importantly it needed to include life skills. To teach children how to be resilient, how to negotiate, what their agency is, to empower them to pursue their dreams and make good decisions. Her work in transforming the education sector in India is hugely impressive. She would not tell you as much, but as she told us story after story it was clear that her Maverick spirit, her desire to create a more equitable world was enacted in her ability to see where the social systems fell short and then work collaboratively with government, non-profit and the private sector to ensure no child falls through the gaps. Suman sees the social layers that Bronfenbrenner's theory highlighted in Chapter 6, and she works through these multiple layers to bring about sustainable and systemic change.

One of her more recent projects is the establishment of an online career guidance portal, making the transition from high school to college, and gradually to the workforce, more accessible, especially for young girls in India. The portal informs adolescent users of 144 different types of careers, in real time, and is gender sensitive. It provides information, social role models, practical guidance and access to scholarships and funding. It is multilingual to accommodate India's many languages, and sustainable through the strong working relationships with various stakeholders involved. What started out as a single idea has developed into a project currently implemented in 15 states across India and impacting the lives of 17 million adolescents. One of the greatest aspects of this initiative is that, like Suman and several of our Mavericks, it is agile, adaptable and future-focused: 'We are preparing children for jobs that will be available in 20 years – we are not just thinking about the now.'

Suman is not done yet. In fact, she has just taken a bold step to embrace a brand new challenge in the hope of being able to make a systemic impact on the education sector in Sierra Leone. We have no doubt she will.

Leading oneself

Maverick leaders are typically comfortable in their own skin. Their life has a meaning. They are doing something that matters to them. They are engaged with the world around them. A good question therefore might be, 'Are you perhaps a bit too comfortable? Is there a degree of complacency creeping into your life? Are you stretching yourself sufficiently?'

There is always a temptation to stay close to whatever has given you your success so far. But every good life moves through phases. It has – and needs – moments of transition, when something new and daring is tried. It may be a different way of behaving, or a different way of thinking, or a different persona. Life itself is a grand experiment.

The Maverick leader is often seen as larger than life. They carry a certain confidence, self-possession, even aura. They don't hold back. They make things happen. Some would say that they lack diplomacy, can sometimes be a bit brusque with others, perhaps because they seem to be absorbed in their work. Their excuse will often be that they 'have more important things to do'. Their life is held together by a strong will and a focus on that part of reality that they want to change.

They know themselves well enough to know that their vices and virtues are bound up in their preference for acting on the world rather than just reflecting upon it. They are most in their element looking outwards at possibilities rather than inwards at doubts. They know full well that their identity as a Maverick is bound up with their preference for praxis rather than analysis. For example, they prefer to lead by example rather than by instruction. For most Maverick leaders, it is not so much the answers – or even the questions – that they bring to the table, as it is the bold and brave *manner* in which they attack a problem.

They know that their reputation for being in a hurry to achieve results in the real world can cause consternation in those around them who would prefer to take things more slowly and carefully. The effective Maverick leader takes care not to give an impression of hubris or arrogance. This is where their emotional intelligence is vital. It alerts them to the effect they may be having on others.

'Know Thyself' is just as potent now as it was 2,500 years ago. Its premise is that self-awareness and self-knowledge equip you to relate better with others and, thereby, live a more fulfilling life. It is an ancient expression of the modern idea that emotional intelligence makes any joint enterprise more effective. As you make better sense of your own emotions, so you become better able to read the emotions of others. For example, noticing – and being able to describe and name – your own emotions, and the situations that give rise to them, enhances your ability to interpret the emotions of others. This empathic intelligence has been shown to be related not only to personal well-being but also to inter-personal effectiveness. It is the skill of mentalization, the extraordinary human ability to use the explanatory model for what is going on in our own mind to read the minds of others – their desires, intentions and beliefs. As we become better at understanding our own thoughts and feelings, so we become more attuned to our fellow humans. It is, in short, the evolutionary blessing of our self-consciousness. We are able to see each other through each other's eyes.

To a large extent, we live the stories we tell about ourselves, and our future is circumscribed by them. Naturally, the stories we tell will inevitably have a strong arbitrary element. We make them up to some extent. We could, if we had wanted, have told ourselves very different stories, and chosen different events around which to tell them. This flexibility of narrative means that we are free, to some extent, to reinterpret our lives. By reshaping our past, we give ourselves the means – and the licence – to become a rather different person. We become the explanation we invent for ourselves. And just as our lives shape our stories, so our stories can reshape our lives.

So, what are the questions that need answers if we are to give a revealing account of our life so far? Here are three sets of powerful questions, both for personal reflection and shared discussion:

- **Calling:** What matters to you? What were you meant to do? To what does your talent point? What always had your name on it?
- **Circumstances:** How did you get to where you are? What experiences made you the person you have become? What obstacles did you have to surmount?
- **Choices:** Which of your decisions in life have defined you? What did you make happen by force of will? What decisions did you choose *not* to make? Which opportunities did you seize – or miss?

Answering these questions opens a window onto your sense of self. But they can also inspire the desire for personal renewal. A good exercise is to return to the same questions but, by answering them differently, create a fresh narrative, paint an alternative portrait, and bring out hidden aspects of your nature. Perhaps it is time to forgive yourself (and others) for past demeanours, release yourself from any lingering feelings of guilt, face up to some of your self-delusions, and start to imagine different scenarios for your future.

Leading the movement

The Maverick leader is often misunderstood or misinterpreted. First impressions can be that he or she is a lone wolf, or a firebrand or a shooting star. They can be seen as quixotic, unpredictable and inconsistent, perhaps even moody, aloof or vain. These perceptions may well be unfair. But people cannot help forming judgements of others, however premature. We are drawn to what is unusual in the other person and then use our imagination to create a portrait.

The implications are important. These initial impressions can harden into firm judgements. They may impair the Maverick leader's ability to attract and enrol advocates to their cause, even among fellow Mavericks. The challenge will be to find ways of negating, or at least neutralizing these early reactions.

Misperception, of course, can flow both ways. It is not as though Maverick leaders themselves don't harbour certain biases. For example, they have a tendency to form generalized judgements of those at different levels in a typical hierarchy. Borrowing from Barry Oshry's terminology, this is how Maverick leaders, in their more cynical state of mind, might characterize the three levels of an organization:

- **tops**: unimaginative, unambitious, indecisive, waiting for retirement to rediscover their humanity
- **middles**: fearful, hamstrung, compliant, seeing barriers where there are none
- **bottoms**: disengaged, fatalistic, alienated, dutiful, doing just enough to get by

These, of course, are unfair caricatures of workplace attitudes. They probably have no more validity than the perception that Mavericks are unreliable oddballs.

The fact remains that Maverick leaders can sometimes find themselves isolated and adrift without the leverage of an effective network to give impetus to their initiatives and projects. This can be fatal. In an organizational setting, loners achieve little. 'Squads' – tight-knit self-responsible groups – are where the action is. So, what's to be done? How, in practical terms, can a Maverick leader, without the crutch of authority or any positional power, rise above inter-personal prejudice and form a 'community of shared commitment'? We shall suggest four conversational gambits for doing so.

The Drucker conversation

The first kind of conversation is what we shall call a 'Drucker conversation' after the social scientist who effectively invented management as a theoretical discipline and not just a practical activity. Peter Drucker believed that one of the most important conversations that a boss can have with a subordinate is one that starts with the boss asking the subordinate, 'How do I need to change if I am to bring out the best in you?' The idea, of course, is that the principal role of any leader is to add value to the activities of their followers. If he or she is not doing so – if the followers are just as effective, or more effective, without such leadership – then the leader is entirely dispensable.

When the subordinate responds to their leader's question with their suggested changes of behaviour, the leader is then free to say, 'Well, if I am to change in line with your suggestions, it would help me to do so if you were to change your own behaviour in the following ways... .' The conversation can then take its natural course as each party commits to modifying its behaviour in the light its counter-party's advice. This is a mature, and very difficult conversation, because it is founded on trust. Each party is speaking candidly and constructively to the other, recognizing the mutual interest of being fair, straightforward and honest.

Drucker proposed this conversation for managers and their subordinates, but our suggestion is that it is equally powerful for any pair of work colleagues. The Maverick leader is not having this conversation with his colleagues as leader to follower, let alone boss to subordinate, but as one human being to another. It is an ice breaker. Not only does it rely upon a degree of trust, it also builds trust. It is an opportunity for those embarking on a difficult mission to open up to each other and share what exactly it is that they most need from one another if they are to excel.

Fair process

The second kind of conversation goes under the name of 'fair process'. This is a conversation that is designed to ensure that all parties to a decision commit to its implementation, even though some of them may believe that it is not the best option on the table. In a community of Mavericks, the chances that there will be unanimity on every important decision are minimal; hence the need for a method that creates unanimity of *action* where there isn't necessarily unanimity of *opinion*. The way that this is achieved is by open, fair and inclusive dialogue. Every party to the decision has an equal and absolute right to have their ideas heard and debated. Better still, every idea is improved upon by the quality of the discussion. If later it is rejected in favour of another idea, then so be it. 'I was heard, I was listened to, I was impressed when others took my idea seriously enough to want to strengthen it further, so why should I resent the fact that it lost out to another idea and withdraw my support simply because other ideas have been found by the group to be better, or at least more favoured? Next time, it could well be *my* idea that wins the backing of everyone, despite some people's misgivings.' This kind of conversation is particularly powerful in settings where opinionated people hold idiosyncratic beliefs about morally serious issues. In other words, Mavericks.

Decentring

The third kind of conversation entails 'decentring', a concept elaborated by Nigel Nicholson, a distinguished evolutionary psychologist. He defines it as a form of 'mental displacement' whereby we 'climb into another person's perspective to understand their narrative; their worldview; their morality play' (Nicholson, 2003). Imagine, for example, a tough meeting in which there are strong disagreements, everyone fights their corner, some home truths are uttered, and powerful emotions are on display. How do we interpret the behaviour? What explanation do we give for what we witnessed?

Decentring consists of four steps:

1 Think back to a particular incident. For example, recall the behaviour of a particular person at a particular moment in the meeting, perhaps saying something that discomforted you. How, at the time, did you interpret it? What label did you place on it? Now think about how *they* would describe their behaviour. What explanation would *they* give for this incident? What might *they* say was their motive?

2 Now use your imagination to become this person. Place yourself in their world and, bringing everything you know about their situation, build a model that makes their behaviour reasonable, understandable and ethically defensible. In other words, try telling the story from *their* point of view, not *yours*.

3 Next, ponder how they might be describing *your* behaviour at the time. What narrative are they constructing to make sense of your interventions, your emotions and your behaviour towards them? Might they have sussed you out? Might they, in fact, have a fairly accurate picture of how you were interpreting them? Might they feel justly offended by your explanation?

4 Consider this: we are unduly influenced by the interpretations we give of each other's behaviour, without sufficiently checking whether our explanations are true and fair, and thereby putting our relationship on a firmer foundation. A lot of organizational behaviour is a response to a misconception of the intentions and motives of others. By decentring and sharing these (unreliable) interpretations with each other, we sweep away false assumptions and defuse at least some of the unhelpful emotion. We begin to see each other as reasonable, conscientious, if sometimes overly sensitive, fellow human beings.

The emotional lives of Maverick leaders could sometimes benefit from a measure of just such collective decentring.

Defensive behaviour

The fourth kind of conversation concerns 'defensive behaviour'. It owes its most elegant formulation to Chris Argyris, whose theory of 'model 1 behaviour' we mentioned earlier, and is based on the need to break through the defensive barriers that people in organizations put up to protect their self-interest and social esteem.

In a corporate setting, where the governing variables tend to be those of achieving goals, winning the argument, suppressing negative feelings and arguing rationally, the pressures on managers will be to stay in control, play safe, give little away, and not place too much trust in others. Honesty, for example, will mean nothing more demanding than not telling any lies; strength will mean putting forward your position simply so as to get your way without showing any sign of weakness; and integrity will mean sticking to your principles, come what may.

Argyris argues that these behaviours, driven by fear and self-protection, are symptoms of what is now called a 'fixed mindset'. For personal and organizational learning to take root, a bolder, more open, more vulnerable set of behaviours is essential.

Honesty will mean saying what you know yet fear to say and encouraging others to do the same; strength will mean putting forward your position and stimulating debate with the aim of finding the truth; and integrity will mean advocating your values and beliefs in a way that invites enquiry and encourages others to do likewise.

In the next chapter we compare different forms of organizational structure and culture and the extent to which they facilitate and support the Maverick leadership. Do they constrain, restrict, present insurmountable barriers to challenge, to experimentation, to connecting ideas and people across the organizational structure? Or are they open to flexing, changing, challenging the status quo, not for the sake it, but to continually do better, to respond to the emerging and dynamic challenges and opportunities that we face?

CHAPTER EIGHT

Maverick forms of organization

In 1987, Guy Singh-Watson founded Riverford, a group of farms in Devon, Cambridgeshire, Hampshire, Yorkshire and France. The business began with Guy, a farmer, delivering his homegrown organic produce to friends in a wheelbarrow. Some 25 years later, it has become a national vegetable box business delivering to more than 50,000 customers a week.

This is Guy's explanation for why Riverford exists:

– to grow and supply the best organic food…
– as part of an independent, challenging and commercially successful business…
– which balances the needs of customers, suppliers, the environment, and wider society…
– and provides fair and rewarding employment to our staff

He summarizes the firm's guiding values in five words:

WE – DO IT – OUR WAY

Under his talented ownership, the market value of the company grew to more than £20 million. He has twice won the BBC Radio 4 Farmer of the Year award. And his products have been named as *The Observer* Ethical Product of the Decade (Riverford, 2021).

In 2018, he felt he had a choice to make. Should he sell the enterprise to venture capitalists who would seek to maximize their short-term returns or should he find another way of managing its future? He was loath to take the former route. It would feel like 'selling one of my children into prostitution'. Instead, he chose to sell 74 per cent of Riverford stock to its 650 employees at a third of its market value. In doing so, he wanted to make a point about business being an innately social activity. His virtue has been amply rewarded. Since then, it has performed spectacularly well, without compromising any of its ethical standards. He himself retained a 26 per cent stake in the business, with all the profits being shared among those who are now the co-owners and co-strategists of the business.

As an entrepreneur himself – and an archetypal Maverick – he recognizes the unique ability of capitalism to drive innovation and wealth creation, but he has huge reservations about how capitalists typically choose to apply their creed. His business embodies his passionate belief that a responsible and successful business model relies ultimately on a humane organizational model. The democratization of his workplace goes hand in hand with the sustainability of his farming practices.

Guy believes strongly that the vibrant anti-capitalist sentiments among so many of the younger generation now coming into the workforce are due primarily to the disempowering culture of the typical workplace. Joe Atkins, who works in the marketing department of Riverford, and relishes its open culture, almost certainly echoes Guy's feelings when he says:

> In a dictatorship, your voice is suppressed. And clearly that happens in so many businesses and sectors, and it is why so many people hate their jobs: they don't feel like they're contributing, they don't feel like they're listened to.

Joe puts the success of Riverford since its democratization down to the fact that, as co-owners, everyone's voice finds expression – and is heard. Everyone has skin in the game. The workplace is, in Gary Hamel's brilliant phrase, a humanocracy (Hamel and Zanini, 2020).

Guy's Maverick instincts are shown not only in his ecological principles but also in his organizational practices:

> I came to relish the challenge of finding my own solutions to agronomic problems rather than following the prevailing belief that the answer to every difficulty lay in a chemical container. Latterly, this has evolved into a belief that we must find a more harmonious and holistic way of living within the limits of our planet.

The organizational challenge

The big lesson is that a single, easily made, though very brave change, such as employee ownership, can liberate new behaviours. To know – *and feel* – that you have skin in the game is to release the Maverick within yourself. As a co-owner, you feel you now have rights and responsibilities, not just tasks and targets. You are free, *but also obliged*, to exercise agency, connect with other Mavericks with their own perspectives and ideas, come up with bold ideas, try them out, risk your reputation, and more generally act as an instrument of change.

Employee ownership and the values of mutualism were Riverford's response to the challenge of making the workplace friendlier to the Maverick spirit. This model works particularly well for a small and growing business. For large corporations, this may not be practical. So what options are there for a business employing tens of thousands to humanize its workplace and create a setting in which Maverick leaders can thrive. In short, what can managers themselves do to rejuvenate their internal culture?

Before considering what other models there might be, we need to consider the legacy models and their imperfections. The future will be as much about discarding obsolete practices as inventing new ones.

The First Machine Age and its bureaucratic culture

Despite its well-documented shortcomings, 20th-century managerialism is still with us.

Its strategy is to maximize the market value of the firm; its structure is a hierarchy of roles with juniors reporting to seniors; and its systems are bureaucratic with clearly defined processes for standardizing most activities. All three of these elements are unsympathetic to the Maverick leader; they constrain Maverick behaviour, and they promote values that are antithetical to Maverick ways of thinking.

The organizational image – or ideal – is a machine. The lore and language of management is mechanical. People are factors of production ('human resources'). The firm is the sum of its parts. All effects have a cause. Plans are drawn up to achieve predictable outcomes. The criterion is efficiency. What matters is measurable. Accordingly, everyone knows what they are expected to achieve and how they are expected to achieve it. They know what counts as success and failure. They know what they are allowed to do. They know what discretion they have.

The beauty of the system is that it is very easy to understand and almost as easy to operate. It places huge value on security, predictability and control. It goes to great lengths to avoid having to deal with uncertainty, ambiguity and judgement. It is assumed that success is assured if everyone simply complies with the rules and stays true to the goals.

In a relatively stable world, it makes eminent sense. Indeed, since the end of the 19th century, when the technology of mass manufacturing came on stream and industrialization was at its zenith, it has been responsible for the greatest improvement in human wealth and welfare in history.

Over the last two or three decades, however, the conditions that made managerialism a rational and wealth-creating activity have gradually disappeared, ironically the direct result of its own success. Most of the world is satiated with products. Services have now become the core activity of high-level economies. Manufacturing is taking a smaller and smaller share. The pace of change has accelerated, driven largely by those enterprises that have invented radically new ways of working. A world that may once have honoured the values of obedience, diligence and expertise has moved imperceptibly into a world that demands initiative, creativity and zeal. The crucial economic factors of production, such as capital, labour and data, are no longer the scarce resource from which competitive advantage is crafted. The precious resources in the 21st century will be human attributes, such as intellectual curiosity, emotional intelligence, entrepreneurial courage and moral integrity. The balance of power has been shifting from hands to head to heart.

The surest sign that managerialism was in difficulty was when the attention of senior executives turned from revenue to cost, and priority was given to such initiatives as downsizing, outsourcing, reorganizing, restructuring, re-engineering, and above all, merging and acquiring – in short, anything to avoid the tiresome business of inventing new products and services that the world wanted to buy. The 'management of change' was the rallying cry, designed to conceal the poverty of corporate imagination. In retrospect, we're now realizing the catastrophic impact on corporate prosperity of these myopic and internally focused tactics, fuelled by desperation and a lack of entrepreneurial zest.

Mavericks will have looked upon these unimaginative initiatives with alarm. But it won't have surprised many of them. After all, the defining attributes of managerialism have always been anathema to Mavericks. For example, this is how most Mavericks regard the tell-tale techniques of managerialism:

- Plans and budgets are a form of superstition, not unlike rain dancing, and inhibit more emergent forms of strategy, such as experimentation.
- Corporate statements of vision and values are synthetic and rarely reflect the genuine aspirations of the organization as a whole.
- Best practices, because they are formulaic, subvert genuinely competitive thinking, and inhibit the development of unique winning practices.
- Financial incentives and performance bonuses are no more than bribes for the greedy and insults to the conscientious.
- Organizational alignment arises from a fear of diversity and debate and serves mainly to inhibit creativity and unconventional thinking.
- Competitive benchmarking is plagiarism.
- Hierarchical structures are unlikely to be any more innovative and far-sighted than any other autocratic system.

In sum, these practices are the antithesis of the originality, resourcefulness and experimental attitudes that define the Maverick personality. If organizations are to move beyond the managerial mindset, they are going to have to become more friendly to – and supportive of – the Maverick mindset.

Both of us have worked with many thousands of executives over very many years and it has always struck us how frustrated most of these highly gifted individuals are with the context in which they work – particularly the command structure, the performance metrics and the plethora of rules. In conversations over coffee in the breaks between workshop sessions, the stories of frustration, muted despair, resignation and thwarted ambition have been many. They know that things could be so much better. They know that the potential of their companies is being squandered for want of a more humane organizational model. Sometimes the frustration finds expression in finger-pointing, placing the blame on those above or below, but the truth is that no one bears more responsibility for the baleful effects of managerialisms than anyone else. The problem is systemic. However, the Maverick leader is the one who says, 'Maybe none of us – or all of us – are to blame, but I will find a way to dismantle the cause of our frustration and replace it with something that brings out the best in us all, even if means ignoring the bureaucratic rituals and focusing on the task in hand.' This places him or her in danger of dismissal, but this they regard as a small price for doing the right thing, which is to prioritize the outcome over the means.

Managerialism in crisis

There would seem to be a growing mass of evidence that something is profoundly wrong about the way work is done in today's economy. It is certainly antithetical to the way Mavericks like to work but it is a deeper problem than simply its inability to tap into the skills of Mavericks.

In 1985, Peter Drucker, perhaps the foremost management thinker of his generation, predicted that within a generation, the business landscape would be transformed from one of choking bureaucracy to one of organization-wide innovation. His optimism would appear to have been misplaced. If anything, bureaucratic assumptions and norms have taken an even tighter hold on most large organizations, whether in the public or private sectors, at least in Western countries.

The cost of surplus bureaucracy in the US economy, for example, has been estimated at over $3 trillion a year (or 17 per cent of GNP) – and climbing (Hamel and Zanini, 2016). The *acquis communautaire*, the body of EU law and obligations, now runs to over 180,000 pages, at a cost of €27 billion a year – and is also irreversibly growing. A fitting epitaph for the demise of managerialism could well be one of Robert Conquest's famous laws: 'The simplest way to explain the behaviour of any bureaucratic organization is to assume that it is controlled by a cabal of its enemies.'

The Maverick hemisphere

The imbalance that characterizes the workplace finds its mirror image in society as a whole. The values of managerialism are not unique or limited to corporate life. They describe and explain some of the most important features of the culture of the 20th century. An explanation for this phenomenon has been put forward by one of the world's leading students of brain research.

Iain McGilchrist, a distinguished psychiatrist and former Fellow of All Souls College, Oxford, has written a celebrated book, *The Master and His Emissary: The divided brain and the making of the Western world*, in which he links the evolving anatomy and physiology of the human brain to the changing features of human culture (McGilchrist, 2019).

Based on a profound understanding of neurological research, he argues that the history of civilization since classical times can, at least partially, be explained by the ebb and flow of the relative power exercised by the two hemispheres of the brain, and more particularly, by the increasing dominance of the left hemisphere: 'The hemispheres need to co-operate, but I believe they are in fact involved in a sort of power struggle, and that this explains many aspects of contemporary Western culture.'

Each hemisphere of the brain, not only in humans but also in other creatures, plays a different role. The left hemisphere is characterized by a narrow, sharply focused attention to detail; by contrast, the right hemisphere features an open and vigilant alertness to the broader reality. Why this duality? What purpose does this division of labour serve? In terms of evolutionary fitness, McGilchrist offers the following illustration:

> Imagine a bird trying to feed on a seed against a background of grit and pebbles. It's got to focus very narrowly and clearly on that little seed and be able to pick it out against that background. But it's also, if it's going to stay alive, got to keep quite a different kind of attention open. It's got to be on the lookout for predators and for friends and conspecifics and whatever else is going on.

Each hemisphere has a different attentional style, each as important and as coherent as the other, with the left paying attention to particulars, and the right giving its attention to the bigger picture. This has been demonstrated vividly in experiments with patients suffering from brain trauma. In one experiment, for example, patients were invited to draw a house. Those that had damage to their right hemisphere focused their attention on all sorts of seemingly irrelevant details, such as the brickwork, or the drainpipes, or the curtains, even though they had drawn the roof upside down; whereas those with damage to their left hemisphere got the basic structure of the house right but with little concern for the detail.

Each hemisphere has its own personality. The left hemisphere deals in mechanical imagery, thinks in terms of cause and effect, reads the world more literally, and privileges self-interest; the right hemisphere is more at home in the living world, possesses empathic skills, connects with others, and is more adaptive. Each hemisphere is stronger for being accompanied by the other. For example, the left is so close to reality that it cannot imagine anything; the right is so distant that it cannot understand or do anything. In combination, imagination and reasoning are a formidable partnership. McGilchrist argues that in classical times the balance of power between both hemispheres was more equal, but modern civilization has fallen victim to a lopsided brain. Business, in particular, is in thrall to the near-sighted, less empathic and less imaginative left hemisphere.

McGilchrist, in examining the Industrial Revolution through this lens, suggests that the invention of the factory, for example, and by implication the accompanying practice of management, 'enabled the left hemisphere to make its most audacious assault yet on the world'. It shows up in its obsession with material things, deterministic explanations, and illusions of control and invincibility. Its instinctive preference is to disown responsibility for its own actions, preferring to invest its energy in the construction of excuses for anti-social, uncooperative behaviour. McGilchrist says of it, 'If the defect might reflect on the self, it does not like to accept it.' The result is that selfishness has been allowed to exercise too much power in the modern world. In other words, the First Machine Age, for all of its success in creating untold wealth, also had the effect of empowering the left hemisphere to inhibit the more creative, playful and improvisational style of the right hemisphere. The result has been a more mechanical, less humane society, with the consequence that the Maverick spirit feels less at home in the world and more up against the system. The instrumental rationality that characterizes the modern world, and particularly the workplace, is extremely difficult to dislodge.

McGilchrist does not pull his punches. He takes a strong moral position on the importance of a balance between the two hemispheres. It is not just that the left hemisphere has strengthened its hold on the mind; it has also sought to inhibit the role of the right hemisphere. McGilchrist laments this development. He believes that it has damaged the quality of life and the chances of human fulfilment.

Einstein once drew a distinction between the intuitive mind that he described as 'a sacred gift', and the rational mind that he saw as 'a faithful servant'. Commenting on this insight, McGilchrist noted, somewhat despairingly, that 'We have created a society that honours the servant but has forgotten the gift.'

The Second Machine Age and its technocratic culture

With the transition moving from management by authority (or hierarchy) to management by knowledge (or meritocracy), data management and analytics are moving centre-stage. The so-called Second Machine Age is based on the premise that more data equates to better decision-making. Competitive advantage is increasingly being seen to be based on analytics, the ability to draw insights from information.

This is a precarious assumption. The so-called Information Age is just as likely to lead to paralysis as insight. Indeed, many executives would admit that most corporate cultures today are characterized by analysis, debate and procrastination more than by intuition, courage and decisive action. As a result, the pace of learning inside the firm often falls short of the pace of change outside. In a fast-changing world, analysis of historical data is a poor guide to effective future action. Paradoxically, the more data we possess and the better informed we become, the slower and more hesitant are the decisions we make. The commodity in shortest supply is the courage to innovate.

Learning is best achieved by acting on the world imaginatively and noticing what happens. In science, this is called experimentation. In music, it is performance. In art, it is the playfulness from which new movements emerge. In jazz, it is improvisation. But in business, the requirement to be 'right first time' is producing a climate of fear and indecision, or what Jeffrey Pfeffer has called 'the knowing–doing gap'. We delay the 'doing' part in the neurotic pursuit of just a bit more 'knowing'. The perverse result of these irrational pressures is that it would seem preferable to get things precisely wrong rather than roughly right.

The challenge is to create a corporate culture that is comfortable trying things out, that possesses a kind of daring-do, that places greater emphasis on discovery than analysis, and that relies more upon iterative processes of exploration. Instead of believing that the future can be plotted intellectually like a journey to a chosen destination, perhaps the art is to be more nomadic, going where the spirit moves us, and, in Robert Frost's phrase, 'taking the road less travelled'. Instead of more thinking, perhaps there should be more action; instead of diligence, greater daring; and instead of 'why me?', an attitude of 'why not?'.

As exploration and disruption become the ruling paradigm, so bureaucracy (relying upon rules and obedience) will be seen to be too inflexible, and meritocracy (relying upon expertise and analysis) too ponderous, with both organizational models being regarded as too inwardly focused.

The Maverick organization and its adhocratic culture

We can now return to the question of what kind of organizational context brings out the Maverick spirit. What adjustments to traditional organizations, for example, would Mavericks find most congenial? Apart from employee ownership, what organizational design options could serve to tap into the Maverick potential of a much larger cross-section of people at work?

A Maverick organization will be pragmatic. It will have a bias in favour of action. It will focus upon capturing opportunities, solving problems and getting results. For this reason alone, it will be relentlessly focused on the external world. Its modus operandi will be adaptation. When 'stuck', the default position will be to conduct an experiment, break the deadlock, let reality be the judge, and make the change. Strategy will emerge from trial and error, rather than analysis and inference. Natural conversations on topics of mutual interest will outnumber formal meetings addressing a pre-set agenda. There will be no hiding places.

Adhocracies have been around, in various forms, for as long as people have joined forces to do things that they could not have done nearly as well alone. In today's economy, you find such cultures in the Accident & Emergency departments of hospitals, in the research labs of universities, in the innovation hubs of companies, in the open offices of new ventures, and in the more innovative departments of professional service firms.

So what are some of the surest symptoms of a Maverick organization?

First, coordination is not achieved through rules or procedures so much as through a shared enthusiasm for solving a particular problem such as capturing a particular market opportunity. The art is to be on the front line close to the action, noticing what is happening, picking up on weak signals, attending to the unexpected and adapting to change. This will mean that as much attention goes on framing the question as answering it. Those who identify the opportunity will typically be those who exploit it.

In WL Gore, a chemical company, you go where your interests take you, you work on projects and initiatives that excite you, and you team up with those who inspire you. In other words, the organization structures itself organically and spontaneously around the problems and questions that bring enterprising employees together. The energy goes to where the unlocked value lies. There is no organization chart of predetermined jobs, roles and positions. Passion is the organizing principle.

Second, strategies get formed and decisions get made in response to the findings of experiments rather than the edicts of executives. Hierarchy barely enters into the process. The guiding factors are empirical discoveries rather than authoritarian plans. It is through conversation that potential solutions are generated and through controlled tests that discriminative evidence is gathered. In the famous words of William James, sometimes described as the father of American psychology: 'Truth *happens* to an idea. It *becomes* true, is *made* true, by events.' As experiments yield up their data, so those ideas that are closest to the truth shape the decisions that are taken.

For example, Costa Coffee, a division of Whitbread, designed a process, Project Marlow, for launching its revolutionary coffee vending machine – a project that is a million miles away from the bureaucratic phase-gate process of innovation in most large companies. The company recruited 38 highly talented people, 'the best in their field', from wherever they could be found, to act as Maverick leaders and, with no knowledge of Whitbread processes and virtually no interference, build the business from scratch (London Business School, 2014).

Third, people are motivated not by financial incentives – bribes, by any other name – or the size of the budget, but by the intrinsic appeal of the work itself. For example, the appeal may lie in the intellectual difficulty of the problem, or the moral worth of the activity, or the sheer conviviality of the team. The assumption is that most people want to do a great piece of work. They want to do something that matters, something of quality, something in which they can take pride, and something that utilizes their special skill. It plays to their desire to go to work not so much to make a living, as to make a life. This recalls Aristotle's concept of *eudaimonia*, or human flourishing, a state of mind which emanates from the pursuit of a fulfilling purpose, the acquisition of virtue, the utilization of one's abilities, and the exercise of one's autonomy.

Fourth, the capital on which returns are being measured is not only financial, but also social and moral. Social capital is the difference between what the group of individuals would achieve working separately and what it is able achieve by working together. It is founded upon emotional intelligence, mutual understanding and trust. Moral capital sets a still higher standard. It is not calculative. It is sceptical of 'economic man'. People are not treated instrumentally as though they are resources. The relationship between colleagues is best characterized as one of reciprocal generosity, a recognition perhaps that it is more blessed to give than receive. Adam Grant, a business professor at the Wharton School, has called this the 'gift relationship'.

Fifth, the performance of the organization is measured in an unconventional manner. It may well be, of course, that the standard instruments, such as the profit and loss statement and the balance sheet, are maintained, if only for legal reasons, but the metrics by which decisions and actions are judged will be radically different.

Most performance measures are comparative. They compare one number with another. For example, in most conventional businesses, there are two bases of comparison: one is the previous year, in which case a good performance is one that improves on last year's results; the other is the plan, in which case a good performance is one that 'makes the numbers' and beats budget. In an adhocracy, the numbers that matter will be comparisons with particular competitors or with some notion of potential, such as untapped internal skills or external market opportunities.

For example, McKinsey's bottom line has long been the increase in the aggregate market value of its client companies over the previous 10 years relative to that of its competitors, such as Bain or Boston Consulting Group.

Given that an adhocracy's core methodology is experimentation, then the ultimate metric will be related to the pace of organizational learning, such as the rate of trial or error, the frequency of disruptive breakthroughs, and the ratio of refuted ideas to corroborated ideas. Profit is a misleading metric if only because it is a lagging indicator. In effect, any particular year's profit reflects, on average, the quality of the decisions made six years earlier. Thus, it comes too late to steer by.

Sixth, it is a 'horizontal' organization, in the sense that it faces outwards to the customer rather than upwards to the boss. Compared to a bureaucracy or a meritocracy, an adhocracy has been turned through 90 degrees. In effect, the organization chart becomes a value chain of activities rather than a pyramid of hierarchical positions.

For example, at Morning Star, a food processing business, you report, not to a boss, but to the person or group of people whose own work depends most crucially on the quality of your work. Periodically, everyone negotiates a contract – a kind of promissory note – with their immediate customer. For most people, this will be an internal customer, but ultimately every chain reaches into the market, to the ultimate user. At Morning Star these contracts play the same role as a budget does in most businesses. They set the parameters of performance and define what must be achieved for a 'good' performance to be claimed. In a sense, the market replaces the executive board as the ultimate driver and director of the business. The role of the board becomes one of coach and counsellor rather than commander and controller.

This is a nice example of the oblique principle: that in business, as well as in life, we do not achieve what we directly aim for, and that success at one thing (say, X) is more likely to follow from the pursuit of another thing (say, Y). An adhocracy will trust in the fact that aiming for a strong return on moral capital is more likely to increase the return on financial capital than vice versa.

The shift to a more adhocratic way of working demands a profound philosophical adjustment of values and beliefs. It means leaving behind the tired and counterproductive assumptions of earlier organizational models. So, what single shift in structure would trigger these six practices?

THE SIX MAVERICK-FRIENDLY PRACTICES

1 Organizing around the problem to be solved rather than the role to be filled.

2 Managing more by experimentation than planning.

3 Motivating people by the intrinsic importance of the work to be done rather than the financial rewards for doing it.

4 Focusing as much on the social and moral attributes of the workplace as on its financial returns.

5 Measuring performance relative to potential rather than to the past or to the plan.

6 Organizing as a value chain linking internal suppliers and customers rather than a reporting structure linking bosses and subordinates.

In a large company, what kind of catalyst could play the part of employee ownership in Guy Singh-Watson's Riverford?

The choice of architecture of a Maverick culture

In 2015, the Dutch bank ING made just such a move. It boldly broke with hierarchical and bureaucratic tradition by organizing the most senior headquarters staff into 13 'tribes' and then dividing these tribes into 350 'squads' of nine people each. The aim was seamless customer service through greater organizational agility and responsiveness. Operations staff and call centre staff were also structured into self-steering teams.

Bart Schlatmann, the Chief Operating Officer of the bank at the time of the transition, expressed the purpose of the change in the following way:

> It is about minimizing handovers and bureaucracy, and empowering people.
> The aim is to build stronger, more rounded professionals out of all our
> people... the key has been adhering to the 'end-to-end principle' and working

in multidisciplinary teams, or squads, that comprise a mix of marketing specialists, product and commercial specialists, user-experience designers, data analysts and IT engineers – all focused on solving the client's needs and united by a common definition of success.

The squads sit together in the same space; there are no managers in control of coordination; cross-functional collaboration is built into the tribal structure; the silos have disappeared. Thus, there is no longer any need for project managers or steering committees, and software releases are spontaneous; many of the walls between the offices have been taken down; meetings are far fewer and more informal; in short, the culture resembles a campus.

Schlatmann describes the culture:

> Our new way of working starts with the squad. One of the first things each squad has to do is write down the purpose of what it is working on. The second thing is to agree on a way of measuring the impact it has on clients. It also decides on how to manage its daily activities.

Transparency is emphasized. Every quarter, every tribe shares its recent achievements and key lessons, whether from success or failure. And it outlines its ambitions for the near-to-medium future and from which other tribes and squads it believes it needs to learn and with which it will need to collaborate.

Peter Jacobs, the Chief Information Officer, has emphasized that ING were as ruthless in letting go of their pre-existing organizational and governance structure as they are passionate in embracing the new order. His colleague, Schlatmann, expressed it thus:

> We gave up traditional hierarchy, formal meetings, overengineering, detailed planning, and excessive 'input steering' in exchange for empowered teams, informal networks, and 'output steering'.

Much of their confidence in doing so lay in their deliberate policy of looking beyond banking for exemplars. For example, they learnt more from the tech companies, particularly Spotify, with whom they continue to work closely, than they could ever have learnt from other financial services firms.

The revolution was not without its pain. When the change of structure was announced, all the senior staff were asked to reapply for positions in the new organization. The criteria for reappointment were essentially cultural rather than technical. Did they have the right mindset? If not, they were let go.

There are aspects of ING's culture that might still constrain the natural ebullience and impatience of many Mavericks, but it is far more congenial to the spirit of the Maverick than the culture it replaced. And, perhaps more than any other large European company, it sets the standard for transforming a bureaucracy into an adhocracy. On all the important criteria, it is outperforming its former self.

In this chapter, we have described the organizational settings in which Mavericks flourish. We contrasted certain organizational designs with others in terms of the importance they place on diversity of opinion and the freedom they extend to those who want to challenge the status quo. In the next chapter, we examine culture at the scale of society. We consider what kind of society is most favourable to the development of the personal characteristics that we have selected as being the defining qualities of Mavericks. After all, societies and cultures differ dramatically in the values they honour, the virtues they promote and the behaviours they admire. Some societies, for example, place particular emphasis on individuality, creativity and self-expression. Others place greater weight on conformity, solidarity and security. How can the Maverick's spirit be developed and put to work in society at large?

CHAPTER NINE

Maverick states of society

What enhances human accomplishment?

It is an astonishing fact that the prosperity of the world would be doubled if everybody were free to live in the country of their choice. Simply by moving location, to wherever they would most like to live, the benefits that material well-being brings to people would be radically improved. The so-called good life would be available to far more people.

Same people. Same world. Same resources. Twice the wealth. Just by moving. How come? Why is location so important? From what would people be escaping? To what would they be drawn? It's not going to be a geographical difference, such as climate; it's going to be a sociocultural difference, such as a sense of opportunity.

Context makes the difference. There are moments in history and places in the world where humans have reached extraordinary states of being. We call this 'civilization'. What we mean by this contentious idea is that, almost accidentally, particular societies at particular times discovered a way of living together that brought out the best in human nature, whether in terms of peaceful co-existence, social interactivity, philosophical speculation, artistic achievement, scientific progress or moral maturity. It is as though a set of circumstances arose, planned as well as unplanned, that played particularly well to the genetic architecture of the human mind. People felt at home in their world. Their higher faculties of creativity and ingenuity, but also their natural inclinations for cooperation and conviviality, found more plentiful expression.

We are inclined to explain human flourishing by pointing to the key features of today's open societies: democratic institutions, basic freedoms, frictionless markets, the rule of law and so on. As an explanation of civilization, this is too narrow. It lacks historical imagination. When we take a broader, more timeless approach, these 21st-century arguments lose some of their power. The astonishing achievements of Ancient Egypt, China, Greece and Rome, for example, require a different explanation.

All sorts of behaviour, whether primitive or civilized, can be rationalized against some set of beliefs. So, the question becomes: what assumptions provide the most reliable account of our better nature? What *should* serve as the starting point for our theory of human well-being, the development of the individual spirit, and the personal discovery of the Maverick within? Our argument for turning to evolutionary theory for an answer is that no other theory of human behaviour has anything like the same empirical weight and explanatory force.

Back to the future

We need to reach back into our evolutionary origins as a species to fully understand the conditions most favourable to self-development. We easily lose touch with who we truly are if we dwell too much on our current concerns. We end up deceiving ourselves. Our rational mind overrides our instinctive knowledge. Or, as Jonathan Haidt expresses it, the rider believes that he is in control of the elephant (2006). For example, our emotional lives only start to make sense when we appreciate the purpose that these emotions served in our early history as a species. We are creatures – and perhaps prisoners – of the mind that we inherited from our earliest ancestors.

Their lives were intensely social. They lived in small bands. They survived and thrived as a result of their cooperative skills and social inclinations. They were expected to give as much as they got. They held together. They mucked in. They did their bit. And they took their turn. It was a cohesive and coherent society. People knew their roles, and they knew what they had a right to expect from others. Social loafing was a source of shame. If anyone opted out of their fair share of work, they were likely to be ostracized. Just

162

as surely, if anyone insisted on getting their own way, or bossed people around, they were playing a precarious game that could easily backfire. Solidarity, alignment and fairness were core values.

Almost everyone discovered quite quickly that if they all signed up to these moral principles, whether they served their immediate self-interest or not, then the group as a whole would flourish. In turn, each individual discovered, sometimes the hard way, that as long as they contributed to the well-being of the community – and were seen to do so – they themselves would benefit, both materially and socially. If, on the other hand, anyone sought to undermine these principles, or gain advantage over others, they risked censure or punishment of some sort. These principles were the foundations of a society of mutual cooperation and support.

Evolution-wise, our behavioural preferences were formed by the consequences to our survival of these behaviours. Those habits and customs that served us well became soft-wired and endure to this day. For as long as humans have lived, the environment in which our character as a species evolved was essentially a social one, characterized above all by reciprocal obligations. This is the setting in which our morality gradually developed.

Our individual nature is bound up with our traditional membership of small, largely self-sufficient groups. As David Sloan Wilson puts it, 'Small groups are a fundamental unit of human social organization' (2019). This was the size of unit best adapted for cooperation and survival. It remains central to our genetic character, and it serves as the setting in which Mavericks feel most at home and perform at their best.

This aspect of our evolutionary heritage contains an important moral lesson. However sophisticated we may believe ourselves to be, we should acknowledge that we are at our most human and most fulfilled when absorbed with others in a shared activity. We jeopardize our sense of well-being by rashly or ignorantly departing too far from our innate evolutionary preferences. The intellect can easily persuade us to discard human traditions that no longer seem to make sense. We may also ignore instinctual feelings that we are unable to rationalize. But we should be careful. In evolutionary terms, our powers of rational thought developed as a tool for influencing others rather than one for enhancing our own decisions.

When we neglect the importance of shared activities in small group settings, and we cast ourselves adrift from others, we risk becoming ill at ease and anxious. Loneliness is an unnatural state. It is in relation to others that we feel most at home in the world. There is, of course, a distinction between being alone and feeling lonesome. But in the absence of joint activity of some sort, life can quickly become meaningless. As has been said, work keeps us sane. We work as much for social cohesion and a sense of belonging as we do for a livelihood. Chronic isolation is injurious to our mental and physical health. During the pandemic of 2020/21, this was the mood state of many millions of people.

In this sense, the individual is an artificial construct. No one can be understood on their own. In the words of John Donne:

No man is an island
Entire of itself,
Every man is a piece of the continent,
A part of the main.

The Maverick leader's sense of responsibility

Examining the evolution of morality and looking for common patterns across different cultures, Jonathan Haidt and Jesse Graham, working in the tradition of cultural anthropologist Richard Schweder, put forward six sets of values as the foundation of a moral community (Haidt, 2012):

- care/harm
- fairness/cheating
- loyalty/betrayal
- order/disorder
- sanctity/degradation, and
- liberty/oppression

These principles were not reached by argument and reasoning. They were forged pragmatically in the furnace of human experience. As a result, they are ambivalent and sometimes contradictory. The obligations we owe to each other as a matter of moral duty arise from these foundational values. The idea is that if each of us commits to meeting these obligations – *knowing that everyone else is bound by the same code of conduct* – we give ourselves the greatest chance of leading prosperous and fulfilling lives. If we all make small sacrifices for the common good, everyone benefits. Typically, Mavericks understand this instinctively. They choose to prioritize their obligations over their rights. They treat morality as the implicit contract we have with one another.

Since the enlightenment, various progressive ideologies have been advanced that challenge this purportedly archaic and moribund social contract, replacing it with something much more radical and utopian. Most of them have chosen to prioritize just one of the six principles and build it into a proselytizing faith:

- socialists chose care
- libertarians chose liberty
- conservatives chose order

The history of the last 100 years is, in part, a tale of the rational distortion of morality, usually in pursuit of an idealized future, whose achievement was worth untold amounts of suffering. Invariably, they did so on the basis of an impeccably rational argument, but one that ignored the pluralism and subtleties of traditional morality.

The most famous and influential post-enlightenment moral theory was utilitarianism. It underpinned most of the ideological movements of the 20th century. Jeremy Bentham and John Stuart Mill, who first formulated the theory, defined 'the good' as whatever maximized happiness across a population of autonomous, self-interested individuals. Economics borrowed this theory of moral behaviour as a foundation for its model of a wealth-creating society.

There is research to suggest that those who study economics become more selfish as a result (Grant, 2013). Perhaps we should not be surprised. The human being that figures most prominently in economic theory is some-one exclusively concerned with their own material advancement. The theory is that if everyone behaves in the same hedonistic and self-interested manner then the welfare of society as a whole is optimized. This is not a philosophy that Mavericks, with their innate sense of duty, find attractive.

Linked with the image of 'economic man', there has been an inflation of human rights – 'what the world owes me' – and a deflation of any equiva-lent responsibility – 'what I owe the world'. Increasingly we are awarding ourselves rights while simultaneously offloading onto governments the responsibility for delivering on these rights. It sometimes seems that only the state is now obliged to act dutifully and behave morally.

Morality does not begin with legislation, or the actions of lawyers, or indeed governments. Rather, the law codifies what, over time, people have come to regard as an obligation that should attach to everybody in society.

Morality evolves, like life itself, by variation and selection. The mutations that introduce new moral ideas into society arise from the singular acts of singular people. Most of these mutations fail to catch on. But some capture the imagination and become contagious. What began as a personal gesture evolves into a more general principle of virtue. Every Slavery Abolition Act first needs its Wilberforce. One role of the Maverick leader is to set the moral standard for what is possible and desirable more generally.

A good society is one in which these kinds of gestures are natural. They are not only made, but they are also noticed, talked about and, if effective, are imitated and popularized. In other words, it is an experimental society in which the evolution of morality is accelerated as a result of greater behavioural variation and more judicious selection. A cultural context is created in which individuals set standards by their behaviour that others choose to follow, and, much later, philosophers and legislators attempt to codify. This resembles the tradition of common law, by which legislation encodes practices that society has come to believe to be just. The general principle here is that morality evolves as a result of behaviour rather than theory, and the good life embodies a sense of duty rather than an assertion of rights.

Maverick leaders don't wait for the 'right' to do something. They have no need of anyone else's 'permission'. They prefer to think in terms of their responsibilities rather than their rights. They are not ideologues, framing abstract schemes for the rescue of humanity. They are pragmatists, trying things out, noticing what happens, and adapting accordingly.

Taking personal responsibility

Mmusi Maimane was the leader of South Africa's opposition Democratic Alliance party between 2015 and 2019. In our conversation with him, he emphasized the duty that citizens bear each other for the state of their own society:

> The thing about great leaders like Nelson Mandela is that people all too easily succumb to the belief that, 'OK, we've got the great man at the top, so the rest of us can carry on with whatever we want to do.' This then creates a state of affairs in which people set aside their activism and surrender their power, even on basic issues, allowing a situation to arise in which the political party becomes God, expected to provide all, and encompass all.

In Mmusi's opinion, the result in South Africa has been a decline in personal responsibility for better outcomes, a diminution in the shared sense of a desired future, and an erosion of confidence that it can be achieved.

Mmusi insists that, in many parts, South Africa is an unbelievably impressive place: 'It really is.' But then you go to another part, and it is depressing, particularly the corruption: 'These problems are not going to be solved purely by politicians. They need business; they need civic society. It's the "values piece" that has gone out the window.'

Without being nationalistic, he believes passionately that South Africa (and indeed Africa as a whole), inspired by its Ubuntu morality, can – and should – offer to the rest of the world a human face in a world that is going digital. 'South Africa needs to restore its position; it needs to recover its values.'

Mmusi draws a parallel with Americans having to leave the United States to discover what it is to be American. South Africans too need to remind themselves of what is special about their own culture. We talked to him just after he had spoken at an international conference. He was struck by the reputation that South African doctors and lawyers enjoyed for their hard work. He couldn't help comparing this image with the self-talk of South Africans themselves: 'We tend to look at ourselves as some backward, corrupt bunch, whereas we are actually an innovative, hardworking and diverse group of people who, for the circumstances that we face, continue to punch above our weight.'

Damaris Parsitau is someone who certainly lives up to Mmusi's idea of a responsible citizen in today's Africa. She is an exemplar of how Mavericks set a fine example of what is possible and desirable in a very challenging society. As the first PhD qualified female professor in both Kenya and Tanzania, a Brookings Institute, Echidna Global Scholar Alumna and Harvard University visiting professor, Damaris has broken through all barriers of expectation of what it means to be a woman in Maasailand, Kenya.

Growing up in the Maasai tribe, where school attendance 'was not usual for girls', Damaris had a father who, despite never setting foot in a classroom himself, promoted and encouraged her continued education. Without any memory of ever meeting a female professor, Damaris decided early on in life that she wanted to be a professor. She saw, from a young age, the vast structural and cultural marginalization that affected her community and decided that she would use her education as a tool to empower herself and others. As a professor of gender and religion studies, Damaris challenges entrenched cultural and religious beliefs that hold girls and woman back in her community. She commented:

> You can't have education and do nothing... I feel like I cannot have an education and just sit down and see suffering... I am moved by pain, I am moved by injustice, I am moved by discrimination and I want to change that.

She had a vision which was larger than herself and spoke of a deep-seated sense of responsibility to help others become educated, particularly girls and women. Damaris sets the example, she lives out her values and so it was no surprise to hear that she was also voted one of 100 most influential Kenyans.

In her closing comments of her interview Damaris reminded us of why her Maverick spirit is so essential in society. She commented, 'Take others with you... don't be the last to break through the barrier.' As testament to this, Damaris has equipped and enabled several other young girls to be selected at some of the top Ivy League universities worldwide. Through setting up structures that encourage girls to continue their education, establishing mentorship programmes, building their networks, arranging skills development initiatives and assisting them in applying for scholarships, Damaris has been the role model for others that she lacked in her own childhood. She is transforming education in her community, and in doing so, transforming the inherent social role and value of girls within her community.

Compare the life led by Damaris under very tough circumstances with that of Nick Hine in a much more benign setting, that of the United Kingdom. Nick has, since 2019, served as a very high-ranking officer in the British armed forces. In what respect is he as much of a Maverick as Damaris? What does Maverick behaviour look like in the setting of the British armed services?

Nick lives by two guiding principles. First, 'If in doubt, do the right thing, even if it doesn't turn out right.' Second, 'If I can make things look different, they feel different; if they feel different, they are different; if they are different, then we are changing the culture.'

Pause, and take in the Maverick spirit that sits beneath both Nick's principles: there is the guiding philosophy of doing good, despite the cost; and there is the importance of incrementally changing the culture. Neither of these is easy to implement, especially for Nick who is autistic and working in a rather rigid and bureaucratic world.

Nick highlighted how we, as people, organizations and cultures, get stuck in habitual patterns of thinking and behaving. We easily fall victim to 'groupthink' and stop asking 'why so?' We become disconnected from the original purpose of our work. We cease challenging our own orthodoxies. He emphasizes the need for neurodiversity, an alternative way of thinking and acting. As someone who has struggled to fit in to society's neurotypical mould, his experiences have shown him that there is another way – a less orthodox, sometimes less accepted, but often more efficient and effective way.

He considers himself a disruptor within his organization. He places particular emphasis on 'being OK' with 'taking risks' and 'taking jumps':

> It's not about burning the house down. It's about trying to take the organization from the place that it is – which is an 18th-century analogue organization (even though it doesn't think of itself like that) – to a 21st-century digital organization where everything is different.

His story reminds us of the importance of avoiding thinking in a linear way when we are trying to change things, even if that means 'breaking a few eggs' along the way. Be willing to use small, simple, consistent acts which, they argue, can start reshaping the bigger picture. How do you do this? 'One conversation at a time.' He uses the dilemma of naval uniforms to highlight this point. He argued for the reduction of the uniforms from 47 different working pieces to just one set of working attire. It cost £100 more, but it was of a higher quality, had better thermal properties, was more comfortable to wear and was better looking... and it was a smashing success. Small, simple, pragmatic steps: if it looks different, it feels different; if it feels different, you are changing the culture. Eloquently, Nick expressed how Mavericks can impact culture in an open society in subtle but powerful ways:

> It was like pinpricks of light. If you – or I – can make enough pinpricks of light on a page, when you stand really close, all you can see is the pinpricks of light. When you stand back, all you can see is light. So, what I'm trying to do is to change the culture of the organization by all these little pinpricks of activity. So that when everybody stands back, they go, 'Oh, blimey, that's all different now.'

The Maverick leader's sense of community

The lesson of evolution to the workplace – *any* workplace – is to recognize man's natural predisposition to cooperate. Mankind is soft-wired to work in small groups. There are exceptions to every rule, of course, but we take risks whenever we part company with the genetic properties of our mind and our naturally preferred ways of working.

What recommendations flow from these observations? First, we should be wary of utilitarian values and the idea that society is no more than the sum of its parts. In particular, we should be sceptical of any top-down plan or ideological remedy, or solution at the level of society. Better, much better, to rely more upon a multiplicity of ideas emerging from an archipelago of small, self-directed groups, within which the bonds of affiliation are strong and between which the rivalry is healthy.

We observe small group creativity at its best under conditions of an emergency. Whenever a company faces an existential crisis – and we all noticed this in many organizations with the onset of the Covid-19 pandemic – the rule book is discarded, plans are shelved, standard procedures are set aside, and hierarchical structures are relaxed. People cease to be bosses and subordinates. Instead, teams form spontaneously around the problems to be solved. Improvisation becomes a critical skill. Status and seniority cease to have their customary authority. Those who feel they can contribute bring their ideas into the conversation. In other words, the problem, not the organization chart, sets the terms of the behaviour.

Of course, as soon as the crisis subsides, most people revert to their former ways of working, as though nothing has been learnt from the experience. Yet, everyone will remember, usually with delight, the level of engagement, empowerment, trust and conviviality that they had witnessed during the emergency. Thereby, in an accidental but most effective manner, nature is reminding us of the efficacy and enjoyment of small group working – and how we ignore it at our peril. In fact, there are two distinct and dysfunctional consequences of ignoring this evolutionary truth:

- First, we leave innovation entirely to the courage and creativity of individuals working on their own, isolated from their fellow beings or from the support of third parties, to come up with ideas and projects that benefit not just themselves, but society as a whole. This is the **entrepreneurial panacea.**

- Second, we derogate all the big issues, including innovation, to a central planning authority to draw upon leading expertise and current states of knowledge to dream up ideas and formulate grand solutions. This is the **meritocratic panacea.**

Both are contrary to the spirit of our evolutionary architecture. Yet, neither policy is short of powerful protagonists and adherents. This division is subtler than a right/left split. It is a profound schism in modern societies. On the one side, there is a conviction that, in an open society, the pursuit of self-interest, reinforced by laissez-faire talent and enthusiasm, automatically advances the common good and can only be corrupted by state interference; on the opposing side, there is an equally dedicated position that, in a complex global society, centralized planning is an essential complement to laissez-faire behaviour. Within the firm, the same split finds expression in reliance either on the 'great man' theory of leadership or on bureaucratic methods of command and control.

One way of finding the middle ground between these extremes has been suggested by Elinor Ostrom, a Nobel Prize-winning economist. She looked for solutions to the seemingly intractable problem of what economists call the 'tragedy of the commons'. How do you avoid a situation in which rational self-interest causes over-exploitation of a finite, shared resource? It may be over-grazing a commonly owned pasture, or over-fishing a commonly owned fishing area. Neither of the standard solutions seemed to be working well. One was to privatize the common resource and thereafter rely upon a competitive market to manage it sustainably; the other was to establish a regulatory framework, supervised by a single authority (Ostrom, 1990).

What Ostrom chose to do was to discover what worked best in practice. Instead of inventing an abstract model, she studied real-world examples of effective practice. For example, she examined the solution discovered by a group of about 100 fishermen plying their trade off the coast of Alanya in Turkey. In the 1970s, frustrated by a free-for-all system that was causing fish stocks to decline and violent clashes between the fishing crews to erupt, the fishermen came to an agreed way forward. The total fishing area was sub-divided into geographical parcels and each year the fishers drew lots to determine which parcel was theirs for the coming year. The parcels rotated among the crews for purposes of fairness. Each of the parcels was big enough to sustain a livelihood for its fishing crew. It was easy to see if anyone was breaking the rules.

Ostrom codified the pragmatic principles that brought success to this and many other communitarian schemes like it. She called them core design principles (CDPs). There are eight of them:

- strong group identity among all those subject to the rules of their own making, and a clear understanding of what these rules mean, by way of rights and obligations
- a strong sense of fairness, reinforced by a transparent equivalence between costs and benefits for each member
- an inclusive process of decision-making on all key issues, avoiding the need for bosses or any kind of hierarchy
- thorough monitoring of the behaviour of all the members to maximize compliance and minimize any gaming of the system
- a system of gently escalating sanctions against members who break rank and abuse the fairness of the system
- a fast and transparent process, conducted by members themselves, for resolving those conflicts or ambiguities that do arise
- sufficient autonomous authority of the group of members themselves to set their own rules without excessive interference by outside authorities
- scale independence of these design principles, in so far as they are nested within larger-scale groupings (for example, the legal system) while retaining their autonomy

Each of these eight principles is based on cooperation and a strong sense of fairness. They work best in groups of fewer than 150 members. We have highlighted them precisely because they are so congenial to Maverick behaviour and so conducive of it. More than any other organizational model, they play upon the inner Maverick, and this is one reason why they work so well.

Compare these principles with those that prevail in more orthodox organizations, in which hierarchy and bureaucracy hold sway. They challenge many of the most popular design principles in most organizations. In large companies, for example, it is rare to find such attention being paid to fairness, affiliation, inclusion, transparency, obligation and agency, all of which are values that trade on the best elements of human nature. Ostrom's CDPs have been shown to work just as well in schools, colleges, charities, volunteer groups and businesses. Her work prompts these questions of any organization or community that harbours ambitions to be more daring, imaginative and resourceful, or, in short, to be more Maverick:

- What rules prevail in *your* organization?
- What are *your* implicit design principles?
- What drives *your* behaviour and culture?
- What implicit values are *your* rules propagating?

When we turn from design principles at the organizational or communal level to behavioural principles at the personal level, what sorts of 'commandments' should be recommended if they are to be in keeping with Ostrom's communitarian values?

Victor Hwang and Greg Horowitt have sought to decode the behaviours that have spawned the most successful innovation hubs in the world, such as Silicon Valley (Hwang and Horowitt, 2012). Their research reinforces the evolutionary idea that innovation is a social process that benefits hugely from the interactivity of small but highly diverse groups. Their description of the behaviour of the key players in these 'oases of innovation' bears an uncanny resemblance to the Mavericks we have chosen to feature in these pages. They speak of breaking the rules and dreaming, opening doors and listening, trusting and being trustworthy, experimenting and iterating together, seeking fairness rather than advantage, and emphasizing the act of giving rather than receiving.

We have distilled their behavioural principles into these six maxims:

1 **Imagine anew...** make discoveries beyond the status quo.
2 **Notice what is surprising...** go to the edge of your experience.
3 **Expand your circle of trust...** take the risk of opening up.
4 **Emulate evolution...** speculate boldly and test rigorously.
5 **Leave your comfort zone...** error is the source of all learning.
6 **Give to receive...** create value before capturing it.

There is no better description of someone who lives by these values than that of... Maverick.

Where business fits in

Can business set higher moral standards than the society it inhabits? Might it contribute to more fulfilling experiences than other social activities? Ought it to lead the way in prototyping a more flourishing society?

In earlier centuries, most people found their identity in the place of their birth, or the neighbourhood in which they grew up, or the place in which they settled down and built their life. To borrow a telling phrase of David Goodhart, they considered themselves to be 'citizens of somewhere' rather than 'anywhere' (Goodhart, 2017). This would have been where they felt most at home in the world. Their identity was bound up with family, community and congregation – what Edmund Burke called the 'little platoons' that gave life its special flavour and meaning (1909). But now, with greater personal mobility, these ties are loosening. Increasingly, the main 'home' of identity, purpose and affiliation is the organization one works for and the job one does. Yet many employers have failed to notice, let alone adapt to, this extraordinary feature of modern life. The assumption is still that work is an economic, not a social activity; that we go to work to make a living, rather than make a life; and that the workplace is no more than a place of work. The emphasis is on efficiency and productivity, rather than shared identity and a common cause.

Times are changing. For perhaps a large majority of people, their work is where they expect to find a purpose to their activity and a true sense of belonging. This puts a heavy demand on the nature of work and the design of the workplace. It must meet more than the financial needs of those who work there. It needs to provide the tools for leading a meaningful life.

Summary

We get closer to the unvarnished truth about human nature by turning to evolutionary theory rather than any other model of man. Only by first making sense of the species to which we belong can we hope to play to our strengths. All our emotions, values and biases have their roots in our evolutionary history. What we regard as 'good', for example, will have strong causal connections with what contributed to our evolutionary fitness.

As a species we continue to evolve, the difference being that our consciously chosen behaviour is playing an ever more important role in the pace and direction of our genetic evolution. We have acquired partial control of our biology. We are increasingly becoming the agent of our own design. This makes it all the more important that we understand better the implications of our major cultural choices. This includes how we choose to work together. By moving towards more inclusive, less extractive modes of working we will be rewarding behaviours that are cooperative and responsible, rather than selfish and short term.

From our evolutionary knowledge, we have robust evidence that the small group is the basic unit of human behaviour – and *cultural progress*. We know that part of the 'secret of our success' as a species, to quote Joseph Henrich, is our natural gift for working cooperatively and empathically (Henrich, 2015). Mavericks intuitively understand this.

Small groups by their nature are neither so large that they need to be structured hierarchically nor so small that they depend upon individual genius. They are a classic case of the wisdom of the middle ground. A post-industrial world that is far less reliant upon scale and efficiency and more favourable to trial and error will also be a world in which Mavericks flourish as never before. The tools for evolving consciously into an ever more humanistic world are in our hands.

In the final chapter, we bring together the insights and experience of our Maverick leaders, the research that supports what it takes to be a Maverick leader, and suggest 15 practices that will enhance the Maverick leader within all of us.

CHAPTER TEN

Becoming a Maverick leader

We all recognize the seeds of the Maverick within ourselves.
Nothing in the Maverick character is entirely foreign to us.
Equally, we recognize those factors that inhibit
or censor our innate Maverick nature.

If we want to do more to shape a better world, step by step, by confronting what we and those around us should be doing better, by acting in our own sphere of influence, we need to give voice to and life to our innate Maverick nature.

There is a concept in economics, politics and social discourse known as 'preference falsification', a phrase coined by Harvard professor Timor Kuran (1997), in which people tailor their choices, their expressed views, to what they believe to be more socially acceptable compared to what they actually think and feel and what is in their better interest. Because people falsify their real preferences, the result is that it becomes even harder to bring about the betterment that so many people need and want. When people conceal their discontent about how things are done, what things are done, or how people are treated, it isolates those who try to challenge and push for betterment.

What is socially acceptable of course has changed radically throughout history. If you go back into the not so distant past, we see that many things that most people now consider to be socially unacceptable were at some point considered acceptable – including eating other people! So what makes something socially acceptable and how does what was once socially acceptable become unacceptable? The answer of course is that our culture determines what is socially acceptable, whether that be our family culture, community culture, organizational culture or national culture. But the question that we really have to ask is, who does our culture best serve and who does it disadvantage, discriminate against, marginalize or victimize? Many national cultures today are, for example, patriarchal. Who does patriarchy serve? Many organizational cultures are hierarchical. Who does hierarchy serve?

The superficial answer to the question of who the patriarchy benefits, is men. This is simplistic to the point of being wrong. The patriarchy benefits some men over some other men, it benefits some men over some women and benefits some women who 'lean in' over some women and some men. Alan Buys explores this question of who the patriarchy benefits in a systemic way (2019). The point is, the patriarchy disbenefits a lot of men and a lot of women when compared to some other cultural systems. Until more men and women are prepared to voice their dissatisfaction with the patriarchy and actively work towards a better cultural system, a system that actually benefits the few over the many is more likely to persist for longer. It requires more of us currently falsifying our preferences by remaining silent or actively supporting a system that disadvantages many to become Maverick leaders.

The same analysis can be applied to the question, who benefits from the organizational hierarchy? The traditional answer is that everyone benefits, because properly organized work, managed and directed by those with the appropriate levels of authority, makes for an efficient and productive organization. Another answer might be that hierarchy, at least as executed through hierarchical behaviour, limits and diminishes the contribution of most people in the organization beyond following instructions.

There is much debate and research into these cultural norms and whom they serve, and in what ways. It is not our purpose to enter into these debates; rather it is to point out that what is socially acceptable always advantages some over others. And each socially accepted norm persists unameliorated, not until some imposing force is overturned, but until those people falsifying their preferences, in compliance with what is socially acceptable, stop doing so and join forces with the ever-present Maverick dissenting voices working for change.

We need to be more resourceful

We break down preference falsification and accelerate change towards a better organization, community or government by stepping up and connecting with others, by generating and deploying greater resources. This is why resourcefulness is one of the four differentiating characterizes of the Maverick leader and why we position it as the first required to build the platform for change. Resourcefulness depends first and foremost on curiosity and we can all be more curious.

Donald Rumsfeld, former US Secretary of Defence, is remembered by many for his reference to 'unknown unknowns', when describing intelligence reports regarding terrorist access to weapons of mass destruction. He said:

> Reports that say that something hasn't happened are always interesting to me, because as we know, there are known knowns; there are things we know we know. We also know there are known unknowns; that is to say we know there are some things we do not know. But there are also unknown unknowns – the ones we don't know we don't know. And if one looks throughout the history of our country and other free countries, it is the latter category that tend to be the difficult ones (Rumsfeld, 2002).

We quote the entire paragraph above because we need to take into account all three categories – known knowns, known unknowns and unknown unknowns – and understand how they can trip us up when we're embarking on change.

Known knowns are not predictors of the future, they are simply accepted wisdom about what has worked or been true in the past. That does not mean that they might not remain true and useful; it means that you have to be aware that they may not remain true and be useful. *Known unknowns* invite assumptions. Assumptions are quick and easy ways of moving on when you know you don't know something. The problem is of course that your assumptions could be wrong. And *unknown unknowns*: how can you manage things you don't even know you don't know? The answer to all these three challenges is to engage with others with curiosity: the prerequisite to resourcefulness.

Curiosity

In Chapter 3 we shared the advice of Ronald Burt, one of the founders of network analysis, who believes creating open and diverse networks to be one of the best predictors of a successful career; the source of success lying in actively seeking out relationships with individuals with whom there is no tie at all, particularly those who have complementary talents and know-how. If we define success as achieving betterment, as opposed to simply wishing for it, then open and diverse networks are critical. So we can identify two activities that all of us can pursue that will give us access to more resources, more people and ideas: build an open and diverse network and engage with curiosity.

BECOMING A MAVERICK LEADER (1)

1 Build an open and diverse network.

2 Engage with your network with curiosity.

Building a diverse and open network

Though it takes conscious effort, a diverse and open network is key to being a Maverick. Here is a summary of how to build an effective social network to help you mobilize transformational positive change.

Who you know

As the saying goes, it's not about what you know, it's about who you know. The more those in your network are different to you, the more potential you have to make change happen. This takes going beyond your comfort zone of talking to people who agree with you. You need to seek out people who challenge what you think and provide new perspectives and information.

Go beyond introductions from friends

Seek out people that no one you know could give you an introduction to. People you would have to cold call. You could also force yourself to cold call someone who can get you to the person you have in mind but cannot get to directly. A diverse and open network is made up of a series of other networks for which you are the only common denominator.

Reciprocity

Influencing and learning are the property of relationships. And relationships are built on give and take. Any effective relationship based on give and take starts with give. By actively giving, contributing towards others' aspirations and goals, their values and fundamental human needs, you build the kind of relationships that you can call upon to support you in your endeavours.

Treat people as individuals

It seems so obvious. Everyone is a unique person with unique needs, aspirations, skillsets and contributions to make. And yet, so often we see people in terms of categories. Even more often, we are told by others what's right and what's wrong with the people we are about to meet. But if you can meet every person with a fresh mindset, an open mind and are willing to explore their aspirations, and share with them yours, so much more can be achieved than a predefined set of assumptions as to what is possible.

Engage your network with curiosity

Curiosity Maverick Keith Coats, the Director of Storytelling at the futurist consultancy Tomorrow Today, had some detailed advice on how to engage people with curiosity:

> Some people have the type of personality that allows them to initiate naturally and seamlessly 'curiosity conversations' – conversations in which they connect, ask questions and come away with deeper insights and understanding. For many however it is not that straightforward. Being intentional around initiating and hosting curiosity conversations is an important mindset and skillset for leaders to cultivate.

The following are some of Keith's simple tips on how to go about this:

1 Identify specific people from whom you would like to learn something. These may be people who are readily accessible or perhaps not, it doesn't really matter. In some cases, the work that goes into gaining this access is half the fun of having curiosity conversations! It might be that the person

you wish to have a conversation with is unknown to you – 'I'd like to talk to an astronaut' for example – so finding someone who knows someone who used to know someone who… you get the picture! If the approach is respectful and you are only asking for 20–30 minutes of their time, most people will be amenable to your approach. Don't think that the people from whom you need to learn something are only those in powerful or prominent positions. The person you have passed every day on your way to work who 'sleeps rough' – stopping to politely converse with them in a curiosity conversation might well yield deeper insights than a conversation with a prominent CEO.

2 Know what the question is you want to ask. In other words, have a focus to your conversation. Having located our astronaut friend, the lead question might be: 'Perspective is so important for leaders everywhere. I am curious to know how being in space impacted your perspective of life on our planet?' It is important that you do your homework as to why you want the conversation and then take care in how you will set it up.

3 Respect the person's time. Stick to the agreed time and be on time! Often, you'll find that the conversation overshoots the allotted time, but this is always at the discretion of the person you are meeting.

4 Avoid taking notes. This is not an interview; it is a conversation. Budget some time immediately after the conversation where you can find a quiet place and transcribe the salient points from the conversation. Do this immediately while the conversation is still fresh in your mind. Make a note of why you sought the conversation in the first place and any other 'surrounding context' to the meeting. In time, when you review past conversations, this additional information could be important.

5 Take note of not only what is said but what is 'not said'. You can learn as much from the unspoken interaction as from the actual conversation. Sadly, there are times when the person might be dismissive and abrupt, where you feel as though you are an unwelcome interruption to their day. Thankfully, however, in the vast majority of curiosity conversations you will encounter individuals who are exceedingly generous with their time and wisdom; those who are warm and equally curious about why it is you want to meet with them. Such curiosity conversations leave an indelible impression.

6 Keep a 'curious conversations journal'. Over time it will become a wonderful resource and reminder of an intentional (and never-ending) journey.

Developing this curiosity conversational discipline will spill over into other encounters you have along the way. After the passing of time, the discipline will (hopefully) morph into a lifelong habit. If you have a leadership team you suspect has become arthritic in their learning attitude and practice, introducing them to curiosity conversations, and then holding them accountable to have such, is a great way to ignite or reignite their own learning journey. In the context of leadership, why is all this so important? Well, leaders who are not learners cannot be adaptive. It is that simple... and it is that challenging!

Some of Keith's intentional curiosity conversations include meeting with:

- a world champion big-wave surfer
- a double-lung heart transplant recipient
- an Afghan woman encountering the ocean for the first time
- a double gold medallist Olympian rower who made a comeback aged 40
- a PhD student researching VR
- an international cricketer
- a transgender person
- a monk who did a 10-year silent retreat
- a leading South African politician
- a business owner whose staff gave exceptional service
- authors of various books that made an impression on his thinking/ perspective
- a 'homeless' person
- someone who had been blind since birth

BECOMING A MAVERICK LEADER (2)

3 Identify people from diverse walks of life to whom you would like to talk.

4 Think of a great question to explore with them relevant to their walk of life and your interests.

5 Using your connections, you will eventually manage to contact them and 90 per cent of them will agree happily to talk to you.

6 Capture the essence of the conversation directly afterwards in your curiosity journal.

The ladder of inference

Another great skill the Maverick leader requires to make the most of the diverse insights and contributions of others is the practice of intelligent advocacy and enquiry. The idea is based on the thinking of Harvard professor Chris Argyris, encapsulated in his 'ladder of inference'.

The ladder of inference is a tool for deepening our understanding of what is going on, through exploring diverse perspectives. The idea is very simple. We can think of reality as some sort of video that we're all watching. We know through our biases that we are very selective about what we see. If we were not, of course, we would just be overloaded and unable to operate. But as we know, our selective filters are different, because of our different experiences, perspectives, skills, etc. Having been selective in what we see, we then add meaning to what we have selected. And then we make assumptions, sometimes consciously, sometimes unconsciously, to explain and fill in gaps. At that point we come to a conclusion, a conclusion about what is going on, what is happening, and then we apply our belief system about what is the right thing to do and from there we go into action. This whole process often happens at speed and subconsciously. What happens is that we end up arguing based on what the right thing to do is – the right action to take – and our positions tend to become polarized.

If you genuinely want be inclusive, to include differences, and understand that there is a benefit to progressing betterment in so doing, instead of arguing in terms of right and wrong, we can use the ladder of inference to enquire and advocate in an intelligent way, to get the best out of our differences.

What does this mean, to enquire intelligently? It means, instead of pounding the table with what we believe is truth, the right, best and proper way to do things, we ask the other person questions to explore their ladder of inference. The first obvious question is: What do you see? Next you can ask: What does this mean to you? Then you can ask: What assumptions have you made? And finally: What is it about what you believe that means you think X or Y, whatever it is, is the right thing to do? The point of this process is that two things are possible. First, by making yourself aware of the other person's ladder of inference, you may actually be persuaded to adapt your approach to be more effective or simply to be more open to the fact you could be wrong, or your colleague could be right, at least to some extent. Second, in obliging your colleague to go through this process, they may be persuaded that in fact they could be wrong; they may have missed something, perhaps one of their assumptions is a little bit lacking in evidence.

None of this is guaranteed to mean you'll reach agreement and harmony, but it does mean two things: 1) *you're more likely to agree*; and 2) *you may find out the source of your disagreement*. For example, if you saw different things, or you made different assumptions, both can be worked on by looking more closely and by testing and checking your different assumptions, through experimentation or seeking more evidence.

Intelligent advocacy, as opposed to intelligent enquiry, is simply doing the same with your own ladder of inference. That is making explicit to others what you saw, what it meant to you, your assumptions, etc, so others can see how you got to where you got to. Again this creates the possibility of finding out where you disagree or indeed persuading your colleague of your point of view. Intelligent advocacy and enquiry is much more likely to lead to new discoveries and effective solutions than simply arguing about who's right and who's wrong.

BECOMING A MAVERICK LEADER (3)

7 Practise the art of intelligent advocacy and enquiry.

We need to be more nonconformist

The second distinguishing characteristic of the Maverick leader is the choiceful challenge of established conventions, norms, rules and procedures. To try and discover new ways of doing things that are more beneficial to more people.

A great way to unleash your nonconformist abilities is to ask the questions that other people are not asking and think the things that other people are not thinking – or at least not admitting. There are two quotes we are very fond of to bring these points alive. The first is from the futurist Jim Dator: 'Any useful idea about the future must appear ridiculous' (1996). Of course there is the caveat that not every ridiculous idea is useful. But if you're not prepared to have and voice your ridiculous ideas you'll never know which ones are useful.

The second quote is from the physicist Richard Feynman: 'I'd rather questions that can't be answered than answers that can't be questioned' (2017).

BECOMING A MAVERICK LEADER (4)

8 Ask the questions other people are not asking and think the things that other people are not thinking.

In thinking about why it is so important to challenge convention, rules, norms, etc, it is worth considering how they come about. Let's take organizational rules for example. Some rules come about because something bad happened and understandably the organization wants to avoid that bad thing happening again in the future. So they establish a set of rules to 'ensure' the bad thing does not happen again. Equally, rules can be established to ensure a good thing that happened, happens again. The problem is two-fold. First, more and more rules are added to the rule book, rules are rarely or never removed from the rule book, and a stifling, expansive and expensive bureaucracy is born. Second, the world changes and the rules that were put in place over time become ineffective or even counterproductive.

The same can be said of norms. There is an apocryphal and often cited experiment that goes as follows (Zabawski, 2011). A bunch of monkeys are placed in a cage. Some juicy bananas are presented in the cage high up, accessible only by climbing a ladder. As soon as one of the monkeys, probably the alpha male, starts to ascend the ladder to grab the bananas, the monkey is rewarded for his efforts by a powerful hosing down with freezing cold water before he reaches the bananas, and consequently he retreats. Being an alpha male, he recovers, attempts the same exercise but unfortunately is met with the same response. After repeated freezing soakings he gives up and the bananas remain untouched. Having observed the repeated soaking, the other monkeys desist from grabbing the bananas.

At this point, the experimenters, in white coats, remove one of the monkeys and introduce a new monkey from the cage. The new monkey instantly sees the bananas and moves towards the ladder. Before he can reach the first rung of the ladder, the other monkeys attack him and drag him back to the furthest corner of the cage to prevent him from climbing the ladder. In order to ensure the new monkey makes no further attempts he is severely beaten for his efforts. What does he learn? That there is a norm, that even when bananas, which are good things, are readily available, simply a few steps away, it is wrong to attempt to retrieve them.

The experiment continues by replacing monkeys until the population of monkeys comprises none who were there when the original freezing hosing down took place. Yet none of the monkeys, all of whom never witnessed the original and only hosing down, ever attempts to reach the bananas. A norm has been established in the cage. Do not attempt to retrieve the bananas! The problem with this is that while that may have been a good norm at one point in time, i.e. that the consequences of attempting to get the bananas outweighed the benefits of the bananas, it may not be true forever. But a norm is forever. Unless the norm is challenged.

This story may seem bizarre and far removed from the world of organizations and business. And yet it is exactly what often happens in how we behave in organizations. When once we followed our instincts and took risks in pursuit of what we valued, we become risk-averse and too frightened to challenge, because of earlier disappointing or harmful results, and a norm is established.

BECOMING A MAVERICK LEADER (5)

9 Question rules and norms; do not simply ask why we have them, but ask what benefits may be possible if we did not have them.

We need to be more experimental

Having challenged the rules, the norms, the conventions, as opposed to simply conforming, we need to recognize that in so doing we enter uncharted territory. To assume that we know for certain what will work better would be tantamount to omniscience. So we need to embrace the road of trial and error. In Chapter 5 on experimentation, we made the point that the art of choosing which experiments to conduct is recognizing the difference between a constraint that has to be complied with, a regulation, a legal requirement, and a convention, or a tradition, or so-called 'best practice', historical practices that are no longer the best way of doing things.

'Bricolage' is a term used by French anthropologists, particularly Claude Lévi-Strauss, to emphasize the importance of improvisation in the creation of a culture or an artefact. He contrasted man's ability to solve problems by 'tinkering around', drawing upon seemingly unrelated ideas and combining them in new patterns, with the more ordered thinking of an engineer who typically proceeds from goals to means. Mavericks are inveterate bricoleurs. They prefer to muddle through to a better place rather than to create plans to achieve a predetermined more certain, but less valuable outcome. They are comfortable with ambiguity, contradictory opinions, and not always knowing the answer. Breakthroughs come about through a skilful coaxing of serendipity:

> We need randomness, mess, adventures, uncertainty, self-discovery, near-traumatic episodes, all those things that make life worth living, compared to the structured, fake, and ineffective life of the empty-suit CEO with a pre-set schedule and an alarm clock (Taleb, 2012).

Good intentions, as the proverb predicts, are more likely to lead to disappointment than triumph. Throughout history, the greatest outcomes have rarely been the result of purposeful action. They are more likely to have been accidents waiting to happen. Conversely, those things that went badly were usually the outcome of deliberation. Disasters were often caused by powerful people coming to decisions based on an inflated sense of their own wisdom. They did not understand what they were doing but felt licensed nevertheless to push ahead with their strategies. The great, unacknowledged truth is that innovation *cannot* be predicted, managed, planned or choreographed. But it does result from experimentation, sometimes.

Experimentation is the alternative to planning. It is the name that scientists give to the art of making skilful mistakes on purpose. Mavericks understand the importance of trying odd things out in the hope that they will thereby bump into unexpected success. Mavericks notice and learn from their mistakes. If anything, they feel enriched rather than defensive when trials lead to errors. This is the logic of anti-fragility. A good system is one that is strengthened by stress, and where, as Taleb has pointed out, 'things gain from disorder'.

Experimentation is entrepreneurship at scale. Once an organization grows beyond, say, 150 employees, the art of innovation is to routinely and conscientiously test a wide variety of bold ideas. 'Betting the farm' is no longer an option. It's too costly a risk. But betting one of the fields on the farm is not only viable, but highly desirable. At any one time, 10 experiments testing 10 ideas in a contained way – one field at a time – becomes part and parcel of running a business rationally... not too dangerous, not too safe.

Experimentation is a numbers game. For every 10 ideas tested, one will come through as a winner. Placing small bets on big ideas allows us to be far braver in the ideas we choose to test. No one is allowed to bet the farm. No single idea is the solution. By containing the experimentation within a small part of the organization, we can afford to fail many times in the search for the breakthrough idea. As long as we are experimenting at a sufficient pace, we can be sure of a continuous stream of breakthrough ideas.

To discover a winning idea, we need at least 10 brilliant concepts worth testing; and to get to these 10 concepts, we need at least 100 conjectures that have potential; and to get to these 100 conjectures, we need 1,000 brainwaves worth discussing. Innovation is a funnel.

Only in a culture that can routinely spawn 1,000 innovative thoughts can we bank on the regular discovery of a winning idea. Mavericks trade on this arithmetic. They intuitively understand Tristan Tzara's counter-intuitive plea, 'Let us try for once not to be right.'

The art of entrepreneurship at scale is to blend bold thinking and rigorous testing. Most companies and communities err on the side of timid ideas and insufficient testing. The timidity arises from a fear of even the smallest failure. Insufficient testing arises from impatience, a false sense of urgency, the pressing need to be seen to be 'doing something'. Experimentation is the art of slowing down, giving creativity whatever time it needs, and then being far more selective of the ideas that eventually get implemented.

The motto of an experimental organization and person should be 'little BIG bets': small-scale experiments coming up with radical market solutions. It looks wasteful, because 999 rejected ideas are needed to get to a single accepted idea, but this is the economics of the ideas marketplace.

BECOMING A MAVERICK LEADER (6)

10 Go to bed each night with at least one idea for an experiment to start the very next day.

11 Every day do something or say something you have never done or said before.

12 Take a frustration or ambition you have, find one or more people who agree with your frustration or ambition, and initiate an experiment.

Strengthening your resolve

Leadership inevitably divides. Because leadership, as opposed to management, by definition involves challenging and proposing something different to the status quo. Management is about running the status quo as efficiently and effectively as possible. Challenging the status quo divides because it separates those who see the status quo as beneficial to them, from those who see the status quo as oppressive or disadvantageous. And those to whom the status quo is advantageous are usually those with the most power, under the status quo, and thus well equipped to robustly resist any attempt to change the status quo. Often such resistance is manifest in less than transparent and fair-minded ways. And this presents the biggest hurdle for the Maverick leader.

Yes, we must connect and create a 'movement' towards change, through using our resourcefulness to connect ideas and people behind a vision better than the status quo. And yes, we must adopt a nonconformist approach to challenge convention, norms and rules. And yes, we need to experiment to navigate the best route through uncharted territory. But without resilience and a compelling sense of purpose, resourcefulness, nonconformity and experimentation will amount to nothing more than armchair radicalism without the ability to persist in the face of resistance.

This is not a self-sacrificial invitation to adopt a lemming-like compulsion to die in a ditch for your cause. To die in a ditch without having made any progress does nothing for your cause. We want our Maverick leaders to live long and make a positive difference.

Expect opposition and embrace it. One of the most common traits among our selection of Maverick leaders is their ability to embrace those who opposed them, to see them as valued people and to recognize how they need to work with them to learn and to change mindsets. We asked Khadim Hussain how he felt about those who opposed him, sometimes with hostility: Was he angry with them? He replied, 'No, I felt sad, I understood that it came from their mindset, their way of thinking, and with a smile on my face, I determined that I would change their mindset.' As Luciano Cirinà put it, who can fail to identify with 'steel workers fighting for greater safety to protect their lives'? People naturally and rightly act to protect their position and the well-being of those they are responsible for – but they also, in time and through discourse, recognize that their well-being is related to the well-being of others. As Mmusi put it, 'How do we bring people who are our oppressors in one sense, to the same space as those who are oppressed, and ask them both to forgo those privileges and fight for the rights of the next generation?'

BECOMING A MAVERICK LEADER (7)

13 Fight your opponent's ideas; embrace your opponents as people.

Higher-order goals and life philosophy

Ultimately, none of what has gone before in this book is of any use, unless the reason for striving to be more Maverick and to lead change is in order to achieve a higher purpose. And what do we mean by a higher purpose? We mean, as we explored in Chapter 6, your higher-order goals and life philosophy.

So this is our final challenge to those of you who want to unleash your Maverick spirit in the service of the greater good. Ask yourself, and keep asking yourself, until you find the answer: What is your higher-order goal and your life philosophy? What is it that you and only you can do better, more of, and persist with, to make the world a better place? If you know the answers to those questions, then you are in a position to adopt and practice all of the approaches, skillsets and tools presented in this book, to use your Maverick spirit for the good of others and the fulfilment of your unique individuality.

BECOMING A MAVERICK LEADER (8)

14 Ask yourself 'What is my life philosophy?'

15 And when you have an answer, ask yourself 'What are my higher-order goals that will guide my every action?'

Summary: becoming a Maverick leader

1 Build an open and diverse network.
2 Engage with your network with curiosity.
3 Identify people from diverse walks of life whom you would like to talk to.
4 Think of a great question to explore with them relevant to their walk of life and your interests.
5 Using your connections, you will eventually manage to contact them and 90 per cent of them will agree happily to talk to you.
6 Capture the essence of the conversation directly afterwards in your curiosity journal.
7 Practise the art of intelligent advocacy and enquiry.
8 Ask the questions other people are not asking and think the things that other people are not thinking.
9 Question rules and norms; do not simply ask why we have them, but ask what benefits may be possible if we did not have them.
10 Go to bed each night with at least one idea for an experiment to start the very next day.
11 Every day do something or say something you have never done or said before.
12 Take a frustration or ambition you have, find one or more people who agree with your frustration or ambition, and initiate an experiment.
13 Fight your opponents' ideas; embrace your opponents as people.
14 Ask yourself 'What is my life philosophy?'
15 And when you have an answer, ask yourself 'What are my higher-order goals that will guide my every action?'

Don't sweat other people's small stuff. Do your BIG stuff.

References

Introduction

Dweck, C and Leggett, E (1988) A social–cognitive approach to motivation and personality, *Psychological Review*, **95** (2), pp 256–73

Hegel, G W F (1820) *Elements of the Philosophy of Right*, ed A W Wood, tr H B Nisbet (1991), Cambridge University Press, Cambridge

Hegel, G W F (1899) *The Philosophy of History*, Colonial Press, New York

Kant, I (1785) *Grundlegung zur Metaphysik der Sitten*, Hartknoch, Leipzig

Kennedy, R F (1966) Day of Affirmation Address, University of Capetown, Cape Town, South Africa, 6 June, John F Kennedy Presidential Library

Patchin, J (2019) 2019 Cyberbullying Data, cyberbullying.org/2019-cyberbullying-data (archived at https://perma.cc/ZF67-RQ48)

World Bank (2018) Nearly half the world lives on less than $5.50 a day, www.worldbank.org/en/news/press-release/2018/10/17/nearly-half-the-world-lives-on-less-than-550-a-day (archived at https://perma.cc/7HQF-RAXZ)

World Health Organization (2021) Obesity, www.who.int/news-room/facts-in-pictures/detail/6-facts-on-obesity (archived at https://perma.cc/2699-3CDY)

Chapter 1

Arendt, H (1958) *The Human Condition*, Chicago University Press, Chicago

Corera, G (2017) NHS cyber-attack was 'launched from North Korea', BBC, 16 June, www.bbc.co.uk/news/technology-40297493 (archived at https://perma.cc/D7ND-XL2A)

Kant, I (1997) *Kant, Lectures on Ethics, Reward and Punishment*, ed P Heath and J B Schneewind, p 55, Cambridge University Press, Cambridge

Oshry, B (2007) *Seeing Systems*, Berrett-Koehler, San Francisco

Stewart, J (2002) The real heroes are dead: A love story, *The New Yorker*, 11 February, www.newyorker.com/magazine/2002/02/11/the-real-heroes-are-dead (archived at https://perma.cc/2NWG-UXBJ)

Chapter 2

Dweck, C and Leggett, E (1988) A social–cognitive approach to motivation and personality, *Psychological Review*, **95** (2), pp 256–73

Elkhorne, J L (1957) Edison: The fabulous drone, *Amateur Radio*, 73 [XLVI] (3), 3 March 1967, p 52

Land, G and Jarman, B (1992) *Breakpoint and Beyond: Mastering the future – today*, HarperCollins, New York

Leslie, I (2015) *Curious: The desire to know and why your future depends on it*, Basic Books, New York

Robinson, O, Demetre, J and Litman, J (2017) Adult life stages and crisis as predictors of curiosity and authenticity: testing inferences from Erikson's lifespan theory, *International Journal of Behavioral Development*, **41** (3), pp 426–31

Sneed, J, Whitbourne, S and Culang, M (2006) Trust, identity, and ego integrity: Modeling Erikson's core stages over 34 years, *Journal of Adult Development*, **13** (3–4), pp 148–57

Chapter 3

Aristotle (1905) *Aristotle's Politics*, Clarendon Press, Oxford

Burt, R (1992) *Structural Holes: The social structure of competition*, Harvard University Press, Boston, MA

Castells, M (2009) *The Information Age: Economy, Society, and Culture*, vol I, *The Rise of the Network Society*

Csikszentmihalyi, M (1990) *Flow: The psychology of optimal experience*, Harper and Row, New York

Dunbar, R (1992) Neocortex size as a constraint on group size in primates, *Journal of Human Evolution*, **22** (6), pp 469–93

Feick, L and Price, L (1987) The market maven: A diffuser of marketplace information, *Journal of Marketing*, **51** (1), January, pp 83–97

Gale, P (2013) *Your Network is Your Net Worth: Unlock the hidden power of connections for wealth, success and happiness in the digital age*, Simon & Schuster, New York

Gladwell, M (2000) *The Tipping Point: How little things can make a big difference*, Little Brown and Company, Boston, MA

Goleman, D (1998) What makes a leader, *Harvard Business Review*, November–December

Granovetter, M S (1973) The strength of weak ties, *American Journal of Sociology*, **78** (6), pp 1360–380

Ibarra, H (2015) *Act Like a Leader, Think Like a Leader*, Harvard Business Review Press, Boston, MA

Koestler, A (1964) *The Act of Creation*, Hutchinson & Co, London

Lieberman, M D (2013) *Social: Why our brains are wired to connect*, Random House, New York

Mulgan, G (1991) *Communication and Control: Networks and the new economies of communication*, Polity Press, Guildford

Smith, E E (2013) Social connection makes a better brain, *The Atlantic*, 29 October, www.theatlantic.com/health/archive/2013/10/social-connection-makes-a-better-brain/280934/ (archived at https://perma.cc/4XLP-8AQ6)

TEDx Talks (2013) The key to transforming yourself: Robert Greene at TEDxBrixton, www.youtube.com/watch?v=gLt_yDvdeLQ (archived at https://perma.cc/4C26-87DP)

Vedres, B and Stark, D (2010) Structural folds: Generative disruption in overlapping groups, *American Journal of Sociology*, **115** (4), January, pp 1150–190

Wilson, E O (2016) Evolution and our inner conflict, in *The Stone Reader*, eds P Catapano and S Critchley, pp 270–74, Liveright Publishing, New York

Chapter 4

Ahmed, S (2016) Feminism and Fragility, Keynote presented at the National Women's Studies Association conference, 13 November, feministkilljoys.com/2016/01/26/feminism-and-fragility/ (archived at https://perma.cc/99H6-KJXJ)

Bandura, A (1997) *Self-efficacy: The exercise of control*, W H Freeman, New York

Hegel, G W F (1820) *Elements of the Philosophy of Right*, ed A W Wood, tr H B Nisbet (1991), Cambridge University Press, Cambridge

Huizinga, J (2016) *Homo Ludens: A study of the play-element in culture*, Angelico Press, Brooklyn, NY

Katharine Birbalsingh @Miss_Snuffy, Michaela pupils SMASH IT!! [Twitter] 22 August 2019, mobile.twitter.com/miss_snuffy/status/1164464651054329857 (archived at https://perma.cc/2M7C-7KBS)

Lieberman, J N (1965) Playfulness and divergent thinking: An investigation of their relationship at the kindergarten level, *Journal of Genetic Psychology*, **107** (2), pp 219–24

Pepler, D and Bierman, K (2018) With a little help from my friends: The importance of peer relationships for social-emotional development, www.prevention.psu.edu/uploads/files/rwjf450248-PeerRelationships.pdf (archived at https://perma.cc/2YDU-7477)

Popper, K (1999) *All Life is Problem Solving*, Routledge, London

Rogers, C (1995) *On Becoming a Person: A therapist's view of psychotherapy*, 2nd edn, Houghton Mifflin, Boston, MA

The Times (2021) Sidney Alford obituary, 19 February, www.thetimes.co.uk/article/sidney-alford-obituary-262tcr08l (archived at https://perma.cc/V9NP-6QFD)

Wallach, M and Kogan, N (1965) A new look at the creativity–intelligence distinction, *Journal of Personality*, **33** (3), pp 348–69

Wolf, B and Zuckerman, P (2012) Deviant heroes: Nonconformists as agents of justice and social change, *Deviant Behavior*, **33**, pp 639–54

Chapter 5

Adams, L (2015) *Learning a new skill is easier said than done*, Gordon Training International, www.gordontraining.com/free-workplace-articles/learning-a-new-skill-is-easier-said-than-done/ (archived at https://perma.cc/F78T-KGDX)

Beamish, J and Trackman, T (2019) *The Creative Brain* [documentary] Netflix

Chase, W and Simon, A (1973) Perception in chess, *Cognitive Psychology*, **4** (1), pp 55–61

Churchill, W (1946) Speech, University of Miami, 26 February

Dweck, C and Leggett, E (1988) A social–cognitive approach to motivation and personality, *Psychological Review*, **95** (2), pp 256–73

Ferguson, A (1767) *An Essay on the History of Civil Society*, London

Ormerod, P (2005) *Why Most Things Fail: Evolution, extinction, and economics*, Faber, London

Piaget, J (1951) *Play, Dreams and Imitation in Childhood*, Routledge and Kegan Paul, London

Ridley, M (2020) Britain will thrive if we side with innovators, *The Times*, www.thetimes.co.uk/article/britain-will-thrive-if-we-side-with-innovators-zl3skcqb8 (archived at https://perma.cc/P4YU-YXG5)

Sandlin, D (2015) The backwards brain bicycle: Smarter every day 133 [video], www.youtube.com/watch?v=MFzDaBzBlL0&t=2s (archived at https://perma.cc/8MBU-JFDC)

Scruton, R, Singer, P, Janaway, C and Tanner, M (2001) *German Philosophers: Kant, Hegel, Schopenhauer, and Nietsche*, Oxford University Press

Taleb, N (2012) *Antifragile: Things that gain from disorder*, Random House, New York

Tetlock, P (2017) *Expert Political Judgment: How good is it? How can we know it?*, Princeton University Press, Princeton, NJ

Chapter 6

Bronfenbrenner, U (1977) Toward an experimental ecology of human development, *American Psychologist*, **32** (7), pp 513–31

Duckworth, A and Gross, J (2014) Self-control and grit: Related but separable determinants of success, *Current Directions in Psychological Science*, **23** (5), pp 319–25

Duckworth, A and Peterson, C (2007) Grit: Perseverance and passion for long-term goals, *Journal of Personality and Social Psychology*, **92** (6), pp 1087–101

Kant, I (1997) *Kant, Lectures on Ethics, Reward and Punishment*, ed P Heath and J B Schneewind, p 55, Cambridge University Press, Cambridge

Masten, A, Best, K and Garmezy, N (1990) Resilience and development: Contributions from the study of children who overcome adversity, *Journal of Development and Psychopathology*, **2** (4), pp 425–44

Chapter 7

Argyris, C (1977) Double loop learning in organizations, *Harvard Business Review*, September

Edelman (2021) Edelman Trust Barometer 2021, www.edelman.com/sites/g/files/aatuss191/files/2021-03/2021%20Edelman%20Trust%20Barometer.pdf (archived at https://perma.cc/3CVM-UQN9)

Ferguson, N (2021) *Doom: The politics of catastrophe*, Allen Lane, London

Mouton, N (2017) A literary perspective on the limits of leadership: Tolstoy's critique of the great man theory, *Leadership*, **15** (1), pp 81–102

Nicholson, N (2003) How to motivate your problem people, *Harvard Business Review*, **81** (1), pp 56–65

Chapter 8

Hamel, G and Zanini, M (2016) The $3 trillion prize for busting bureaucracy (and how to claim it), www.garyhamel.com/sites/default/files/uploads/three-trillion-dollars.pdf (archived at https://perma.cc/5MTH-78LN)

Hamel, G and Zanini, M (2020) *Humanocracy: Creating organizations as amazing as the people inside them*, Harvard Business Review Press, Boston, MA

London Business School (2014) Costa Coffee: Project Marlow – Saving the world from mediocre coffee [case study], www.youtube.com/watch?v=0wLjM9BYUYs (archived at https://perma.cc/S6PQ-7KA6)

McGilchrist, I (2019) *The Master and His Emissary: The divided brain and the making of the western world*, Yale University Press, New Haven, CT

Riverford (2021) Ethics and ethos: Who is Guy Singh-Watson?, www.riverford.co.uk/ethics-and-ethos/who-is-guy-singh-watson (archived at https://perma.cc/9PER-TZRK)

Chapter 9

Burke, E (1909) *Reflections on the French Revolution*, The Harvard Classics [XXIV] (Part 3)

Donne, J (1624) *Devotions upon Emergent Occasions: Meditation XVII*

Goodhart, D (2017) Britain's hidden divide: The anywheres vs the somewheres, BBC Newsnight [video], www.youtube.com/watch?v=jva7nThOp81 (archived at https://perma.cc/H5AT-VA2R)

Grant, A (2013) Does studying economics breed greed? *Psychology Today*, 22 October, www.psychologytoday.com/gb/blog/give-and-take/201310/does-studying-economics-breed-greed (archived at https://perma.cc/NRS7-FT5Y)

Haidt, J (2006) *The Happiness Hypothesis: Finding modern truth in ancient wisdom*, Basic Books, London

Haidt, J (2012) *The Righteous Mind: Why good people are divided by politics and religion*, Penguin Random House, New York

Henrich, J (2015) *The Secret of Our Success*, Princeton University Press, Princeton, NJ

Hwang, V and Horowitt, G (2012) *Rainforest: The secret to building the next Silicon Valley*, Regenwald, Los Altos Hills, CA

Ostrom, E (1990) *Governing the Commons: The evolution of institutions for collective action*, Cambridge University Press, Cambridge

Wilson, D (2019) *This View of Life: Completing the Darwinian Revolution*, Vintage Books, New York

Chapter 10

Buys, A (2019) The benefits of patriarchy, Feminist Masculinity, 6 November, feministmasculinity.com/home/2019/11/6/the-benefits-of-patriarchy (archived at https://perma.cc/9Q35-J7KM)

Dator, J (1996) Futures studies as applied knowledge, in *New Thinking for a New Millenium*, ed R Slaughter, pp 105–15, Routledge, London

Feynman, R (2017) @ProfFeynman, I would rather have questions that can't be answered than answers that can't be questioned [Twitter] 18 March 2017, twitter.com/proffeynman/status/842912536915730432?lang=en (archived at https://perma.cc/G26H-Q9L6)

Kuran, T (1997) *Private Truths, Public Lies: The social consequences of preference falsification*, Harvard University Press, Boston, MA

Rumsfeld, D (2002) White House Security Briefing, 12 February 2002, www.c-span.org/video/?168646-1/defense-department-briefing (archived at https://perma.cc/V8DS-9YQL)

Taleb, N (2012) *Antifragile: Things that gain from disorder*, Random House, New York

Zabawski, E (2011) From the Editor, *Tribology and Lubrication Technology*, December, 67 (12), digitaleditions.walsworth.com/publication/?i=89390&article_id=894924& view=articleBrowser&ver=html5 (archived at https://perma.cc/G26H-Q9L6)

INDEX

The index is filed in alphabetical, word-by-word order. Acronyms and Mc are filed as presented; numbers are filed as spelt out; page locators in *italics* denote information within tables or figures.

acquis communautaire (EU) 150
action focus 154
activation (active life) 32–33
adaptivity 8–9, 11, 127, 136, 151
adhocracies 153–57
adolescence 41, 65, 136
adulthood 41, 42
advocacy *84, 185*
AKD Solutions 45
Alford, Sidney 74–76, 77
Alford Technologies 75
Amazon 95
anger 25–27
armed services (Ministry of Defence) 17–18, 75, 168–69
Ashta No Kai 65
Assicurazioni Generali 114–16, 121
assumptions 179, 181, 184–85
Atkins, Joe 146
authenticity 73, 76, 83, 117, 133
authoritarian leadership 74, 126
autonomy 10, 24, 85, 134, 155, 165, 172
awakenings 20–21

Bangalore Blade 75
belief 5, *9, 13*, 17–33, 31, *111, 129*–30
   see also self-belief
belonging 52–57, 60, 62, 87, 164, 174
best practice 92, 93, 149, 187
bias 58, 128, 139, 174, 184
Birbalsingh, Katharine 69, 70–74, 77
Black Lives Matter movement 131–32
black people (narrative) 28, 45–46, 71, 95, 114, 131–32
blank canvas approach 80–81, 113
Boot Banger 75
bottom line principle (McKinsey) 156
bottoms organizational level 26, 139
brain function 59–61, 99, 100–01, 150–52
bricolage 187–88
Brown, Michael Jr 131
Brown, Michael Sr 131
budgeting 135–36, 149, 156
bullying 1, 87

bureaucratic organizations 2, 97, 124, 147–50, 155, 171

calling 20, 126, 138
capital 58–59
   moral 155, 157
   social 59–68, 155, 157, 162–63
   see also ideas generation; networking (connection); relationships
capitalism 135, 146
career guidance portals 136
categorical imperative 7
Centre for Creative Leadership (CCL) 55–56
centres of excellence 78
challenging 4, 30, 78–79, 86, 190
change 148
change agents 130
change methodologies 3
chess playing 98
childhood development 40, 41, 96, 116
choices 138
chronosystems 120
circumstances 138
Cirinà, Luciano 114–16, 121, 190
civilization 7, 82, 123, 150–51, 161–62
clicking points 103
cognitive dissonance 42
collaboration 60, 85–87, 136, 158
   see also coordination
community, sense of 170–73
company man archetype 56
competence 44
conscious 103
conditioning 7, 130
confidence 44–45, 137–38
   see also self-confidence
conformity 7, 71, 77
   see also nonconformity
connection (networking) 56, 57–58, 59–68, 74, 78, 95, 180–83
   see also relationships; social capital
conscious competence 103
conscious competence model 101–04
conscious incompetence 102–03

constraints 92–93, 187
control (self-control) 108, 117
control experiments 91
conversation transcriptions 182
conversations 140, 181–83
    see also dialogue
coordination 154
    see also collaboration
core design principles 172
Costa Coffee 155
Covid-19 pandemic 127, 134, 164, 170
Coyaji, Dr Banoo 65
Craggs, Andy 52–57, 68
Creative Centre for Community Mobilization
        (CRECCOM) 126, 127
creative genius 36–37
creativity 36–38, 51–52, 55–56, 59, 79–80,
        82–83, 96–97, 100–01, 170
crises (emergencies) 20, 41–42, 43, 48, 134,
        170
Csikszentmihalyi, Mihaly 51–52
culture (environment) 7–9, 23, 83, 97,
        124–26, 158, 178, 189
curiosity 46–47, 84, 96–98, 180, 181–83
curious conversation journals 182
cyberattacks 17–18

Dean Witter 21–22, 27
decentring 141–42
decision-making 80, 138, 141, 152–53,
        154–55, 172
default network 60–61
defensive behaviour 125, 142–43
Dell 95
Democratic Alliance 114, 166
democratization 146–47
destructive organizational structures 26
Deutsche Bank 79–81
development stages 35–48
    adolescence 65, 136
    early childhood 96, 119
    young people 1, 78
deviance 85–87
dialogue 10, 141
    see also conversations
Dioplex 75
disciplined pluralism (variation and selection)
        99–100, 166
disenfranchisement (disengagement) 2, 112,
        139
Disney (Walt Disney) 54, 56
diversity 51, 52, 61, 64, 116, 125, 180–81, 184
doing 92–93
    see also practical activity

Drucker conversation 140
Duggal, Guatam 113–14
Dunbar, Robin (Dunbar's Number) 60

early childhood 40, 41, 96, 119
economic capital 59
economic theory 165
Edison, Thomas 37
education 22, 23–25, 65, 69–75, 105–07,
        117–18, 120–21, 126–27, 136–37,
        167–68
Egg 54–55, 56
eight stages of development 41–42, 47–48
Ekine, Adefunke 22, 27
El-Hadad, Janna 78–79, 109
Ellfers, Joost 50
emergencies (crises) 20, 41–42, 43, 48, 134,
        170
emotional environment 110–13
emotional intelligence (quotient) 61, 125,
        137–38, 148, 155
emotions 110–13, 162
empathy 57, 84, 138, 151
engagement 22, 56, 61, 78
    see also disenfranchisement (disengagement)
entrepreneurial panacea 170
entrepreneurialism 10, 58–59, 65, 146, 148,
        188, 189
environment (culture) 7–9, 23, 83, 97,
        124–26, 158, 178, 189
Ericsson, Anders 51
Erikson, Erik 41–42, 47–48
eudaimonia 155
eureka ideas 94
evolutionary theory 95, 162–64, 174–75
example setting 73, 124, 137
exclusion 58, 112
exosystems 119
expectation setting 71, 73
experimental learning 5–6, 23, 31, 78–79, 81,
        84, 87–104, 111, 153–56, 186–89
    and adaptive organizations 9
expertise (experts) 63, 98–100
external resourcefulness 49, 57–58

fail forwards 39
failures (mistakes) 37, 38–40, 93–94, 97, 188,
        189
fair process 141
fairness 172
fear 11, 102–03, 112, 143
feedback 22, 40, 44, 62, 100
first machine age (managerialism) 147–50,
        152

fixed mindset 143
flow 51–52, 66
Fluxx 35, 78, 101
followership 133–34
Ford, Giles 79–83
Foreman, Giles 81
48 Laws of Power, The (Greene) 50
freedom 7, 35, 82, 97

Gate Crasher 75
Gauss, Carl Friedrich 38–39
Generali 114–16, 121
generative factor 110–13
gifts 59
goal setting 106–08
   higher-order (superordinate) 116–18, 121, 191
   lower-level 117
GRACE Association Pakistan 106
Greene, Robert 49–51
grit 107, 108, 116–18, 121
group identity 172
group membership 163–64, 172
groupthink 169
growth mindset 11

hackathons 129
Harvard Business School 23
hazards of existence *see* emergencies (crises)
Hegel, Georg Wilhelm Friedrich 7, 69, 92
helpless responses 38, 39–40, 44, 102, 128
hierarchical behaviour 11, 83, *84*
hierarchical goal formation 107, 108
hierarchical organizations 124–26, 127–28, 149
higher-order goals 107–08, 116–18, 121, 191
Hine, Nick 17–18, 27, 168–69
homophily 67–68
honesty 142–43
horizontal organizations 156
hubris 99, 137
Huizinga, Johan 82
humanocracies 146–47
Hussain, Khadim 4, 23–24, 27, 105–06, 107, 108, 109, 190
hypotheses 22, 87, 90–91, 93
Hytner, Richard 55

ideas generation 59, 185
impulse 7
incentive systems 128, 149, 155
inclusivity 58, 126, 136, 141, 172, 174, 184
individuality 85, 159, 181, 191
infancy 41

influencers 61–62
Information Age 153
ING 157–59
innovation 7, 79–80, 94, 110–11, 170–71, 173, 188–89
innovation hubs 154, 173
inquiry 25–27, *84*
intangible assets 59
intelligent advocacy 185
internal conflict 42
internal locus of control 73
internal resourcefulness 49–52
intrinsic motivation 155, 157
invisible walls 86
invitational leadership 126
isolation 66, 79, 87, 112, 113, 140, 164, 170
   see also loneliness

Johnson & Johnson 67, 78
justice system 18–21, 27, 78, 131

Kant, Immanuel 7, 33, 116
Kennedy, Robert F 1, 28, 133
knowing–doing gap 153
known knows 179
known unknowns 179

labelling (stereotyping) 58, 67
ladder of inference 184–85
late adulthood 41, 42
leadership selection 125
learning 22–23, 40, 44, 46–47, 94, 97, 101–04
learnt helplessness 128
left brain hemisphere 151–52
Let Maasai Girls Learn 120
Lewis, Annmarie 18–21, 27, 78, 109
life philosophies 96, 108–09, 115, 116–18, 191
lightbulb moments 94
London Business School 23, 55–56, 57, 81
loneliness 163–64
   see also isolation
Lopez, Oscar Corona 22–23, 27, 89–92, 109
lower-level goals 107, 108, 117

machine age 147–49, 152–53
macrosystems 119
Maimane, Mmusi Aloysias 114, 116, 166–67
male mindset 3, 29, 66–67, 186
managerialism (first machine age) 147–50, 152
manufacturing sector 148

market mavens 63
mastery-mindset 38–40, 44, 51–52, 103–04
mavens 63
Maverick, Samuel 4, 32
McKinsey 156
measurement systems 91, 155–56, 157
medicine, and experimentation 92–93
mentalization 138
meritocratic panacea 171
mesosystems 119
Michaela Community School 69, 70–74
microsystems 119
middle adulthood 41
middle managers (middles) 81, 139
mindset 11, 94, 98, 143, 181, 190
    male 3, 29, 66–67, 186
    mastery 38–40, 44, 51–52, 103–04
    performance 38, 40, 44, 97, 102
Ministry of Defence (armed services) 17–18,
    75, 168–69
mistakes (failures) 37, 38–40, 93–94, 97, 188,
    189
Mizukami, Yusuke 57–58
model 1 behaviour 125, 142
Modi, Armene 24–25, 27, 64–65
moral capital 59, 155, 157
morality 102, 141, 148, 163, 164–66, 167
Morgan Grenfell boardroom 79
Morgan Stanley 21–22, 27
Morning Star 156
motivation, intrinsic 155, 157
National Health Service 17
neocortex 60
network effect 129
network strength 63–65
networking (connection) 56, 57–58, 59–68,
    74, 78, 95, 180–83
    see also relationships; social capital
'no', use of 36–37
non-hierarchical leadership 126–29, 157–59
nonconformity 5, 9, 13, 31, 69–87, 111,
    185–87, 190
    see also conformity
Norman, Andre 28, 109, 129–33
norms 69, 70, 83, 178, 186–87
North Korea 17

obesity 1
Ofsted 70
Ogilvy 30
online bullying 1
open networks 65, 180, 181
operational networking 62
organizational generative factor 110–13

organizations
    adaptivity of 8–9
    behaviour of 83, 84
    bureaucratic 2, 97, 124, 147–50, 155, 171
    culture of (environment) 7–9, 23, 83, 97,
        124–26, 158, 178, 189
    hierarchical 124–26, 127–28, 149
    horizontal 156
    levels of (hierarchies) 26, 81, 139, 178
    rules of 186
Osama, Samar 3, 29, 66–67
Oshry, Barry 25–27
Ostrom, Elinor 171–72

pandemic, Covid-19 127, 134, 164, 170
Parsitau, Damaris Seleina 120–21, 167–68
passiveness 128
paternalism 71
patriarchies 178
Peace Education 24–25
peer group relationships 78
people and planet mindset 4, 42–43, 109
performance mindset 38, 40, 44, 94, 97, 102
personal behavioural principles 173
personal networking 62
personal responsibility 70, 166–69
personhood 72–73, 83, 85
planning 99, 149, 157, 171
playfulness 37, 79–83, 84, 96–98, 153
pluralism 12, 99–100
powerlessness 112, 133
practical activity 51–52
    see also doing
preference falsification 177, 179
prefrontal cortex 100
preschool age 41
prison system 1, 18–19, 28, 131–32
problem focus 154, 157
profit 156
programme/ project management 3
Project Marlow 155
purpose 188

questioning 18, 42, 79, 84, 89–91, 154, 182,
    184, 185–86
quitting 130–31

Rainmakers Group, The 20
Rainmakers Worldwide 20
rapport 57, 66
reciprocity 59, 155, 163, 181
recognition of existence 29–30
recruitment 23, 30–31, 89–91, 155
    referrals 64

relationships 11, 113–14, 115–16, 119–20, 135
  peer group 78
  see also networking (connection); social
    capital
Rescorla, Rick 21–22, 27
resilience 118–20, 190
resistance 18, 24, *84*, 87, 190–91
resolution *84*, *190–91*
resourcefulness 4, 5, 9, 13, 31, 49–68, *84*,
  111, 179
right brain hemisphere 151
Riverford 145–47
role-modelling 3, 74, 168
Royal Armament Research and Development
  Establishment 75
rules, organizational 186
Rumsfeld, Donald 179

Saatchi and Saatchi 55, 56
Sachdeva, Suman 136–37
Sahni, Urvashi 117–18
Samati, Madalo 126–27
school age 41
schooling *see* education
second machine age 152–53
self 135
self-awareness 61, 138
self-belief 72, 102
self-confidence 44, 126, 133
self-control 108, 117
self-doubt 38, 102–03
self-efficacy 72–73
self-esteem 72
self-leadership 132–33
services sector 148
Siddiqa, Nasrin 77
significant others 61–62, 87
Silverstein, Hannah 35–36, 78, 101, 102
Singh-Watson, Guy 145–46
social belonging 52–57, 60, 62, 87, 164, 174
social capital 59–68, 155, 157, 162–63
  see also ideas generation; networking
    (connection); relationships
social deviance 85–87
social ecological systems theory 119
social inclusion 58, 126, 136, 141, 172, 174,
  184
social media 59, 91
socially acceptable behaviour 177–78
Sony 54, 56
Spotify 158
squads 140, 157–59
status quo 69, 86, 190

stereotyping 58, 67
strategic influencers 61–62
strategic networking 62
strategy formation 154–55
strength 142, 143
strong network ties 64
structural network folds 66–67
structural network holes 65, 66–67
succession planning 127
superordinate (higher-order) goals 107–08,
  116–18, 121, 191
supplier-customer link 156, 157
Sutherland, Rory 30

technocracy 152–53
technology 1, 62, 148
10, 000-hour rule 51
Thomas, Akin 45–46, 109
tops organizational level 139
traditional leadership 2, 83, 128, 134
tragedy of the commons 171
transparency 43, 158, 172, 190
trial and error 94–96, 135–37
trust 63, 82, 116, 127–28, 140, 173
Twin Towers attack 21–22

unconscious competence 103–04
unconscious incompetence 102
undeterred characteristic 5, 6, 9, 14, 23–24,
  31–32, 57, 105–21
unknown unknowns 179
unspoken interactions 182
utilitarianism 165, 170

variation and selection 99–100, 166
Vera, Rik 4, 42–43, 95, 109
vision statements 149
Voice, The 90
volunteering 11, 54, 60, 106, 172

Wall Street Journal 53
Walt Disney 54, 56
water-lined shaped charge system 75
Watson Wyatt (WW) 53–54, 56
weak network ties 64–65
well-being 1, 74, 138, 161, 190–91
'why am I here' 25–27
WL Gore 154
work 55, 174

young adulthood 41
young people 1, 78
youth justice 18–21, 27, 78, 131

WHAT
PHIL●SOPHY
CAN TEACH Y●U
AB●UT BEING A

BETTER
LEADER

Alison Reynolds
Dominic Houlder
Jules Goddard
David Lewis

KoganPage